Hilary Putnam

Philosophy Now

Series Editor: John Shand

This is a fresh and vital series of new introductions to today's most read, discussed and important philosophers. Combining rigorous analysis with authoritative exposition, each book gives a clear, comprehensive and enthralling access to the ideas of those philosophers who have made a truly fundamental and original contribution to the subject. Together the volumes comprise a remarkable gallery of the thinkers who have been at the forefront of philosophical ideas.

Published

Donald Davidson
Marc Joseph

Nelson Goodman
Daniel Cohnitz & Marcus Rossberg

Saul Kripke
G. W. Fitch

David Lewis
Daniel Nolan

John McDowell
Tim Thornton

Hilary Putnam
Maximilian de Gaynesford

Wilfrid Sellars
Willem A. deVries

Forthcoming

David Armstrong
Stephen Mumford

Thomas Nagel
Alan Thomas

John Rawls
Catherine Audard

Peter Strawson
Clifford Brown

Bernard Williams
Mark Jenkins

Hilary Putnam

Maximilian de Gaynesford

McGill-Queen's University Press
Montreal & Kingston • Ithaca

ISBN 0-7735-3086-X (hardcover)
ISBN 0-7735-3087-8 (paperback)

Legal deposit first quarter 2006
Bibliothèque nationale du Québec

Published simultaneously outside North America
by Acumen Publishing Limited

McGill-Queen's University Press acknowledges the financial support of
the Government of Canada through the Book Publishing Development
Program (BPIDP) for its activities.

Library and Archives Canada Cataloguing in Publication

De Gaynesford, Maximilian
    Hilary Putnam / Maximilian de Gaynesford.

Includes bibliographical references and index.
ISBN 0-7735-3086-X (cloth)
ISBN 0-7735-3087-8 (pbk.)

    1. Putnam, Hilary. 2. Philosophy, American--20th century.
I. Title.

B945.P874D44 2006   191   C2005-906274-6

Typeset by Newgen Imaging Systems (P) Ltd, Chennai, India
Printed and bound by Cromwell Press, Trowbridge.

Contents

v

Preface

This book is principally for readers interested in modern philosophy who may know little about what precise developments have characterized the subject in the past fifty years, but who wish to learn more, and are prepared to do so via engagement with the writings of a leading and representative figure.

I have tried to explain what distinguishes the contributions made by Hilary Putnam from those of his immediate philosophical ancestors and descendants, and to maintain continuity of theme. The treatment is cumulative. The first part describes salient elements of the philosophical context in which Putnam has worked, elements which have helped develop the character of his thought, the second subject of discussion, a character which has in turn determined the particular contents of his work, those arguments and conclusions which define his main contributions to philosophy and to which the latter parts of the book are devoted.

The main argument of the book is that we should interpret Putnam in a new way. Current debates place undue emphasis on peripheral matters, tending to distort, ignore or hide his most significant contributions. His principal concern is with the question of how it is possible for our thought and talk to be about reality. He has contributed greatly to our awareness of the depths to which the philosophical problems run here, of the value of certain approaches to the questions arising, and of the emptiness of others. This venerable issue, the problem of intentionality, constantly recurs in Putnam's range of immediate concerns, unifies his work, and provides the considerable variety of his writings with a central and dominant theme.

Hilary Putnam

I am most grateful to James Conant, Bob Hale, Dermot Moran and Axel Müller for encouragement and advice. The book is dedicated to my brother, oldest and most cherished companion in argument.

M de G
13 August 2005
Temple Cloud, Cornwall

Chapter 1

Introduction

> I am not writing philosophy for the next historical epoch and for our
> post-human descendants; I am writing for human beings in the present
> period.　　Hilary Putnam, *Meaning and Knowledge* (1976a (v): 63)

Philosophy experiences few seismic shifts in the course of centuries.
Hilary Putnam has been responsible for at least two in a single generation: functionalism about mental phenomena, and externalism about
meaning. Major thinkers epitomize the possibilities of the art and
sometimes change them. Putnam has had that kind of dramatic influence on the interpretation of quantum mechanics, on the formulation
of alternative versions of realism, on the relative status of logic and
mathematics, on the development of current pragmatist approaches to
philosophical problems, and on the clarification of the conceptual
settings within which various social scientific investigations take
place. His enquiries into the history, methods, aims and role of
philosophy have stimulated a more widespread and purposeful self-
questioning among its practitioners than could have been predicted
even ten years ago.

This book attempts to satisfy curiosity and stimulate thought about
Putnam's contributions to philosophy, insisting on the importance of
the effect of the whole and opposing the usual emphasis on certain
leading papers. For the primary hermeneutic problem posed by his
work, the question which drives the present enquiry, is the problem of
integrity. How are unity, wholeness and consistency manifest in this
constantly developing body of philosophical argument and writing?

The book is not restricted to the study of what makes Putnam
distinctive as a philosopher however. As the quoted passage indicates,
his interventions in philosophical debate are of a kind that privilege
the present. And this makes current overall context a subject in its
own right, an area of separable interest, and not mere background. To

represent Putnam accurately, therefore, we need not an intellectual portrait alone, but a portrait within a landscape. With this aim in mind, the book exposes his thinking gradually, first examining the fundamental determinants, features of context and character, and then drawing towards the essential contents.

Stimulus

Why interpret Putnam critically? Partly because, of all contemporary philosophers, he is most aptly described as a public thinker. He has reflected his generation to itself, supplying to conscious awareness and the attentive eye those fresh perspectives on old concerns that represent a common intellectual outlook in process of formation. Moreover, he has been effective in doing so, being one of the most influential thinkers of recent times, a philosopher whose authority stretches far beyond the confines of the discipline. This is the more surprising since philosophy matters about as little to our age as poetry does. So Putnam is significant above all because, being unusually sensitive to present conditions, unusually driven to thinking through them, and unusually direct in talking about them, he makes philosophy itself matter.

Other reasons for interpreting Putnam critically look to the future. Our intellectual landscape is very different from that of even a half-century ago, both in its overall shape and in its details. Philosophy at present is in ferment and undergoing yet further changes. If we are to understand how and why this is so, it is to Putnam's work in particular that our attention should be drawn. This is not just because several important transformations can be traced to his writings, though this would be reason enough. More pressingly, Putnam has made the search for the desired shape of future philosophy his particular task. He has spent his career in uneasy relation to his own heritage, so-called "analytic philosophy", asking what the genuine problems are and how we are to tackle them effectively. Much that we should now be attending to has been indicated by him.

These goals motivate. But it is no less stimulating philosophically to survey internal movements, and particularly to discern in the course of Putnam's career the radical effects of discoveries he himself has made. Frequently tearing up the plans projected by his own hard-won earlier findings, his intellectual consistency is measured less by stability of view than by a constant willingness to begin searching anew with fresh guidelines and constraints. This has earned him admiration and puzzlement in equal measure, often from the same quarter.[1] Of all philosophers, Putnam is least likely to be accused of passing off as hard thought mere reshuffles of bias. Some, it must be admitted, are irritated by this irregular reinvention. It is not hard to see why once we register the charge most commonly laid against Putnam by his critics: that he presents a "moving target".[2] But this complaint betrays a comically belligerent conception of the philosophical task. Prey that fails to keep still long enough to be shot down is understandably a source of frustration. Yet there is no obligation to reserve all parts of the philosophical landscape for killing fields. And we certainly have no reason to choose Putnam as our target, so long as we do not mistake him for the truth. Tracking him takes us by unfrequented routes to remarkable places. The costs of pursuit are more than met by the rewards of insight.

Sources

Pursuing a philosopher with so many twists to his career requires immersion in the writing. There is a great deal of this in Putnam's case. Since the mid-1950s, his influence has been central to the generation of research in most areas of philosophy, not just in each of the genera (logic, metaphysics, epistemology), but in most of the species also (philosophy of science, of mathematics, of language and of mind; latterly social and political philosophy). This influence reflects a generous outpouring of ideas in lectures, talks, papers and books. If one were to set about digesting as many of Putnam's papers as would furnish an ambitious tutorial – four per week, say – it would take a full and restless year to cover the material drawn on in this book.

Putnam's published writings in book form comprise (so far) fourteen volumes. There have been differences in output-volume, and certain rhythms to the flow. Thus the years 1962–67 were particularly high, followed by a low between 1968 and 1972. The years 1981–83, 1986–1994 and 1999–2002 were more productive still, with periods of lesser output in between, especially 1995–98.

Putnam is not a writer of monographs. One more or less helpful way to distinguish his books is between collections of papers on the one hand, and collections of lecture series on the other. The former are like compilations of disparate songs recorded by a single artist over some specific period. Five books belong to this first group: *Mathematics,*

Matter and Method (1975), *Mind, Language and Reality* (1975), *Realism and Reason* (1983), *Realism with a Human Face* (1990) and *Words and Life* (1994). The second group, collections of lecture series, are more like songs grouped by a single artist under some specific overarching theme. There are nine books in this category: *Meaning and the Moral Sciences* (the John Locke Lectures for 1976), *Reason, Truth and History* (lectures given at Frankfurt in 1980), *The Many Faces of Realism* (the Paul Carus lectures for 1986), *Representation and Reality* (the Whidden Lectures for 1987), *Renewing Philosophy* (the Gifford Lectures for 1990), *Pragmatism: An Open Question* (the *Lezione Italiane* Lectures for 1992), *The Three-Fold Cord* (the Dewey Lectures for 1994), *The Collapse of the Fact/Value Distinction and Other Essays* (the Rosenthal Lectures for 2000), and *Ethics without Ontology* (the Hermes and Spinoza Lectures for 2001).

Method

With so much to attend to, something has to give. Interpretative criticism is first and foremost a matter of close, engaged reading; and that has been my main concern. This book does not offer a history of the criticisms Putnam has received at various points in his career, nor lengthy contrasts to his views.[3] It is not a work of piety, and so it registers faults where perceived and pertinent. But its fundamental critical goal is interpretative. This aim is modest; it will be achieved if (but only if) the interpretation stimulates or provokes readers to go on to read widely for themselves in Putnam's writings.

The challenge is to present Putnam accurately but accessibly. The usual methods are employed: description, elucidation, comment and critical evaluation. But there are particular problems in drawing Putnam within reach, given the width and diversity of his interests. It is impossible to deal accurately and confidently with any one part of the vast array of his writings without some grasp of the whole. So the key to introducing Putnam lies in mapping the entire spread of his philosophical writings.

It helps that, as a thinker, Putnam is powerfully of a piece. Deeper than any of the surface diversity with which commentaries and complaints have made us familiar, there is a clearly perceptible unity to the work, achieved through repeated engagements with a small set of hard problems: how are we to account for the directedness of experience, thought and language towards the empirical world? And how are we to account for the effect that the world has, in turn, on our experience, thought and use of language? The centrality of these questions to his work has been the spur to reviewing it as a whole and the backbone of this interpretation. So our interpretative criticism will stress essential continuity in the depths at the expense of instability on the surface; it will focus on the core concerns to which Putnam's main ideas have contributed, not on the sets of mutually exclusive claims formulated on the way; and it will highlight what was retained in each move from one stage to another, rather than what was discarded. Above all, it will treat Putnam's current and culminating position as the correct perspective from which to view his central contributions to philosophy, rather than the position held at each or indeed at any single earlier stage of his development. By foregrounding the basic integrity of his work, I hope to present an account that is both true to Putnam and helpful to his readers.

Structure

Putnam's career has spanned one of the most momentous periods of change in the history of science and of philosophy. Like most thinkers who make an original contribution to the world in such circumstances, Putnam had to struggle for release from a cramping environment. To understand him, therefore, we need to be attentive to historical context and particularly the intellectual culture in which his thinking is situated. Without losing sight of his unique and defined presence, sufficient weight must be given to the various external pressures in relation to which he developed his own approach, and to the various internal pressures in relation to which he in turn formulated his original ideas. So what follows has been structured with this primary goal in mind: to present Putnam's contributions in a comprehensible manner by attending to their determinants. In effect, this means moving through the context of his thinking and its character to its contents.

The first part of the book consists of a sketched survey of Putnam's career, and an account of the intellectual climate in which he came to philosophy. The focus is on features of overall context up to the point in time when he was having as much of an effect on contemporary philosophizing as it was having on him.

The second part identifies certain core issues that initially stimulated Putnam and have remained of central concern throughout his career, together with the various methods and argumentative forms to which he has had constant recourse. These issues and methods, which have given character to Putnam's thought and structure to his career, are themselves given character and structure by the place they occupy in contemporary debate. So by investigating them, we gain a sense of the ways in which Putnam's contributions to philosophy have been embedded within recent history of philosophy.

The third and fourth parts of the book survey Putnam's thinking from the 1950s to the present. Three dominant themes run through the discussion. First, Putnam's relation to the philosophy of science, and particularly problems concerning the status of mathematics and logic, the interpretation of quantum mechanics, and the nature of scientific theorizing. Secondly, Putnam's contributions to the philosophy of language, and particularly issues arising in the theory of reference and of meaning. Thirdly, Putnam's relation to the philosophy of mind, and particularly problems concerning the nature of mental phenomena. The argument throughout is simple: Putnam's development depended on a growing appreciation of the importance of intentionality to philosophy, of questions about how it is even possible for subjects and the world to relate, of how a subject's representations can be about the world, of how the world can inform and justify those representations. The ordering in these latter parts of the book is partly chronological and partly topic-based. Over a series of case studies in the areas of philosophy of science, of mind and of language, the argumentative stance is centred first on interpretation and then on application. The aim is to move the reader constantly from questions about what Putnam thought, when and why, to questions about whether he was right. So the focus on discrete issues provides several opportunities to begin evaluating Putnam's work critically.

By singling out what determines the stages of Putnam's development, we discern the thematic patterns of his work, and thereby come to appreciate something of the depths of the philosophical tradition within which it is embedded. For if anything continues to bind the various strands of analytic philosophy, it is an underlying focus on intentionality issues and a unifying appreciation of their unique importance. Since we too are rooted in these depths no less than Putnam himself, we stand to learn something about ourselves, as well as about him, in pursuing this enquiry further.

Part I

Context

Chapter 2

Overview

Find a writer who is indubitably an American in every pulse-beat, snort and adenoid, an American who has something new and peculiarly American to say and who says it in an unmistakable American way, and nine times out of ten you will find that he has some sort of connection with the gargantuan and inordinate abattoir by Lake Michigan.   H. L. Mencken (Dedmon 1953: 283)[1]

Hilary Putnam was born in Chicago in 1926, the son of an author and translator (Samuel Putnam).[2] When he arrived there from New York six years later, Milton Friedman found Chicago to be a "new, raw city bursting with energy, far less sophisticated than New York, but for that very reason far more tolerant of diversity, of heterodox ideas" (Atlas 2000: 6). There is no particular reason to expect instructive parallels between philosophers and their native cities. But the reflection is irresistible in this case. Putnam has an unmistakably American way of doing philosophy and of writing it. Moreover, his approach to the subject has always been open-minded and his voice dissenting, unorthodox, nonconformist.

Putnam moved with his family to Philadelphia in 1934. He remained in the city for his undergraduate studies in mathematics and philosophy at the University of Pennsylvania, graduating in 1948. He then transferred to Los Angeles, where he was supervised in his doctoral work at UCLA by Hans Reichenbach (1891–1953). Reichenbach was later identified by Putnam as one of "the two philosophers who have had the greatest influence on my own philosophical work" (Putnam 1975e: 153). His teacher's areas of specialization included probability theory. Indeed, it was on probability that Reichenbach wrote his doctoral dissertation at the University of Erlangen. A generation later, he supervised Putnam's dissertation on the same subject. Putnam gained his doctorate in 1951 with a dissertation on the application of the concept of probability to finite sequences. The essay was first published nearly forty years later, accompanied by a new authorial introduction (Putnam 1951).

Mathematics and mind

Putnam's first teaching appointments were in mathematics, initially at Northwestern University and then at Princeton. In the late 1950s, along with Martin Davis and Julia Robinson, he answered a number of decision problems related to the tenth of the twenty puzzles bequeathed to posterity by David Hilbert (1862–1943), the German mathematician and advocate of formalism (see Putnam 1975b; 1958; 1960c; 1961b; Davis 1962; 1963; 1973; Robinson 1972a,b; Church 1971).

This relation is emblematic of deeper connections. For as we shall see, the research programme advanced by Hilbert was entirely commensurate with that taught to Putnam by his logical positivist supervisors: a set of assumptions and procedures that were largely responsible for structuring the debates to which his early work contributed. In Hilbert's proof theory, for example, observable facts are the only facts there are, and propositions verifiable by observation and experiment are the only real propositions. And Hilbert was himself concerned to draw parallels between this view and contemporary versions of instrumentalism in his paper "The Foundations of Mathematics" (1967).[3]

The decision problems tackled by Putnam concerned "Diophantine equations".[4] These were named after Diophantus of Alexandria, the third-century Greek mathematician largely responsible for separating Greek algebra from geometric methods, and for introducing symbolic form to denote recurring quantities, operations and powers. His work focused on indeterminate equations, and it was in the margins of a copy of his *Arithmetica* that Fermat notoriously claimed to have proved his last theorem. This was a so-called "impossibility theorem", stating that if $n > 2$, the equation $x^n + y^n = z^n$ cannot be solved in positive integers x, y, z. And an impossibility theorem also lay at the heart of the problems with which Putnam and his colleagues dealt in a series of papers from 1958 onwards.[5]

Also in the late 1950s, Putnam was laying out the features of *functionalism*, a decisively new approach to theories of mental phenomena. The basic idea contrasts the function of a thing with the matter of which it is constituted, and claims that the former is more important than the latter. So the question "how?" becomes more significant than the question "what?" The basic argument for regarding this approach as correct for mental phenomena comes in two steps. First, show that it is the approach to take when accounting for phenomena associated with computing machines. Secondly, show that there is a sufficiently deep and relevant analogy between computing machines and minds to justify the claim that whatever approach should be taken in accounting for the former should be taken in accounting for the latter. John Searle has called the mind–machine analogy "one of the most exciting developments in the entire two-thousand-year history of materialism" (Searle 1992: 43).

We can describe a computer in terms of its software and ignore whatever particular hardware enables it to realize the programs it runs. We concentrate instead on what it does, and in particular its input and output relations. Mental phenomena should be treated in the same way, according to functionalism. The result is that such phenomena are defined in terms of what they are typically caused by and what other mental states or behaviour they typically cause. The question of what constitutes particular minds becomes irrelevant, or at least only as relevant as it ever is to ask what sort of hardware enables some particular model of computing machine to carry out its characteristic and defining functions.

Geometry and realism

While engaged in this work, Putnam took up a post in the philosophy of science at the Massachusetts Institute of Technology (1961). From there, he published a number of papers establishing a robust *realism* in the philosophy of science.

Realism is an elastic term – a useful (perhaps necessary) feature of the word, so long as it is used with care. The basic feature common to all forms of realism is the claim that the nature and existence of whatever things are in question are independent of the nature and existence of minds. But this is to raise more questions than it answers, and the realist's first task is to satisfy curiosity by being more specific. Most importantly, one is never a realist *simpliciter*, but a realist (a) about some subject-matter (e.g. material substance, abstract objects, values) and (b) to some degree – such things are absolutely, or largely, or in some significant way, mind-independent. An increasingly common view holds that "Realism" is "a term with so many applications as to be almost vacuous" (Fowler 2003: 212). But we can reject this message of despair if we set these and related parameters.

There are, of course, many reasons why an entity might be counted as either dependent on, or independent of, minds. But two instances, applied here to the structure of the world, will be of prime importance in what follows. Suppose we argue that the structure of the world is as it would be even if human beings had never theorized about it; moreover, that it is as it is no matter how human beings do theorize about it. Or suppose we argue that the truth about the structure of the world is such that it might be, or might have been, beyond our ability to know about it; that the truth might intelligibly outstrip the evidence. Then we are arguing for a form of realism about the world's structure.

Perhaps the most important instance of Putnam's realism in these years was his intervention in debates on the structure of physical geometry and relativity theory. Prompted in some degree by the directions taken by Reichenbach and certain logical positivists, attempts were made to give detailed form to a *conventionalism* associated with the French philosopher and mathematician Jules Henri Poincaré (1854–1912). On this view, the axioms of geometry are mind-dependent in a particular way: they are conventions freely entered into by human beings and in the end a matter of our own choice, either as individuals or as communities.[6]

Putnam denied that a view of this sort could accurately represent the nature and function of axioms of geometry (Putnam 1959; 1962c; 1963a; 1965a; 1974c; 1975e). It is not up to us whether we should adopt Euclidean or non-Euclidean geometry. There are facts of the matter about which is true. The world should be described by a physical geometry whose curvature changes with time. It is as stating basic empirical properties of space that the axioms of geometry should be regarded.

Meaning and truth

In 1965, Putnam moved to Harvard, the university which had functioned as the summit and source of pragmatism in America. Putnam remained at Harvard until his retirement thirty-five years later, a colleague throughout that time of W. V. O. Quine (1908–2000), who had similar special interests in mathematics and science. Quine is the second of the two philosophers Putnam considers to have had the greatest influence on his work (Putnam 1975e: 153). They were joined in 1968 by Nelson Goodman (1906–98), who published his *Languages of Art* that same year. Goodman's arguments concerning the way pictures are "about" objects and states of affairs tied in with Putnam's thinking on the ways that experiences, thoughts and words are "about" the things they represent.

Putnam went on to hold personal chairs at Harvard in Modern Mathematics and Mathematical Logic. In his first decade there, he helped establish *externalism* (sometimes called *anti-individualism*) as an influential position in the philosophy of mind and language. The slogan Putnam coined for this view is that " 'meanings' just ain't in the head" (Putnam 1975f: 227). The original idea was that what anyone means by a particular type of word, namely terms for natural kinds (e.g. "water"), depends essentially on features of the world they are situated in, and not (or not simply) on features peculiar to them as individuals. But the view has been made to extend to other kinds of word, and beyond what is meant to what is thought and what is experienced. The "Twin-Earth" story Putnam used to launch the original position continues to dominate discussion of the issues arising. It stands as a paradigm thought-experiment: clear, focused, attention-grabbing.

The appearance of more extreme versions of realism in the early 1970s prompted Putnam to think closely about his own long-term advocacy of that position. (Putnam's early realism is often called "scientific"; he himself has disliked the epithet because it smacks of scientism – the view that all knowledge worthy of the name is part of science; Putnam 1976a: 19–20.) Previously he held a view of truth which allowed for the possibility that a scientific theory might *really* be *false* even though it was plausible, simple, conservative, complete, consistent, an accurate predictor of all observations – in other words, *ideal*. Halfway through the decade, he began lecturing publicly on modifications to, and then retractions from, this view.

He came to regard his earlier, radically non-epistemic, version of realism as incoherent for reasons akin to those provided by advocates of verificationism, a position whose tempting features he had long battled against. Realism of this sort implies that an ideal theory lacks something, but is quite unable to say what it lacks; it distances what is held to be verified from what is held to be true without sufficient reason or due cause.

Some early signs of change are present in his John Locke Lectures at Oxford in the spring of 1976 where he took issue with Hartry Field's views as expressed in his 1972 paper "Tarski's Theory of Truth" (Field

2001: 3–26; Putnam 1978a: 9–80). Putnam's adjustments were made in what he described as "intense interaction" with the views of Quine (particularly his doctrines of "indeterminacy of radical translation" and "ontological relativity"), of Goodman (his version of non-realism) and of the Oxford philosopher Michael Dummett (1925–; his anti-realist or verificationist semantics) (Putnam 1978a: vii–ix; 1–6; 1999 (iii)). As a result, Putnam began to emphasize the extent to which the world is to be regarded as dependent on the representations we have of it. But his views continued to change over the next decade, so we should only with great caution follow the standard practice of labelling this his "internal realism" period. If the name is taken to denote some settled position, it fits ill with the developing views expressed by him over these years.

Differing perspectives

Coinciding with this time, which amounted to a period of intense self-criticism, Putnam became increasingly critical of the kinds of philosophy associated with mainstream American philosophy departments.

Perhaps scandalously, no non-misleading names are in common use for this brand of thought. The phrases "analytic philosophy" and "Anglo-American philosophy" are intersubstitutable in current usage without significant change of meaning. The latter name is particularly inaccurate since the roots and early manifestations of this approach are as German–Austrian as they are English. "Analytic philosophy" is the standard label and it will be used here, but with the following caution. Analytic philosophers disagree fiercely among themselves, not only about which answers succeed in resolving which philosophical problem, but also about what the questions are, and even what the goal of philosophy is or should be. It is not to be assumed that there is some one method of analysis to which all proponents subscribe, or that all proponents suppose any philosophical problem can be resolved by analysis alone.

Launched into analytic philosophy in the 1940s, the period of its consolidation in America, Putnam's work was initially both stimulated and guided by this style, quickly becoming recognized as paradigmatic of the approach, and thus in turn stimulating and guiding its progress. Gradually, Putnam began to register unease with the foundational problems and guiding methodologies of analytic philosophy. His concerns stimulated a flood of writing in this period: nine of his sixteen major books and collections are centrally concerned with related themes.

Putnam perceived in the tradition of American *pragmatism* a possible antidote to the moribund character and debilitating effects of analytic philosophy. He has collaborated in papers on the subject with his wife, Ruth Anna, a scholar of the tradition. "I join the pragmatists in utterly rejecting the idea that there is a set of substantive necessary truths that it is the purpose of philosophy to discover" (Putnam 2004a (i): 16). On this view, philosophical reflections have no special status in contrast to everyday thinking. Science should be taken "at face value – without philosophical reinterpretation" (Putnam 1976a (iii): 37). There is no special metaphysical realm of objects and facts for which we need a privileged science and method (philosophy). Philosophy is falsely characterized when treated as a discipline limited to the acquisition of knowledge and the discovery of truths. Philosophy is principally an *activity*, one that is distinguished from other things that we might do, not simply by being more particularly reflective, critical, evaluative and transformative, but by being principally concerned with our life as a whole.

Pragmatism finds various different but interrelated ways of placing emphasis on practice. Charles Sanders Peirce (1839–1914) is perhaps best known for his advocacy of one very strong version of the doctrine: "Consider what effects, which might have conceivably practical bearings, we conceive the object of our conception to have. Then, our conception of these effects is the whole of our conception of the object" (Peirce 1933: vol. 5, 5.402). A weaker version has been advanced with regard to the accuracy of systems of representation. Such systems evolve in practice as new ways are found to make them useful. This might suggest that at the heart of our notion of what makes representational systems accurate is the likelihood of their being successful, together with our appreciation of that likelihood.

A third version can be illustrated by appeal to meaning. In practice, we place great emphasis on procedures for recognizing and concurring with the use of words and other kinds of symbol. This suggests that deeply embedded in our notion of the meaning of such symbols is appreciation of the kinds of situation in which their application is justified, together with recognition of the practical consequences of endorsing their application.

Putnam's interests in pragmatism drew him increasingly to the works of another Harvard philosopher, William James (1842–1910).

He was also influenced by the writings of John Dewey (1859–1952), once chair of the Department of Philosophy, Psychology and Education in Putnam's birthplace. It is Dewey's championing of forms of thinking that are indispensable in everyday life, together with his entreaty that we should take the essential variety of such forms seriously, that has made Putnam include him in his "list of 'heroes'" (Putnam 2004a: 4). The version of pragmatism that Putnam defends, "pragmatic pluralism", combines a Wittgensteinian point with Deweyan application; at its heart is

> the recognition that it is no accident that in everyday language we employ many different kinds of discourses, discourses subject to different standards and possessing different kinds of applications, with different logical and grammatical features – different 'language games' in Wittgenstein's sense – no accident because it is an illusion that there could be just one sort of language game which could be sufficient for the description of all of reality.
>
> (Putnam 2004a (i): 22–3)

The pragmatist influence is particularly marked in Putnam's approach to ethics, a subject to which he has given increasing attention latterly. The point of engaging in ethical activity is essentially the same, whether that activity take the form of reflective thought or immediate action: to "improve the way we deal with specific evils, with the hunger and violence and inequality that mar our world". We should not search for – nor regret the lack of – "universal truths that will infallibly guide all future generations" (Putnam 2004a (i): 31–2). The point of reflective thought on the subject is avowedly not to codify our best practices in some form of moral textbook nor to "distil" a list of principles and maxims out of behaviour intuited by some means or other to be ideal.

Intentionality

In this late period, Putnam began assembling the results of separate investigations made throughout his career on various problems of *intentionality*. (For major instances see Putnam 1960a; 1965b,d,e; 1973a; 1974b; 1975b,c,d,e,f; 1983a; 1991a; 1992a.) But for infrequent lapses, our experience is of the world, it is of the world that we often think, and it is for the express purpose of speaking about the world that our language is generally put to use. What must be true of the world, and of us, and of the relation holding between the world and us, that this should be possible? This is the basic problem of intentionality.

Putnam retired from Harvard in 2000 but has continued to write and lecture on these themes. The main purpose of his most recent publications has been not to offer new key ideas, but to substantiate those of which he has remained convinced. This has meant drawing synchronic connections between those ideas as they occur in particular contested areas of philosophy and as they occur (or may be made to occur) in similar form in other areas, even beyond philosophy. It has also meant drawing diachronic connections between those ideas as they occur now and as they have occurred in the past.

So one collection of essays, appearing in 2002, presents a view Putnam has held for some time: that the alleged dichotomy between statements of fact and statements of value is bogus. It does so by noting the implications of this conclusion (for the science of economics in particular), and by rehearsing the history of debate on the subject. A second collection, appearing in 2004, proceeds in a similar way. Putnam's current position on the intentionality of thought and talk is focused on ethics and narrowed down to the implications for how we should live. Intentionality will not sustain the kinds of (deflationary or inflationary) metaphysics on which ethics has often been thought to depend: an ontology of scheme-independent objects joined to us in what we think and say by uniquely determinate referential relations. Putnam deals with the history of various proposals about what those scheme-independent objects might be ("Goodness" or "The Good", for example), before discussing the implications for ethics of intentionality correctly conceived.

Chapter 3

Analytic philosophy

> In a way it is wrong, or merely academic, to talk of the *influence* of
> European thought on American thought, since the latter is continuous
> with the former. But in so far as the American intellectual conceived of
> the continuity as being an influence, it no doubt was exactly that, and,
> in being that, it was, in its time, useful.
>
> Lionel Trilling, "The Situation of the American Intellectual
> at the Present Time" (2000: 286)

This artful, calculated comment is the centrepiece of an essay written
in 1952, the year after Hilary Putnam completed his doctoral work.
The judgement expresses one, quite influential, point of view concerning American intellectual life at the time his career was launched.

The remark is worth pondering: Putnam's thinking developed
within a context that was itself undergoing significant change. The
immediate task is to relate his career to philosophy as he found it. And
Trilling's comment neatly establishes the basic contours of that
encounter, features whose implications and motive force have played
themselves out in recurrent themes throughout Putnam's career.

Crisis

Consider first the cunning with which Trilling's judgement is delivered. He plays with the disquieting thought that the difference
between something's being plain wrong and its being academic is of
minimal significance (itself *merely* academic?) only to hurry us past for
the bold claim: that American thought has up to now been simply continuous with European thought. And of what value has the European
influence been? Before we can reach Trilling's evaluation, we have to
negotiate a series of sub-clauses, confident that the pile-up is preparing us for a gratifyingly vigorous adjective. "Useful", when it finally
arrives, is deeply, humorously, disappointing.

But shuttle back and the passage bares its teeth: the brief encounter with "merely academic" has primed us for another conclusion. It ranks the useless together with the academic and what is (almost) plain wrong so as to encourage us to prize the useful, by contrast, more highly. Decoded in this way, the comment comes to something more nuanced. Being useful, European influence has been unexciting, perhaps, but positive nonetheless, worthwhile, perhaps even significant. So Trilling encourages us to see the postwar American intellectual as on the one hand beset by certain anxieties of influence, and on the other as driven by the urge to be useful. The past tense in the quoted passage adds a third element, preparing us for Trilling's view that American intellectual life is going through a vivid turning point, a crisis. In his opinion, the tide of European influence is on the ebb: it is no longer "a large, definitive, conscious experience of the American intellectual".

European influence, the virtues of usefulness, the experience of crisis. If these three themes and the moods they reflect were distinctive of the context in which American intellectuals in general found themselves in the 1950s, they are certainly most deeply rooted in the philosophy of that period. And Putnam could stand as the paradigm example, for at the time he was receiving his philosophical education, European influence predominantly meant "analytic philosophy", a label coined in the 1930s but not in regular use until the 1950s.[1] (It is tempting to infer that this was the point at which a large enough number of people recognized that they shared a common philosophical outlook; but a more negative conclusion is equally consistent with the facts: that the name only caught on when the need to identify a target was sufficiently widely appreciated.[2]) And it would be hard to overestimate the impact of the forms of analytic philosophy converging on American philosophy departments during the 1930s and 1940s. By the early 1950s, then, the question of European influence on American philosophy had become pressing; what is the nature of that influence? What is its value? What response should it evoke? And in so far as these are questions about the nature and value of analytic philosophy, they have continued to haunt Putnam.

The influence is particular as well as general since Putnam regarded the European and analytic philosopher Reichenbach as having had the greatest impact on his philosophical work (Putnam 1975e: 153). Another celebrated émigré, Rudolph Carnap, also had a direct influence on Putnam. Their impact on Putnam and on other philosophers was as diverse as their philosophical interests. But with Reichenbach and Putnam specifically in mind, it is important to stress views on space and time, particularly as they relate to philosophy of geometry, the implications of relativity theory, and the problem of the physical basis for the existence of irreversible processes.[3] And central to the Carnap–Putnam relationship were the project of inductive logic, views on the nature of meaning in natural language, and the overall approach to the theory of meaning bequeathed by Carnap to his students and successors which came to be known as "California Semantics" (Putnam 1963b,c; 1970b; 1975d; 1975f).

Trilling's two other themes bear on Putnam in the light of his relationship to European influence and to its specific manifestation as analytic philosophy. The virtues particular to usefulness are appealing to him precisely because they helped articulate his dissatisfaction with analytic philosophy, or at least as that style of thought was expressed when he was a student and under the guidance of a major proponent. These virtues have had their share of philosophical attention largely as a result of pragmatism and the confluence of its various forms in America under the prompting of Peirce, William James and Dewey. The urge to be useful is reflected in Putnam's commitment to making philosophical thought practical, purposeful, efficient.

Finally, the experience of crisis in intellectual life is reflected in diverse ways in Putnam's writing. Each speaks to a questioning of modes of thought in their general aspect and in their particular characteristics, a scrutiny of those types of philosophy associated historically with a predominantly European setting, and of those types associated with the irruption of analytic philosophy into America. This sense of, and appreciation for, intellectual crisis has affected Putnam's own thought in a number of ways: for example, in his preparedness to treat models of philosophical thinking as contingent, adaptive, subject to constant pressure. His approach is particularly sensitive to the subjection or distortion that can occur when one way of thinking is brought into connection with another. Putnam has responded by regarding vulnerability to change as not only a fact, but welcome.

In short, we cannot hope to understand Putnam's philosophical career without attributing due significance to the themes identified by Trilling as pressing quite generally on American intellectuals of the time. To recall the phrase with which Putnam launches one of his most important discussions of contemporary philosophy, "We start, then, with a cultural situation" (Putnam 1975d: 2).

Hilary Putnam

The method of analysis

There were several strands to what became generally known after the Second World War as "analytic philosophy", and considerable interweaving of the filaments. But that name came to seem the most convenient overall description, both because of what it implied and what it left open.

All its proponents could be expected to agree that the methods and progress of philosophy depended on processes of analysis. But the name did not imply commitment to any particular notion of what those processes were, or of whether indeed there was more than one, or of exactly how the problems of philosophy could be made to surrender to that analysis, or of which problems would thereby be resolved and which justifiably ignored, having lost their status as real problems. There was (and is) considerable disagreement about these matters among philosophers accurately described as "analytic". And these deep differences of opinion have been responsible for stimulating much of Putnam's own most significant work. But whatever the differences dividing the great representatives of the approach and their disciples, there exists a wide consensus that rests on more or less wholehearted endorsement of the following principles.

Knowledge is acquired through relevant experience, careful observation, controlled experiment, together with the appropriate use of reason, logic and calculation. To enable sound reasoning, we develop logically connected structures of rules, laws and generalizations which are at best demonstrable and at least supported by high degrees of confirmation. It is only by being public and communicable that any statement with a claim to being true can count as such. Many of these statements must also be in some way testable, capable of verification or falsification, by methods that are open to and endorsed by relevant experts in the community. Personal intuitions and dogmatic assertions are as dubious as self-styled pieces of knowledge whose sources or means of justification turn out to be non-natural or non-rational. The natural and applied sciences represent the most successful application of these methods. The laws they establish as governing the behaviour of inanimate bodies, animals and plants constitute exemplary conclusions. But these principles also apply to abstract disciplines, such as logic and mathematics, and stretch beyond the social sciences to the discovery of moral and aesthetic norms and principles. Not all questions are in principle answerable, perhaps; but those that are not are little or nothing to us.

These principles bear a striking resemblance to standard Enlightenment doctrines, of course: only slight modification is necessary to make possible translation from one set to the other.[4] So we are still somewhat in the dark as to what is particularly distinctive about analytic philosophy. It would be hard to find a self-description that better captured what all adherents tend to say when pressed than this: philosophers in the analytic tradition "think that the best way to promote profitable discussion is to be as clear as possible with oneself about what one sees and judges, to try and establish the essential discriminations in the field of interest, and to state them as clearly as one can (for disagreement if necessary)" (Leavis 1948: 1).[5] But the fact that something is amiss becomes clearly apparent when we note that the person articulating this code of practice is not even a philosopher, let alone an analytic philosopher, and that he is regulating not philosophical method but the practice of literary criticism. The difficulty is not with the code itself. For there are good reasons to achieve a simple style of writing which plainly represents the content and connectives of one's argument, and avoids unnecessary awkwardness and obscurity.[6] Indeed, some of the reasons for promoting a form of this sort are clearly ethical: the style that pronounces judgement should expose itself to judgement. The problem is rather with the use of the code to define and delimit a certain way of doing philosophy: clarity and openness to disagreement are features common to a large number of activities, and not even just academic disciplines. If this is the best that advocates of analytic philosophy can produce by way of self-definition, then that manner of philosophizing begins to appear as a style in search of a character, a defining form that lacks delimiting content.[7]

Frege, Moore, Russell

This was not always the case. Analytic philosophy was once as rigorous in defining itself as it was in defining the problems it wrestled with.

The fundamentals of the approach are to be found in the successes in logical analysis achieved by Gottlob Frege (1848–1925) and others in the project of deducing the fundamental principles of mathematics from purely logical laws. This project required considerable work in logic and in the philosophy of language because its basic dimension was semantic. It propounded a thesis about the meaning of mathematical statements that required their systematic translation into a

21

formal language that accurately represented logical relations. On Frege's own view, for example, statements about natural numbers are about the extensions of certain concepts. So the number 9 is to be analysed as the extension of the concept that pertains to all and only those concepts that apply to exactly nine objects. Analyses of this sort could only be achieved by developing new logical apparatus. But once forged, this apparatus could be used to solve a large number of philosophical problems.

One optimistic and generalized version of this analytic approach was represented by G. E. Moore (1873–1958), a Cambridge philosopher who taught in America during the Second World War and had a deep influence on subsequent developments there. Analysis for him meant getting clear about the meaning of disputed questions in philosophy. Moore's version was optimistic because he believed such questions would be answered once their meaning was clarified:

> The work of analysis and distinction is often very difficult: we may often fail to make the necessary discovery, even though we make a definite attempt to do so. But I am inclined to think that in many cases a resolute attempt would be sufficient to ensure success; so that, if only this attempt were made, many of the most glaring difficulties and disagreements in philosophy would disappear.   (Moore 1993, preface to 1st edn: 33)

Moreover, Moore held that our ordinary uses of language are in sufficiently good order not just to provide evidence of what is the case, but also perspicuously to represent it once the analysis is achieved. Moore's version was generalized because he did not suppose that resolution of the problems of philosophy depended on one unique or privileged process of analysis.

The first question on which he tried out the approach was the nature of what there is. His target here was the idealism of F. H. Bradley (1846–1924) and T. H. Green (1836–82), which claimed that reality is an un-dissectable unity and spiritual in nature. In his refutation, Moore argued that reality is a plurality, made up of an indefinite multiplicity of things which themselves fall into different kinds: mental, material, abstract. Within philosophical circles, his method of analysis is strongly associated with his attempts to bring down to earth those flights of abstract theorizing that contradict common sense. But his analytic approach reached its widest audience with the publication of his *Principia Ethica* in 1903, an event that John Maynard Keynes described as "exciting, exhilarating, the beginning of a renaissance, the opening of a new heaven on earth (Keynes 1949: 81–2).

Others took an equally enthusiastic view of the nature and competence of analysis, prompted in large part by the following thoughts. If mathematical statements can be translated into formal language, then so can ordinary sentences. This process of analysis is revealing: it will disclose the deep logical form underlying the surface grammar of such sentences. And logical form is surely more basic: it is what ordinary sentences are trying to express. Moreover, this analytic process is powerful: it will turn the oddities and confusions of surface grammar into clear, precise, transparent representations. It will be obvious exactly what it is that ordinary sentences are trying to express. Finally, this analytic process is useful, in particular for philosophy, whose problems have been expressed in ordinary language and often inherit its quirks and muddles. If philosophical puzzles were to be analysed and expressed so as to reveal their logical form, they would become more tractable; some even might simply evaporate.

Bertrand Russell (1872–1971) exemplifies this version of the analytic approach. In the first years of the twentieth century, he became increasingly confident of the potential of specifically logical analyses in clarifying and resolving philosophical puzzles. In order to show that the problems of pure mathematics reduce to problems in pure logic, it had been necessary to find a systematic way of translating statements of the former into the language of the latter, and in particular to find a logical redefinition of relations such as "implication" and terms such as "proposition", "constant" and "variable". The aim was to show that, behind the whole variety of forms of reasoning which in the past had been called pure mathematics, there lies something very simple: a logical form consisting of propositions containing variables and logical constants which assert "p implies q". Russell became convinced that those selfsame tools of logical analysis could be applied to language. They would reveal what lies beneath the surface of ordinary usage: the logical form of what is being said, consisting again of propositions related by implication. And this would have spectacular consequences for philosophy, whose problems are, after all, framed using language. The whole variety of such problems could be reduced by logical analysis to their clearest form: the logical form of what is being asserted. And then it would be a relatively straightforward matter to resolve them.

Russell showed off this approach in one of the founding documents of analytic philosophy: the paper "On Denoting" of 1905. We tend to assume that there must be an object for any meaningful and grammatically correct referring expression: the object for which it stands. This is straightforward enough for proper names such as "Elizabeth Windsor". But what is the object corresponding to "the queen of New York" or "the round square"? Some were tempted to treat the problem as one of ontology – of what kinds of item we should admit into our lists of things that "are" or "have being". For one way to solve the problem consistently with the initial assumption is just to say that there are unreal objects; that a member of the class of things that "are" is the subclass of nonexistents, and that these items simply have being to a lower degree than items that exist. So suppose there is such an unreal object corresponding to "the queen of New York"; then it is in virtue of standing in a certain relation to this object that the phrase has the meaning it does. Russell resisted not only this solution but also this way of conceiving the problem. In his view, it was not an ontological problem at all and so should not be resolved by ontological means. Exploiting his method of analysis, he offered an alternative conception of the problem and an alternative solution equally consistent with the initial assumption.

The problem, in Russell's view, was essentially one of logic. Problematic phrases such as "the queen of New York" generate contradictions unless their true logical form is recognized. Consider two sentences, (a) "Round squares do not exist"; (b) "The queen of New York exists".

(1) Sentence (a) is true; sentence (b) is false.
(2) (Given (1)), sentences (a)–(b) must be meaningful.
(3) Sentences (a)–(b) are subject–predicate sentences.
(4) Subject–predicate sentences are true (false) iff there is an object to which the subject-term refers, and that object has (does not have) the property expressed by the predicate.
(5) (Given (1)–(4)), there must be objects to which the subject-terms of sentences (a)–(b) refer.
(6) No objects have the property of not existing; if there are objects to which the subject-terms of these meaningful sentences refer, then they exist.
(7) (Given (5)–(6)), sentence (a) must be false; sentence (b) must be true.

Since the truth-values of these sentences have been reversed, a contradiction has been generated. In Russell's view, this is just one of several contradictions which will always arise in systems that treat phrases such as "the queen of New York" as having the logical form their surface grammar suggests instead of the logical form they actually have.[8] So his solution is similarly logical and not ontological. Surface grammar tells us that phrases such as "the queen of New York" are *bona fide* denoting phrases and possible subjects in a subject–predicate sentence. That is why, in line with the initial assumption, their having the meaning they do seems to call for a corresponding object. But analysis of sentences containing this phrase and of the propositions they express reveals that their underlying logical form is not that of denoting phrases at all, but of existential statements (e.g. "There is exactly one queen of New York") which can be conjoined with other predicative sentences to form those of the kind we have examined (i.e. "There is exactly one queen of New York, and she exists"). It is not necessary to find corresponding objects to explain the meaning of *non*-denoting phrases: they may get their meaning in other ways. So we need not be embarrassed by the fact that there is no object corresponding to "the queen of New York". Indeed, once the logical form of the problematic sentence is revealed, it bears its truth-value plainly on its face: the first conjunct is false; there is no queen of New York.

Thus an apparently deep philosophical problem with implications for ontology stands revealed as a merely misleading feature of surface grammar. And the means by which this revelation is achieved are those advocated by Russell as at the heart of philosophical method: the analysis of language using the tools of logic. The methodology associated with this approach came to maturity with the impact of the early work of Ludwig Wittgenstein (1889–1951) on a mainly Austrian and English audience in the 1920s. America received the full impact of these ideas with Hitler's rise to power in 1933.

European influence

The migration of intellectuals which followed the disastrous political developments in Germany has greatly contributed to an exchange of the various standards of civilisation; and I for one cannot but be grateful to a fate which led me into various countries, not as a traveller, but as a teacher and collaborator in the education of youth . . . I have seen that the logistic approach to philosophy is not bound to a certain type of mind, or of milieu or of educational system, but represents a most successful clarification of ideas, by which all forms of scientific pursuit will profit.

(Reichenbach 1947: v)

This is Reichenbach's ringing endorsement of the intellectual developments associated with his exile in America. It was published in the Preface of his *Elements of Symbolic Logic* in 1947, the year before Putnam arrived as one of his pupils. This formative association between a major representative of European analytic philosophy and a rising star of American philosophy was representative of changes that had been under way in American philosophy departments since 1933. Putnam himself would later echo Reichenbach's judgement, noting specifically in relation to the enforced exile of philosophers like his teacher that "it is amply clear . . . that the toleration of philosophical and scientific speculation brings rich rewards and that its suppression leads to sterility" (Putnam 1963c: 304).

The "disastrous political developments" to which Reichenbach refers had caused major positivist thinkers and analytic philosophers, many of them Jewish or Marxist–Socialist, to emigrate in successive waves over the next decade. Moritz Schlick (1882–1936) was murdered in 1936 on the steps of his own university in Vienna by a deranged doctoral student later exonerated by the Nazi authorities. Reichenbach left Germany in 1933 and eventually found his way to California. He was joined there in 1941 by Alfred Tarski (1901–83), whose parents had been killed by the Nazis. Rudolf Carnap (1891–1970) left Prague for Chicago in 1936; he succeeded to Reichenbach's chair at UCLA in 1954 on the latter's death. Among other celebrated émigrés of similar stamp were Herbert Feigl (1890–1945) who had been the first to leave Germany for America in 1931; Friedrich Waismann (1896–1959) and Otto Neurath (1882–1945), who both went to Oxford; Kurt Gödel (1906–78), who left Vienna for Princeton in 1939; and Carl Hempel (1905–97), who left Berlin for Brussels in 1934, then emigrated to America in 1939 on whose East Coast he remained until moving to Pittsburgh in 1977. The arrival of these forceful thinkers focused the attention of philosophers in America on logical analysis, mathematical logic and philosophy of science. Analytic philosophy steadily gained the upper hand, taking hold of departments throughout much of the country in a grip that lasted throughout the second half of the century and shows few signs of relaxation in the new millennium.

American philosophy departments had previously been characterized by the pluriformity of their attachments and the sheer variety of the approaches that they took to philosophy. Beyond this, Kantian idealism had exercised a certain hold. Critical realism was heralded by the publication of a book with that title (1916) by Roy Wood Sellars (1880–1973), and of *Essays in Critical Realism* (1920), to which

George Santayana (1863–1952) contributed. Finally, pragmatism was at its height in American philosophy in the early part of the century, continuing to influence debate considerably in the interwar period. William James and John Dewey were particularly influential figures in this tradition. The pragmatist approach would come to be of vital importance to Putnam much later in his career. (On pragmatism: Putnam 1974b; 1992b (i)–(iii); 1992d; 1994b; 2004a *passim*. On James: Putnam 1988b; 1989a; 1992b (i)–(iii). On Dewey: Putnam 1990c; 1992a; 1993c; 2004a (i)–(v).) Its conception of philosophy and of its goals was naturalist, which concurred with the views of Reichenbach and his associates. All agreed that the findings of the natural sciences should be accorded the deepest respect. But Dewey developed a broad conception of the natural, one which included other features of human life besides those facts about it discoverable by science. Indeed, this conception allowed him to reject for naturalist reasons any fundamental dichotomy between facts and values, and to extend equal respect to all endeavours that shed light on aspects of human life. During the early parts of his career, Putnam was as heavily influenced as other American philosophers by the considerably less generous model of naturalism and of what it is possible to think about philosophically brought over by Reichenbach and others, and then passed on to their students. This was the broadly positivist conception of analytic philosophy characteristic of the Vienna Circle.

Viennese positivism

The positivist tradition was strong in Vienna. A new professorship in the philosophy of the inductive sciences had been created there in 1895 and the physicist Ernst Mach (1838–1916) appointed to it. His work on the science of mechanics drew sharp contrasts between science and speculative metaphysics, with the former standing for the fruitful reduction of the strange to the familiar, and the latter for the barren replication of myths and false seemings as a defence against the inevitable disillusion effected by science-based progress.[9] Mach was succeeded in his chair (1902) by another renowned physicist: Ludwig Boltzman (1844–1906). Both promoted the view that the aim of philosophy was not simply to show how the temptations to the metaphysics of German Romanticism and Idealism might be resisted, but to analyse scientific concepts and to clarify the logic of science.

Given these directives, it is easy to see why this approach would later acquire the label *logical positivism.*

Neurath began holding discussions with scientists, mathematicians and philosophers on related topics in Vienna from 1907; members of the so-called *"Ur-Kreis"* or "prehistoric circle" included the mathematician Hans Hahn (1879–1934; appointed to a chair in mathematics at Vienna in 1921) and the physicist Philip Frank (1884–1966) (Feigl 1981). In 1922, Schlick inherited Mach's chair and the group gathered around him, meeting regularly for discussion in the interwar years. The members comprised about twenty regulars, all of whom had scientific or mathematical training. They included many of those who would later emigrate: Carnap (taught by Frege), Neurath (a fellow student of Hahn and Frank), Waismann (taught by Hahn and Schlick), Feigl (taught by Schlick), Gödel. Others were not members of the group but closely associated with it. Reichenbach, for example, was a Berlin scientific philosopher (alongside Hempel and Einstein), but was associated with the circle through his friendship with Carnap. The "Vienna Circle" was so designated and publicly announced as such in 1929 with the publication of a manifesto by Carnap and Neurath; Schlick was the dedicatee. Only two visitors were ever invited to join the group before it was disbanded in 1938: the Oxford philosopher A. J. Ayer (1910–89) and W. V. O. Quine, who attended meetings before following Carnap to Prague and Tarski to Warsaw in 1933. Something of the flavour of the group is given by a student's account of his introduction to Neurath: "Neurath's first question was: 'What is your study?' I answered 'Philosophy'. 'Do you read mathematics, physics?' 'No,' I said, 'pure philosophy'. 'Do you devote yourself to anything as dirty as that? Why not straight theology?'" The student continues: "I was shocked but in less than an hour had already fallen under Neurath's spell" (Neurath & Cohen 1973: 46). The Vienna Circle was particularly sensitive to two sources of stimulation: the problems posed by Einstein's theory of relativity, and the approach taken by Ludwig Wittgenstein's *Tractatus Logico-Philosophicus* (1921). Characteristic of this group was the belief that philosophy consists in the logical clarification of thoughts by analysis, and the conviction that the residue cannot be a list of substantial philosophical propositions. For philosophizing over ancient and apparently deep puzzles results in one of two outcomes: in suitably clarified questions that may now be turned over to the natural sciences for resolution, or in questions about which nothing at all can be said.

The philosophical implications of relativity theory spoke most clearly for the first outcome. Philosophers had been awed by Kant's apparent demonstration that the fundamental laws of Newtonian mechanics (inertia; conservation of matter; equality of action and reaction) were not only true but knowable *a priori*: that is, without relying on any justification by the character of one's experience. But these laws are not even universally valid, let alone *a priori*, in the conception of space, time and motion brought about by Einstein's revolution in physics.

Several explanations for the second outcome were prevalent, but the two most common were Wittgenstein's position in the *Tractatus* and that which came to be known as *verificationism*. The former requires silence about those questions that are meaningful only in one mode (what can be shown) but seem to call inappropriately for resolution in another mode (what can be said). The latter requires dismissal of those questions that are not meaningful in any mode, there being neither the means of observation nor the forms of reasoning to ascertain the truth about them. This position (which we will examine more closely in Chapter 4) is most commonly identified with the logical positivism of the Vienna Circle. But Putnam himself has argued that it was formulated much earlier, within the pragmatist tradition, by Charles Sanders Peirce (Putnam 1974b: 272–90; esp. 272). And there does indeed appear to be a verificationist aspect to Peirce's view that the meaning of an "intellectual conception" is identical with the sum of its practical consequences. Putnam's view here reflects an interpretation of the history of philosophy which has far broader coverage. He has claimed that pragmatism beat analytic philosophy to the post on a key issue essential to the way many characterize the latter enterprise. It is pragmatism that should count as "the first philosophy dedicated to the proposition that theory of meaning can solve or dissolve the traditional problems of philosophy" (Putnam 1974b: 272).

But the links with pragmatism should not be exaggerated. Any naturalism which might be consistent with the *Tractatus* conception or with verificationism will contrast deeply with that held by pragmatists such as Dewey. According to the former, the only endeavours that truly shed light on human life are the natural sciences. Philosophy is little more than a clearing house, preparatory to scientific work. In so far as we can even make sense of other features of human life, such as values, it is because they reflect facts that it is the business of science to investigate. Those questions that science cannot investigate after philosophy has rendered them down to their clearest form – questions raised by traditional metaphysics, or by religious statements, for example – are all equally and simply meaningless.

The logical positivism dominating Putnam's philosophical education sprang from developments of positions taken early on in analytic philosophy. The positivist's emphasis on sense-experience, observation and the central position of scientific methods and results was an obvious point of contact with the style of anti-idealism adopted by Moore and Russell. Their view that the truths of mathematics are analytic grew out of the logicism associated with Frege and Russell, that mathematics is reducible to logic. Their claim that physical objects were logical constructions out of sense-data had been anticipated by Russell. Their view that linguistic analysis comprises all that is characteristically philosophical was motivated by successes achieved early in the century, basing philosophical analysis on various kinds of reduction to logical form. Their claim that all meaningful sentences are either analytic (true in virtue of meaning alone), contradictory or empirical grew out of Wittgenstein's view (in the *Tractatus* period) that such sentences are either tautologous, contradictory or synthetic (true in virtue of both meaning and the way the world is).

These views have implications for the nature and value of philosophy; its possible purposes and likely achievements; what methods are proper to it; the relative roles of philosophy, the natural sciences and other ways of gathering intelligence about human life; the nature and role of observation in science; the nature of meaning and what philosophy has to offer in elucidating it; how we are to understand the relation between facts and values, between descriptions and evaluative judgements. And these topics have in turn been central concerns for Putnam throughout his career.

Part II

Character

Chapter 4

Structural issues

> He saw that he was confronted, actually, with two propositions. The
> first was simple: "The circumstances are such that I must concentrate
> on so-and-so". The second was less simple: "The circumstances *have
> been so contrived as to suggest* that I must concentrate on so-and-so".
> In pursuing the first proposition he must, at least, not lose sight of the
> second.
>
> Michael Innes, *Death at the President's Lodging* (1958: 18–19)

Midway through his career, Putnam reflected on its beginnings. He
stressed four basic issues on which he had been most susceptible to
influence: realism, rationality, meaning and intentionality (Putnam
1975e: 153–91). Their combination produced a fifth: a function-based
approach. Each issue speaks of the impact of European philosophers in
general and of positivists such as Reichenbach in particular. Each
expresses themes that, in isolation and in combination, provide structure to his philosophical contributions.

In retrospect, Putnam's thinking has been susceptible to two kinds
of basic stimulus and inspiration. What we might call the "core influences" were positions taken on basic issues that affected his thinking
at its heart; "structural influences" were positions taken on basic
issues that shaped and organized his thinking, but not in quite so fundamental a way. Of the five issues just mentioned, a function-based
approach and intentionality belong to the first set, and realism, rationality and meaning to the second. In order to appreciate the role
that the core influences played, we must first examine the structural
influences.

Putnam has responded to the influences on him in various ways.
Some could later be endorsed as true guides: they showed the way to
genuine philosophical problems on which it is necessary to concentrate. Other influences turned out to be mere contrivances: they made
it seem that there were philosophical problems in areas where actually
there are none. Like Michael Innes's detective in the epigraph,

however, Putnam seems to have regarded the contrived second category as almost as interesting and important as the veridical first; certainly, he has kept his eye constantly upon it.

We might hazard a guess as to why this should be. Contrivances have less to say about the issues philosophy ought directly to be concerned with. But they are much more revealing about the nature and enterprise of philosophizing itself. This is for the same reason that, in certain kinds of novel, we stand to learn a good deal about the character of unreliable narrators from the false stories they tell. Where reliable narrators enable us to say what is going on, unreliable narrators cause us to ask "Why *would* this character present what is genuinely going on as if it were not, and vice versa?" And the answers reveal psychological determinants that narrators, reliable or unreliable, might otherwise hide: for example, aspects of their character and of what motivates them. Similarly, if we want to know what characterizes some particular way of doing philosophy, we should ask "Why *would* this approach present what is genuinely problematic as if it were not, and vice versa?" The answer will reveal things that the approach itself almost certainly renders opaque: for example, what stimulates or induces it. This is itself a philosophical question and one that feeds into the deeper issue of how philosophy should be done.

Both questions are of interest to Putnam. More specifically, he enquires into what *does* stimulate and inform analytic philosophy, what gives it the character it has, so as to judge it by what *should*. Thus it is necessary to gain acquaintance with both categories of influence on his work: the veridical influences that present genuine problems, and the illusory influences that present contrived problems.

Realism

Access to the first area of influence may be gained through problems in the philosophy of mathematics, and particularly what the theory of knowledge should say about the existence of several possible systems of geometry. Putnam spent considerable time on this problem, although he ended in a different place from that indicated by the direction in which Reichenbach had been travelling.

The problem received its contemporary form as a result of discoveries in geometry that seemed to call for modification, if not rejection, of the position taken by Kant. In Kant's view, the axioms of geometry as described by Euclid are necessary (they could not but have been true) *a priori* (knowable independently of the character of experience) but not analytic (true in virtue of their meaning alone). Kant came to the conclusion that the axioms are synthetic on the grounds that geometric proofs are spatiotemporal objects and need to be appreciated as such. Hence the reasoning by which these axioms are arrived at depends not just on the purely logical analysis of concepts, but on what he called "construction in pure intuition" (Kant 1933: A 715–17; B 743–45; see Friedman 1992: 55–95). One problem arose with the invention of non-Euclidean systems of geometry and different sets of axioms. Suppose we want to determine which of these mathematically possible but incompatible systems actually holds for the space of physics. If Kant is right and geometry is *a priori*, we will not be able to appeal to experience.

One option is to renounce the *a priori* claim and try to determine which system is correct by making physical measurements: Gauss advocated this approach. But most philosophers resisted so wholesale a rejection of the Kantian doctrine and looked instead for alternative, non-experiential, reasons for preferring one system of geometry over another. This was the context in which the conventionalism advanced by Poincaré in his *Science and Hypothesis* (1905) came to prominence. The view was motivated by his observation that physicists are able to ascribe any possible but incompatible systems of geometry to physical space consistently with whatever facts are observed to obtain. In order to accommodate differences, they need only make suitable adjustments to various secondary laws within any system, such as those describing mechanics, optics and the rules for measuring length.

On the conventionalist approach, the axioms of geometry are conventions governing the description of space whose adoption is governed by their utility in furthering the purpose of that description. Since these axioms do not state fundamental empirical properties of space – the world does not possess an "intrinsic" metric (length, for example, is not an "intrinsic" property of physical objects) – the difference between representing space in Euclidean and non-Euclidean terms admits certain empirical constraints but is in the end a matter of choice.[1] If the equality of different time sequences can only be understood relative to some particular system, as seems to be the case, then it may seem that such equality is itself to be defined by convention and not determined by empirical facts of the matter. Thus choosing which set of geometric axioms to adopt is not unlike choosing whether to register one's weight in kilos or pounds, one's height in centimetres or feet, one's land in metres or yards, one's drink in litres or pints. It is quite consistent with the overall view to claim that our choice is constrained empirically: good reasons may exist for choosing one system over the other. Thus the metric system may be simpler to apply than the imperial, guaranteeing its eventual domination. But the basic point remains: it is up to us which system we should choose, and it would make no sense to worry about which of them is *true*.

The logical positivists were more than tempted by the idea that twentieth-century revolutions in physics supported conventionalism. Of course, this general view in the philosophy of science pre-dated the discovery in physics of the general theory of relativity. Some changes had to be made as a result. For example, Poincaré had argued that, though a convention like any other, Euclidean geometry would always be preferred by physicists because of its simplicity. He was wrong in this contingent aspect of his theory: the simplicity gained for physics by using non-Euclidean axioms in expressing the general theory of relativity justified adoption of a more complex geometry. But the overall position remained widely held.

Putnam began developing a realist position to counter this view: one that stressed the mind-independence of the axioms of geometry. To be more specific, he claimed that the axioms of geometry should be regarded as stating fundamental empirical properties of space; that the truth about these axioms might intelligibly transcend the evidence for them; that it makes a good deal of sense to ask whether Euclidean or non-Euclidean geometry is true; that the world should be described by a physical geometry whose curvature changes with time; and that this is not a matter of choice. In detailed exposition, Putnam was not confronting Reichenbach's wary defence of conventionalism but Adolf Grünbaum's (1923–) keen espousal of the thesis (*Philosophical Problems of Space and Time* of 1963).[2] Grünbaum based his argument on the claim that continuous physical space and time are metrically amorphous. Putnam agreed that there are elements of decision and choice in science, in particular as regards aspects of history (e.g. the initial acceptance of explanatory theories) and features of terminology (e.g. the shapes and sounds of the words formulating those theories). But convention has no more part to play than this ultimately rather trivial role. So if this is all conventionalism comes to, it is a trivial thesis. If it gives convention a more significant role, it is a false thesis.

Putnam's realism concerning the axioms of geometry gave expression to aspects of a developing realist perspective that characterized his approach to philosophy of science in the first part of his career:

> The statements of science are in my view either true or false (although it is often the case that we don't know which) and their truth or falsity does not consist in their being highly derived ways of describing regularities in human experience. Reality is not a part of the human mind; rather the human mind is a part – and a small part at that – of reality.   (Putnam 1975a: vii)

On this view, it is the proper aim of science to formulate true theories that depict the structure of the world. The best explanation of why the history of science has progressed and achieved its various successes is partly that our theories have depicted this structure with ever-increasing accuracy, and partly that this structure is (largely) independent of human theorizing. There are three basic features of this realism that are particularly worth noting.

First, scientific statements purport to express truths about states of affairs only some of which concern the human mind. Hence it is not their business to rest content with merely advancing opinion, nor with stating truths that merely represent how things are in a particular mind or minds in general, nor with expressing emotional responses to states of affairs, whether those states concern human minds or not.

Secondly, the truths expressed by scientific statements might intelligibly transcend our ability to know about them. Hence such truths are not limited to those for which evidence of their truth exists, let alone those over which we have and are able to exercise relevant abilities – for example, the ability to recognize as evidence whatever counts as such; to gather and assemble that evidence into a coherent and consistent whole; to draw sound conclusions from that evidence by valid argument forms; and so on.

Thirdly, the truths about states of affairs expressed by scientific statements are such that they would hold whether or not, and however, humans had ever theorized about them. Hence those truths are not limited to those for which we have, or might have, theories. To be sure, reality (which includes human minds) is of such a sort that its accurate description requires the methods and concepts distinctive of the various investigative sciences and of theoretical science. But the nature and existence of reality is independent of such descriptions: it would exist, and exist as it is, without them.

Rationality

A second Reichenbachian project influencing Putnam – and one most closely related to Carnap – was the attempt to clarify the philosophical foundations of two related topics: induction and probability. Indeed, Putnam has described Carnap's work on inductive logic as having "the sort of importance . . . that Frege's work had for deductive logic in the first years of this century" (Putnam 1963c: 294). Reichenbach advanced a version of the frequency theory of induction. Induction is a satisfactory means of drawing justified conclusions, he thought, even though there can be no fully satisfactory and final proof of this. It is to be analysed empirically through calculations on discovered frequencies, for probabilities are not assigned by evenly distributing the total possible number of outcomes. If it had been correct to estimate probabilities in this manner, we might have been justified in coming to conclusions about probabilities without reflection on the character of our experience. But the probability of an event having some outcome is to be estimated instead as the converging limit of a long series of such events. As such, knowledge of that probability cannot be gained independently of experience.

Putnam found these and immediately related topics sufficiently important to focus his doctoral work on them. In later papers, he stressed that the purpose of inductive logic is to construct a universal learning machine (Putnam 1963c: 293–304). And this provides a direct link between his early attention to problems of induction and probability and his later work on mental phenomena. The development of his functionalist approach came about through his attempts to modify Turing machines (computers scanning a potentially infinite linear tape) so as to create a plausible analogy between their workings and mental processes such as preferring. The modification proceeded by conceiving of such machines not simply as finite and equipped to interact with the environment, but as rational agents. And the model of rationality Putnam used was determined partly by inductive logic.[3] So the ability to estimate the probability of states of affairs was of maximal importance in the conception of modified Turing machines, and hence in the conception of functionalism itself.

Meaning

The third area of philosophical influence on Putnam's career concerns the verifiability theory of meaning. It is worth getting clear about the complex of issues involved because they had a major impact on Putnam's thinking and on that of his contemporaries.

Theories have been taken to count as verifiability theories if they claim that the meaningfulness of a statement and its verifiability in principle are taken to imply each other. Versions of this claim, which came to be known as the "verification principle", held a central place in logical positivism and in the discussions of the Vienna Circle. Advocates often supposed, with more incaution than good reason, that they had the full endorsement of Wittgenstein's *Tractatus*. The relationship between the two is a complex issue and bears on what follows. *Tractatus* states: "To understand a proposition means to know what is the case, if it is true" (§4.024). This has seemed to some to express a theory of meaning that bypasses what can be verified in order to ground itself in what is true. Truth plausibly makes for a deeper underpinning than verification, for, plausibly, nothing can be verified unless it is true, but something can be true and yet not even in principle be verifiable. Hence, although one courts anachronism in saying this, the *Tractatus* could be interpreted as supporting something akin to a so-called *truth-conditional* theory of meaning, rather than a verificationist one.[4]

But the question is not settled so easily. Combined with the view that the truth of a proposition cannot transcend our ability to verify or falsify it, this claim might actually express a version of verificationism. And there are other parts of the *Tractatus* (e.g. "In order to discover whether the picture is true or false we must compare it with reality" (§2.223); "[The picture] is like a scale applied to reality" (§§4.024; 2.1512)) that support a reading of the following sort: to understand a proposition is to know its meaning; to know its meaning is to know what is the case if it is true; to know what is the case if it is true is to verify or falsify it by seeing how it squares with reality; and hence the meaningfulness of a proposition depends on its being verifiable or falsifiable. This interpretation goes some way towards the kind of verificationism advocated by members of the Vienna Circle – the kind to be described in a moment. But not all the way. For although it makes an unverifiable proposition meaningless, it does not identify the meaning of a proposition with its method of verification. Only considerably later, and for a comparatively short time, did Wittgenstein hold this much stronger form of verificationism (Wittgenstein 1975: 66–7; 77).[5]

The verification principle was a subject on which Reichenbach had written shortly after leaving Germany (1938; see Reichenbach 1949). Although he was thoroughly imbued with the spirit of logical positivism, he wanted to distance himself from what he regarded as its unfortunate narrowness, a constriction resulting from too severe an interpretation of the verification principle. (This was largely why he preferred to call himself a logical empiricist.) For the principle as stated may seem very strong: it tells us that unless a statement is verifiable in principle, it is not meaningful. But there is much that it does not say. It does not claim that a statement must be verifiable *simpliciter*, nor that any "in principle" verifiability be conclusive. It leaves open what should be counted as verification and what processes should be regarded as necessary for it. Although it tells us something about what it is for a statement to have meaning, it does not tell us what meaning any statement has. The method by which a statement is verified is a procedure for showing that it has a meaning; it is not necessarily identical with that meaning. And finally, it leaves open whether statements acquire their meaning individually, being verifiable one by one, or collectively, being verifiable as a set or group.

Weaker versions of the principle exploit these gaps; stronger versions close them. The former option is taken by those who think of the principle as formulating useful secondary advice. It reminds us of the significance of relations between what we can meaningfully say and what we can justifiably think. It helps us to articulate a healthy scepticism concerning the intelligibility of statements that are such that nothing whatsoever would count as evidence for or against them. In Wittgenstein's view, it is precisely for this reason that we should be suspicious of the suggestion (Russell's) that the world might have been created five minutes ago (Wittgenstein 1958, II, xi: 221).

A. J. Ayer opted for the latter approach in *Language, Truth and Logic* (1936), his famous advertisement for what the Vienna Circle was about, or at least one particular take on what it stood for.[6] First, he restricts the means of verification to appeals either to the meaning of words and their grammatical structure, or (in)directly to foundational forms of sense-experience such as perception of publicly observable objects and properties. Secondly, he identifies the meaning of a statement with the method of its verification. Thirdly, he represents individual statements as gaining their meaning and being verified individually. Appeals to sense-experience are arbitrated by the exact sciences and, by extension, the social sciences. By constricting the verification principle in these ways, Ayer secures science's pole position concerning what can meaningfully be said and justifiably thought. We can appreciate this by becoming aware of the use Ayer made of the principle, of the function he gave it. So consider this schematic representation of his underlying argument:

(1) The truth/falsity and knowability of any statement is either a matter of its meaning alone (which in Ayer's view meant it was also analytic and necessary), or of meaning together with the way the world is (which in Ayer's view meant it was also synthetic and contingent).

(2) (Given (1)), any meaningful statement must be either analytic–necessary or synthetic–contingent.

(3) (Verifiability criterion) Any statement whose truth/falsity and knowability depend on both meaning and the way the world is (i.e. synthetic–contingent) must be capable of being verified or falsified by experience, where a statement is verified if is possible for experience to render it probable (see Ayer 1946: 35–8).

Now consider kinds of non-analytic statement about which science could have little or nothing to say, such as "philosophy affords us knowledge of a reality transcending the world of science and common sense"; "the world of sense-experience is altogether unreal"; "God exists"; "death is an evil". Call these statements, which exceed the bounds of science, "meta-scientific".

(4) Meta-scientific statements do not purport to be true/false and knowable as a matter of meaning alone.

(5) (Given (1) and (4)), meta-scientific statements cannot be analytic.

(6) Meta-scientific statements do not purport to be verifable or falsifiable by experience.

(7) (Given (1), (3) and (6)), meta-scientific statements cannot be synthetic–contingent.

(8) (Given (2), (5) and (7)), meta-scientific statements cannot be meaningful.

Anti-verificationism

By the time Putnam was thinking about these matters, verification-ism (and from now on its narrow form alone is meant) was beset by challenges. Most poignantly, the verification principle seems unable to meet its own standards for meaningfulness, for the principle could hardly be said to be true in virtue of its meaning and grammatical structure alone. But precisely what foundational sense-experiences could it appeal to for its verification? Furthermore, some had begun to feel that "what the verificationists were propounding was not an analysis of meaning but a persuasive redefinition", as Putnam would later put it (Putnam 1971: 352).

One reason for thinking this is that verificationism must deny differences in meaning where they appear to exist. Suppose that what is meaningful about a theory is a function of what empirical results would verify or falsify it. Then two theories with the same such means of verification must mean the same. But this is false: two such theories might actually be different, to the extent that one would be consistent with the denial of the other (Putnam 1971: 351–6). The case to which Putnam appeals is Vaihinger's hypothesis that the observable world is exactly as if it were made up of electrons even though it may not be. In terms of their verification, two theories are alike: the same empirical results would verify–falsify whether the world really is made up out of electrons as would verify–falsify whether the world merely appears to be constructed in that way. But it is easy to see that they do not amount to the same theory: the latter is true in possible situations where the former is false.

Another reason for thinking that verificationists simply changed the meaning of "meaning" instead of analysing it is that their view clearly constricts what it is for a statement to be meaningless. For suppose we adopt a concept, "MEANING", under the verificationist definition; it is such that the "meaning" of a sentence is its method of verification. It follows that whatever statements are unverifiable either by their grammar and semantics or by empirical testing are without "meaning", and hence are "meaning"-less. But the concepts "MEANING" and "MEANING"-LESS are supposed to be synonymous with our usual concepts. So we are supposed to treat statements that are "meaning"-less as we would treat those that are meaningless: as pseudo-statements, in other words, statements lacking all sense whatsoever. And that is simply a trick in Putnam's opinion. For all we need hold is that "meaning"-less statements are untestable:

> If to call metaphysical propositions "meaningless" were only to assert that these propositions are empirically untestable, it would be harmless (the metaphysicians always *said* that their assertions were neither empirically testable nor tautologies); but, of course, it is not harmless, because the Positivist hopes that we will

accept his redefinition of the term "meaning", *while retaining the pejorative connotations of being "meaningless" in the customary (linguistic) sense, i.e. being literally without sense.* Since, for example, theses which are literally without sense cannot be debated or discussed, anyone who says that metaphysical philosophy is "meaningless" feels free to reject it *in toto* without constructing arguments against it. If "God exists" is meaningless, then Hume's careful examination of the arguments for and against it in the *Dialogues on Natural Religion* was unnecessary; indeed, how could there *be* arguments for and against a *meaningless sentence?* (Putnam 1965d: 122–3)

This view can be applied in various ways; here is one fairly clear instance:

every term that has an established place in English syntax and an established use has meaning – that's how we *use* the word "meaning". The word "God", for example, certainly has meaning. It does not follow that it belongs in science – but it does not belong *not* because it is "nonsignificant", but just for the obvious reason – that there are no scientific procedures for determining whether or not God exists or what properties He has if He does exist. Whether or not the word should be employed as it is in non-scientific contexts is another question. (Putnam 1965c: 236)

So the verification principle demarcates the boundaries of science, not the boundaries of meaningfulness, still less the meaning of any particular concept or word.

Challenges of this sort seemed to call for further work on verificationism, perhaps even for modification of the central theses. But in 1950 Quine published his epoch-making paper "Two Dogmas of Empiricism", persuading many who would otherwise have been content or willing to carry out the necessary repairs that the structure itself should be condemned (Quine 1953). Putnam has described the paper as raising issues that "go to the very center of philosophy". It is because of this, rather than because of his role in seeing off logical positivism, that Quine's work has been identified by Putnam as of fundamental importance to his own philosophical thought.[7]

Quine revealed debilitating flaws in each of the restrictions of the principle and in a way that revealed a radically different conception. The distinction between statements that are to be verified by appeal to meaning alone and those dependent on appeals to the character of experience is one instance of a distinction that must be abandoned: that between analytic and synthetic statements.[8] The claim that we should identify the meaning of a statement with its method of verification assumes that the concept of a statement's meaning is in sufficiently good order that *something* at least can be identified with it; but this is not the case. The idea that statements acquire their meaning individually falls to the same consideration. The claim that statements can be *verified* individually is false. In a phrase that became famous, Quine argued that "our statements about the external world face the tribunal of sense experience not individually but only as a corporate body" (Quine 1953: 41). There is little or nothing of systematic interest about individual statements. Putnam has made regular use of one instance of this overall claim: "that it is not an isolated sentence that has a method of verification, but a whole theory" (Putnam 1965d: 123).

Although Quine's attack seemed wholly to undermine logical positivism, many of its central tenets were left standing. Indeed Quine himself developed a view that strengthened them, a view that influenced Putnam greatly. The old analytic–synthetic distinction implied that there are statements true in virtue of meaning alone (basic mathematical and logical statements were taken as the paradigm). This claim supported in its turn the view that there are statements that are *knowable* in virtue of knowing their meaning alone. If this is so, then in neither case is appeal to experience necessary. Thus the distinction insulates a whole class of statements from empirical science: those whose truth and ability to be known are radically non-empirical. Quine abandoned the distinction, declaring that no statements are entirely insulated in this way. Given their interrelations, some statements are more vulnerable than others to revision in the light of experience, but none are immune.

Hence Quine's view expresses a commitment to empiricism, to the competence of science and to the nature and role of philosophy that any logical positivist would have been happy to endorse. Putnam has been particularly influenced by Quine's account of empirical revisability and by his treatment of collective assessment. He has stressed the importance of one specific instance of collective assessment in relation to philosophy of science. It is whole theories rather than isolated statements that have methods of verification; empirical tests are constructed in such a way that large groups of sentences figure in them.

Putnam has been keen to identify and root out verificationist ways of thinking in specific areas of philosophy. The philosophy of mind is one example, where there have been constant attempts to treat everyday psychological terms such as "pain" as theoretical terms referring to neuro-physiological states of the brain. In Putnam's diagnosis, views of this sort were made almost irresistible by a particular disposition in philosophy for which verificationism was largely responsible: a background against which it was possible quite generally to disguise plausible redefinitions as genuine analyses of ordinary concepts (Putnam 1969: 441–51).

The main message Putnam read from the demise of logical positivism and the verifiability theory is that (mis)use of the term "meaning" is one of the easiest, but least successful, ways of "establishing" philosophical propositions in analytic philosophy (Putnam 1965d: 122). Hence it is not surprising to find that he has devoted a considerable part of his career to establishing correct understanding of the correct use for the term. Indeed, the paper for which he is arguably best known is entitled "The Meaning of 'Meaning'" (Putnam 1975f; see also 1954a,b; 1959; 1961a; 1962c,d; 1965b,d; 1967d; 1968; 1970b; 1973a; 1974b,c; 1975b,d,e,f; 1976; 1978a,b; 1979a; 1981a; 1983c,d; 1986b; 1988a; 1989b; 1990b; 1992a). This work preceded his overt hostility to aspects of analytic philosophy, but it is no less indicative of a strongly critical attitude to the approach.

Chapter 5

Core issues

> When we examine what we should say when, what words we should use in what situations, we are looking not *merely* at words (or "meanings", whatever they may be) but also at the realities we use the words to talk about: we are using a sharpened awareness of words to sharpen our perception of, though not as the final arbiter of, the phenomena.
>
> J. L. Austin, *A Plea for Excuses* (1979: 182)

Realism, rationality and meaning are three basic issues on which, as he himself acknowledged, Putnam was most deeply influenced by the philosophical context in which he found himself. Having examined these structural influences, we are now in a position to appreciate two even more fundamental sources of inspiration and stimulus: ideas concerning the core topics of intentionality and a function-based approach.

Intentionality

Putnam's overall concerns in the first part of his career, no less than the second, are expressed by the quoted passage from John Austin (1911–60). How must we and the world be, and how must we be connected up with the world, if we are to perceive it, think about it, talk about it? And in particular, what should we make of the concepts and words we have at our disposal for thinking and talking about the world – what are the "arbiters" here, and how do they operate?

It may seem immediately surprising to draw this connection with Austin, who was on the face of it a very different kind of philosopher from Putnam. Austin, it may appear, was much more inclined (even committed) to piecemeal analyses of linguistic usage, much less subject to the influence of verificationism and the science-focused philosophical programme of Viennese positivism. But Putnam has admired Austin throughout his career, and if we are to understand him we need to know why. Latterly, he has argued for "the importance of being Austin" and has identified him as the first advocate of an approach that provides the solution to various significant model-theoretic problems (Putnam 1999 (ii), (xii)). But as early as 1960 (the year of Austin's death), Putnam was praising him for his "healthy-minded" way of doing philosophy (Putnam 1960a: 76; the immediate stimulus for this praise was Austin's equation of statements with "logical constructions" out of the makings of statements). And the clue to his underlying good opinion of Austin, one that is most revealing about Putnam himself, is to be found in a book review written a little later. There, Putnam commends Austin specifically for his attempts to encourage "a new kind of science of language" (Putnam 1975i: 136).[1]

This was a striking thing for Putnam to have said. It is accurate enough, expressing an interpretation of what Austin was about that agrees substantially with that offered by Austin's own Oxford colleagues. (When Gilbert Ryle (1900–1976) described Austin's "almost botanical classifications of locution-types" as more appropriate for "a future *Principia Grammatica*" than for philosophy, his tone may have been facetious, but his point was not; Ryle 1971: vol. 1, 273). But the notion that Austin was aiming at a new kind of science of language before his early death contrasted sharply with the way he was generally regarded at that time outside Oxford, and particularly in America. It was commonly assumed that he was a denigrator of science, overly impressed by common speech on the one hand, and on the other overly discouraged by failures in our attempts to understand anything else. These charges, commonly laid against a supposed homogeneous group of "Oxford" or "Ordinary Language" philosophers, stemmed originally from those frustrated in a quite indiscriminate way by the directions being taken by post-Russellian analytic philosophy, including Russell himself (1959: 214–19; 241–2; 254), frustrations that were publicized through Ernest Gellner's widely read but deeply inaccurate polemic *Words and Things* (1959).

That the standard interpretation was not simply unsympathetic but quite uncomprehending is plain enough even from the short passage quoted in the epigraph to this chapter. And therein lies the clue to Putnam's respect. First, we are not to abdicate from the attempt to understand reality but to take it as our goal. Secondly, we are not to use common speech *simpliciter* but a sharpened awareness of words and concepts as our tool. Thirdly, we are not to treat this awareness as if it were our *only* tool. Fully understanding Putnam at any particular point in his career requires sensitivity to the way these Austinian tenets are made manifest throughout it.[2] The traditional problems of philosophy concern the relationship between thought and reality. Attention to language is necessary for the improvement of philosophical practice. And we cannot solve intentionality problems by attending to language alone (by exposing them as "pseudo-problems", for example); genuine philosophical problems exist, and we need a variety of tools to solve them.[3]

Reference problems

One particular intentionality problem with which those who had a major influence on Putnam were concerned was the problem of reference under the impact of revolutions and major changes in scientific understanding.

Scientists do not simply overturn old views of some subject-matter and replace them with new ones. They also add, subtract and perhaps modify the concepts used to make statements expressing those old and new views. Indeed, such changes to our overall conceptual set may be necessary if theory change is to be made possible. And if these changes affect the meaning associated with the concepts involved, they affect their reference also. The result is that a good deal of roughly philosophical work is left over. As Putnam noted in 1964 of one specific case, "The conceptual structure of quantum mechanics today is as unhealthy as the conceptual structure of the calculus was at the time Berkeley's famous criticism was issued" (Putnam 1964c: 159). In dealing with the issues arising, much depends on how we think that concepts relate to meaning: whether or not we think that concepts change as a result of science depends on how we think they are associated with meaning in the first place. And this is at root an intentionality problem, a question of how it is possible for concepts to refer at all. Major difficulties that go to the heart of philosophy arise here.

For instance, suppose we think of the meaning of the concept STRAIGHT LINE in such a way that (a) any two straight lines mutually perpendicular to a third cannot meet, and (b) the path of a light ray is a straight line. As a result of various discoveries and consequent theory construction, physicists now widely accept that two light-ray paths mutually perpendicular to a third *can* meet. So something is in error, and it makes a great deal of difference where we lay the blame.

Suppose the fault is said to lie with us: we thought that (a) and (b) followed from or gave the meaning of the concept, but we were wrong.

Then the upshot of scientific investigation would be a change in us, not in our concepts: we now have a better idea of what they mean. This explanation tells us something that is, on the face of it, quite surprising about concepts. Although we use them constantly and might appear to be responsible for them, they are in fact such that we may not know what they mean. Of course, we are accustomed to the idea of individuals being in difficulties of this sort: children learning their first language; adults acquiring technical concepts. But it is remarkably difficult to get used to the idea that all of us, for centuries, might have been entirely wrong about the meaning of a simple concept in everyday and significant use. And although we may become reconciled to the idea of an ignorant past, it is very hard to contemplate what the idea implies: the possibility of an ignorant present and future. For suppose in the light of present physics we understand the concept STRAIGHT LINE consistently with (b) and renounce (a). It is always possible that future physics will reveal (b) to be inconsistent with other claims that we think of as following from or giving the meaning of the concept. Hence the concept is such that we still do not, and may never, know its meaning.

Alternatively, we might suppose that the concept itself is to blame. The result of scientific investigation would be to show that the original concept is confused or inconsistent and to replace it with a modified or entirely different concept (perhaps using the same word to express the concept, perhaps not). But this explanation is incomplete as it stands, and there are several ways to fill out the picture. It might be said that the meaning of the original concept was given by both (a) and (b). Now physics seems to have shown that nothing satisfies both conditions. So on this interpretation, there never was anything for the concept STRAIGHT LINE to refer to. This does not make it exactly like the concept (if such it is) ROUND SQUARE since it is not obvious that there could never have been something that satisfied both (a) and (b). But for practical purposes, this is a distinction with little actual difference. And the upshot is surprising. When previously we spoke of straight lines, we were simply talking nonsense, if we were saying anything at all. So we could talk of geometric theories which make use of the concept much as we now talk of the caloric theory of heat, of phlogiston theory and of electromagnetic ether.

Another way of completing the explanation would be to say that the meaning of the original concept was given by (a) rather than (b). Current physics seems to have shown that we need a concept whose meaning is given by (b) rather than (a). So there has always been something for the concept STRAIGHT LINE to refer to. It is just that the concept has changed, and in this fairly precise sense: the "something" in question, the reference of the concept, is now different. What makes this interpretation surprising is that it leaves the change of concept unmotivated, and hence unexplained. For either we still have a use for a concept whose meaning is given by (a) or we do not. In the one case we retain the old concept, in the other we discard it. But either way, we need a new concept to capture (b) and a new word to express that concept. So in neither case would the reference of the concept be different; in neither case would the concept itself have changed. And that makes a good deal of difference to the way we understand the impact of science. We tend to think that scientific investigation has taught us something about straight lines by showing that two light-ray paths mutually perpendicular to a third can meet. But that cannot be the case on this interpretation. For it claims in effect that the words "straight line" are ambiguous. As soon as we are clear about which concept they express, one whose meaning is given by (a) or by (b), we will see that the claim is either false or a truism, the mere definition of the concept in use. Thus in neither case is this claim something we have learnt from science.

The problem of reference under the impact of science and the background issues to which it calls attention have been a constant concern of Putnam's throughout his career. The problems expand and ramify, but they can be traced back to the underlying issue of how intentionality is possible.

If science informs, corrects or changes our concepts and not simply our use of them, then the means by which we think and speak about the world are in an important sense quite independent of us. And this independence might be thought to make intentionality hard to understand. Given this distancing of means, how is it we are able to bring concepts to bear on the world in such a way as to enable us to think and speak about it?

Alternatively, this independence might be regarded as the most important factor in explaining why intentionality is possible. Given the independence of the world, its objectivity, how else could it be accurately represented for us in our thought and talk *except* by means that are themselves independent of us?

Putnam began formulating a response to intentionality problems, and specifically those that changes in science had created for the subject of reference in the 1960s and early 1970s. It is useful to note parallels between his developing ideas and the work of his Harvard colleague Nelson Goodman, who focused on the intentionality of one kind of representation in particular, namely depiction or pictorial representation. In the Oxford John Locke Lectures that eventually became *Languages of Art* (1968), Goodman argued that accounts of depiction should be dependent on accounts of reference. Now Goodman is explicit about the extent to which his arguments owe to Peirce's application of pragmatism to the theory of signs (Peirce 1983: vol. 2, 2.246–2.305) and to philosophical debates about depiction whose source is Peirce: debates centring on various attempts to subsume theories of art under theories of meaning, specifically under a general semiotic theory (Langer 1957; Morris 1946). So we can see in this influence on Putnam early signs of sensitivity to pragmatist modes of thought that would become steadily more overt in his later writing.

Goodman's starting-point was the claim that the verb "represents" is multiply ambiguous. The way to understand what it is for a picture to be "of" something is to think of the way that a name is "about" the bearer corresponding to this label, and the way that a predicate is "about" the class of objects whose members correspond to this description (Goodman 1968: 22). Indeed, he claimed that these ways of thinking express an identity between reference and depiction, and do not merely exploit parallels or analogous features. For a picture that depicts an object "refers to and, more particularly, denotes it". Hence denotation should be regarded as "the core of representation" (*ibid.*: 5).

Denotation itself should be understood as the product of a symbol system, a set of rules established by convention that correlates symbols with their denotata. So a picture is a character in a dense symbol system; pictures in general take their place as one particular kind of character in one specific variety of symbol system. And just as the "meaning" (semantic content) of a written or spoken text is not determined or constrained by the shapes and sounds and colours of its surface, so the "meaning" (pictorial content) of a painting is not determined or constrained by its surface features. In both cases, meaning is determined by systems of conventions, the choice of which is in important senses quite arbitrary. So we might think there is some "right" way to depict objects: realistically, for example, or literally, or naturalistically. Or we might think that one painter depicts objects more realistically, or literally, or naturalistically than another. But we would simply be expressing our allegiance to what is, for us, the customary way of depicting objects, a way that has no more legitimacy or objectivity than this: it fits into an overall representational system which influential artists have found agreeable, have endorsed and have persuaded us to accept (Goodman 1968: 38).

As we shall see, several aspects of this position are reflected, either positively or negatively, in Putnam's developing approach to intentionality. Two features in particular are common to both. First, the attempt to account for intentionality more generally by giving priority to the task of becoming clear about how language can be "of" the world. Secondly, the interest in and emphasis on the rules governing language, particularly in its use to state scientific facts, to express scientific discoveries, and to describe what has changed and what has remained the same through crises in scientific theorizing. Matters of dispute centre on the nature and competence of the conventions associated with language use; specifically, what role they play in correlating names with their referents, and precisely what may legitimately be described as "arbitrary" about them. Finally, Goodman's position can be cited as one source for Putnam's view, developed through the mid-1970s and early 1980s, that there are a number of possible representational systems, and that several issues central to philosophical debate are determined by whichever such system sets the standards at a given time for a given culture or enterprise. The principal issue of this sort concerns what counts as a "realistic" representation, either specifically for some subject-matter (such as pictorial representation) or generally for any enterprise with a claim to the label. But one application is of particular interest to Putnam: namely, what counts as a satisfactory scientific theory of some subject-matter.

A function-based approach

Two of the previous topics – meaning and intentionality – combine to form a fifth, equally dominant structurally in Putnam's early contributions to philosophy. This is his tendency towards a function-based approach, understood broadly as any approach to philosophical issues that subordinates other queries about the relevant phenomena (e.g. "what is their constitution?") to the question "what is their use, their function, their role?"[4] In developing this approach, Putnam was particularly influenced by aspects of the later Wittgenstein. The tendency to think of the later Wittgenstein as more or less focused on issues in the philosophy of language and mind causes us to miss an obvious and strong point of connection with Putnam: between 1929 and 1944, about half his writings were centred in the philosophy of mathematics (Hacker 1996: 86).

One way to conceive of the intentional relation between what we say and what is the case – between propositions (or the statements expressing them) and the world – is as based on a particular kind of straightforward one-to-one correspondence. This was Wittgenstein's own view in the *Tractatus*. As he would later summarize the view (which acquired the label "Augustinian" after the passage quoted from Augustine's *Confessions*, I, viii) before taking each of its aspects to task: "The individual words in language name objects – sentences are combinations of such names. – In this picture of language we find the roots of the following idea: Every word has a meaning. This meaning is correlated with the word. It is the object for which the word stands" (Wittgenstein 1958, §1: 2). This view combines intentionality with meaning in the simplest way: the meaning of an expression is the object it is of, about, or stands for. It expresses an approach to both topics that has tightly gripped philosophical imagination and seems if anything to have strengthened its appeal.

On a closer view, the Tractarian approach has the following detailed form. The sense of propositions and of the statements expressing them are the states of affairs they represent – the proposition is true if objects are arranged as it says they are, and false if not. The sense of propositions is determined by the meaning of their simplest con-stituents, conceived of as names. The meaning of these names is given by the objects they stand for or represent. Unless a name is "of", "for", or "about" some object, it will lack meaning. Moreover, any statements in which such an "empty name" occurs will be similarly without mean-ing, and any propositions expressed by those statements will lack sense (Wittgenstein 1922: §§4.0311, 5.473, 6.53). Hence it is on the intentional relation that the very possibility of propositions and of meaning depends.

This conception can be criticized in various ways. Consider the three-part idea which in the quoted passage Wittgenstein identifies as at the root of the view. The combination of the first and third claims faces the problem that some words have no object to stand for and yet, so it seems, are not thereby rendered entirely meaningless. Depending on one's view of fiction, names such as "Pegasus" and "Father Christmas" are perhaps examples. Moreover, to think of the object for which a word stands as its meaning seems simply to confuse different kinds of item – rather as if one were to be asked to think of the entity for which "US Government" stands as some particular object, such as a specific building or person. But the aspect of this approach that stimulated the late Wittgenstein's most concentrated desire to revise is its picture of intentionality, and specifically its way of redrawing the referential relations that exist between words and reality. "For a *large* class of cases – though not for all – in which we employ the word 'meaning' it can be defined thus: the meaning of a word is its use in language" (Wittgenstein 1958: §43: 20). In this later view, the meaning of an expression depends not on a one-to-one representational relation with an object but on its use, its rule-governed function. More specifically, *whether* the expression has a meaning at all depends on whether it has established employment in performing linguistic acts. And *what* meaning the expression has depends on how it is, and how it can be, employed.

It is plausible to suppose that we learn the meaning of expressions in our first language by learning how they function, how they can be used. Moreover, it is by observing the employment of expressions that anthropologists and field-linguists learn languages new to them. And Wittgenstein certainly draws on this evidence to support his claims. But these aspects of his argument can confuse. His view goes deeper than the claim that we elucidate the meaning of words by describing their functioning. That would be compatible with claiming that use is merely a convenient way of getting at meaning, whereas on his view, so it seems, there is no more to be "got at" than use. Hence use does not simply elucidate the meaning of words; it elucidates the concept MEANING itself. Wittgenstein rejected the notion that he was thereby offering a "theory" of meaning. But his claims certainly presuppose an account of that concept, and one exhausted by the notion of use, of employment, of function.[5]

What Putnam called Wittgenstein's "functional conception of language" is an instance of a broader strategy with deep relevance for understanding much of their overall methodology. We would not expect to learn how to play chess by associating the pieces with objects. We learn the game instead by learning how the pieces function, what moves are permissible for each, what situations prompt which moves, which moves produce what results, and so on. In the same way, Putnam argues, we should not expect to learn much about various philosophical subjects by associating their elements with objects; we should attend instead to the ways they function.

Applications

One example of a function-based approach in operation is Putnam's view in the 1960s of the analytic–synthetic distinction. As we have seen, his enquiry is based on the idea that the only fruitful questions are those directed at use and use-value: "What happens to a statement when it is analytic? What do people do with it? What point is there to having a separate class of statements called analytic statements? Why mark these off from all the others? What do you do with the statements so marked?" (Putnam 1962c: 35; the strategy can be found throughout pp. 33–69). And he uses a functionalist argument to ground meaning on the network of beliefs composing our conceptual scheme, stressing:

> the extent to which the meaning of an individual word is a function of its place in the network, and the impossibility of separating, in the actual use of a word, that part of the use which reflects the "meaning" of the word and that part of the use which reflects deeply embedded collateral information.
>
> (Putnam 1962c: 40–41)

Another example is Putnam's function-based treatment of problems concerning minds in the late 1950s and early 1960s. Associating mental phenomena with the particular ways in which minded beings are constituted tells us little about either. We should ask instead about how such phenomena function, what relations exist between different kinds of mental state and event, what circumstances prompt which such states and events, which such states and events produce what kinds of behaviour, and so on. (See Putnam 1957c; 1960b; 1962d; 1963d; 1964b; 1965c; 1967e,f; 1968; 1973b,c; 1975b,g; 1981a (ii), (iv); 1983e,m; 1984c; 1985b; 1986c,e; 1988a *passim*; 1998d; 1991a; 1992a (i)–(iv); 1992e; 1999 *passim*.)

Putnam occasionally put the point in terms recalling an Aristotelian distinction: for us, the question should be not "what is our intellectual *matter*?" but "what is our intellectual *form*?" (Putnam 1973b: 302). He has been particularly keen to note the Wittgensteinian aspect of his own methodology in relation to two specific aspects of philosophy of mind: concepts and understanding. In his view, Wittgenstein showed that language is not just a conventional sign-system but the means by which concepts are used. And the question of how concepts are used is of more central interest to philosophy than the question of what they are. Equally important is Wittgenstein's insistence that one's understanding of a linguistic expression and of one's own thoughts is not to be regarded as an occurrence but an ability (Putnam 1975d: 1–32; esp. 3–13).

Putnam recognized earlier than most that Wittgenstein's function-based conception of language, if adopted, would deeply affect not only our approach to semantic questions, but our conception of intentionality:

> Wittgenstein believed that the concepts of REFERENCE and TRUTH were not really of much use in philosophy, and that one should ask, not "what do our words refer to?" (as if that could be separated from the language we employ), but "how do we *use* our words?" – what *functions* they have in human activity, and how those functions change, overlap, are taught and learned, is in the center of the investigation. (Putnam 1975i: 135)

The contrast here is perhaps not quite accurately expressed: Wittgenstein did not mean to *replace* reference and truth with use, but to show how focusing on use is the way to elucidate reference and truth. However, the main point is clear: paying due attention to functional relations rather than to one-to-one correlations between words and objects is the way to make problems in semantics tractable.

Since these problems are so deeply interconnected with intentionality, we would expect their solutions to bear on the question of how our experiences, thought and talk relate to the world. For suppose we acknowledge the function-based point: it is incoherent to think of reference as a single determinate one-to-one relation between us and the world. Then intentionality cannot be conceived of as depending on any such relation. This raises two major questions: what difference this makes to analytic philosophy, and what should be said about intentionality.

The first question is easy enough to answer: conceiving of intentionality in a function-based way requires that we renounce many of the most venerable approaches to the subject. We cannot follow the Lockean tradition, built on the claim that thoughts and words are related in virtue of mediating mental items ("ideas") derived from the senses; nor the closely related tradition that regards the mediating work as done by the senses themselves and their modes; nor the tradition that depicted the intentional relation in terms of causal links between thoughts/words and reality, one instance of which is the behaviourist view that intentionality is a matter of stimulus and verbal response. All such traditions are vitiated by their common source: that intentionality is made possible by the fact that (a) what one thinks and what one means is an object of some sort (whether a concrete material object, or a psychological object, or an abstract object); and that (b) the nature and identity of that object determines the nature and identity of an object in reality as the object one is thinking about or means (whether by resembling the object, or representing it in some other way, or by being in some causal relation to it). (a) and (b) account for intentionality, on this view, because it is in virtue of them that the thinking subject and the statements he or she produces are connected to the world.

The second question – how then *are* we to conceive of intentionality? – is considerably more difficult. What should philosophers impressed by the function-based approach say? This is the question on which Putnam's attention has been concentrated throughout his career, prompting the thought that "a function-based approach" is the way his distinctive contribution should be labelled if it is to be identified at all by name. Putnam's response has developed interdependently with his responses to the other issues raised in this chapter: realism, rationality and meaning. We shall examine that response in what follows.

Chapter 6

Intentionality

If the dull substance of my flesh were thought,
Injurious distance should not stop my way,
For then despite of space I would be brought,
From limits far remote, where thou dost stay.
No matter then although my foot did stand
Upon the farthest earth removed from thee,
For nimble thought can jump both land and sea
As soon as think the place where he would be.

William Shakespeare, Sonnet 44

The emotive force of these lines depends upon our recognition and ready acceptance of intentionality, of the relations that are possible between thought and reality. Putnam has given this phenomenon the greatest possible significance: "I see philosophy as a field which has certain central questions, for example, the relation between thought and reality" (Putnam 1975b: xvii). He goes on to "mention some questions about which I have *not* written, the relation between freedom and responsibility, and the nature of the good life". This passage was written thirty years ago; since then, Putnam has written on these latter subjects also, showing in each case how answers to such metaphysical and ethical questions depend on answers to intentionality questions.[1] Thus his later work has strengthened rather than diluted the emphasis he placed earlier on the connection between thought and reality, making intentionality issues *uniquely* central to philosophy.

Analytic philosophy

Putnam never expresses his indebtedness to the context in which he came to philosophy more precisely than when he describes intentional relations as at the very centre of the field of questions defining the subject. For this is the way in which, if only implicitly, thinkers responsible for launching and sustaining analytic philosophy have characteristically regarded philosophy itself.

Various familiar attempts to define analytic philosophy have failed because they appeal to some position (atomism; Russellian anti-idealism; positivism; and so on) as its defining feature, or some prospectus (usually some interpretation of "the linguistic turn"[2]), when in fact that position or prospectus is either not embraced by all advocates of analytic philosophy, or is embraced by non-advocates. Michael Dummett, for example, has attracted widespread criticism for his approach-based definition of analytic philosophy: as a school that treats the philosophical account of language as the basic approach to solving philosophical problems (Dummett 1993; Glock 1997). Stressing the centrality of intentionality problems does not make this mistake. There is no one position on them or approach to solving them that is regarded as definitive of analytical philosophy. What is definitive of the school and its evolution, enabling it to survive periodic radical changes in direction and structure, is rather a conviction about the importance of intentionality, an evolving sensitivity for the nature of the problems to which it gives rise, and a constant commitment to solving them.[3] This is not (of course) to say that *only* analytic philosophers have been concerned with intentionality questions, nor that analytic philosophers have *only* been concerned with intentionality questions. But it is to claim that these questions have a centrality for analytic philosophers that they do not have for other philosophers, and that other questions do not have such centrality for analytic philosophers.

The basic problem of intentionality (what must be true of us, of the world, and of the intentional relation, that it is possible for it to hold between us?) gives rise to various subsidiary questions on which Putnam has focused. We can distinguish here between questions about the *terms* of the relation between experience–thought–talk and reality, and questions about the *relation* itself (indeed, whether it *is* a relation, as it appears to be). Questions heading in the first direction ask about what kinds of item these "things" must be for our experience, thought and talk to be about them, and what kinds of item *we* must be to be capable of experiencing such things, of thinking about them, of speaking about them. Questions leading in the second direction ask about what kind of relation (or whatever) this "of"-ness, this reference, this "about"-ness, is; about what must be the case if it is to be even possible. The two directions are almost certainly deeply interdependent. We can have little sense of what kind of relation this is unless and until we know something of the items it relates; but equally, we can have little to say about the terms of the relation unless and until we know something of the relation itself.

These various questions are subject to further division, giving rise to a number of sub-issues, each of which then ramifies in its turn. The most important interrelated questions to be raised individually and collectively in what follows are these:

(a) What must be the case if *this* experience, *this* thought, *this* use of language is to be about *that* object, *that* state of affairs, *that* action, process or state?

(b) Are we dealing here with two quite distinct ontological domains, of mind and world, of thought and objects, of meaning and syntax, or with the same domain differently conceptualized?

(c) Is intentionality a relation, and, if so, is it an internal or an external relation – does the existence and identity of a particular experience (or a thought or a statement) depend on being related to the things it is about, or not?

(d) What is it about mental processes of thinking and meaning things that gives content to the bare logic and syntax of a language so that what is said is about what we intend it to be about?

(e) Must one's thoughts and statements be *directly* about things in the world to be about them at all, or must they be mediated through representations of the world?

(f) How do intentional relations make understanding possible – how can it be that A knows what properties are being assigned to which things by B's utterance?

(g) How must thoughts and statements be related to states of affairs if the latter are to make the former true?

(h) When one thinks what is false, one thinks what is not the case; how then can one be thinking about anything at all?

(i) What kinds of thing can we (not) experience, think and speak about?

(j) What kinds of thing are (not) able to do the experiencing, thinking, speaking?

The main stages of Putnam's development can be interpreted as a discovery of several basic features, necessary resources for answering these questions.

Putnam inherited from the founders of analytic philosophy and their successors a conviction of the importance of intentionality and a sense of the several basic problems to which it gives rise. (See Putnam

1960a; 1965b,d,e; 1973a; 1974b; 1975b,c,d,e; 1976a,b,c; 1983a; 1991a; 1992a (i).) Since these distinguishable questions have structured his contributions to philosophy, it is worth considering something of the history of each – in relation to analytic philosophy, on the one hand, and in relation to his writings, on the other. The overall aim is to give substance to the interpretative claims just made.

No-object problems

Within the history of analytic philosophy, the most familiar problem which an account of intentionality must settle is the one responsible for stimulating Bertrand Russell to his classic paper "On Denoting". How is it possible for us to experience or think or speak when there is no corresponding object, nothing for us to have experiences of, nothing for us to think or speak about?

Intuitively, there must be things our experiences are *of* if they are to have content and not be simply empty. And in the same way, we might suppose that if our thoughts are to be significant rather than negligible, perhaps even for our thoughts to be thoughts at all, there must be things they are *about*. Finally, it seems that there must be things our concepts and our uses of language to express those concepts *refer to* if they are to be meaningful and not mere sounds. In a sentence such as "Sammy the Cat is thin as a rake", for example, there must be a bearer for the subject-term: that is, the thing to which the label "Sammy the Cat" attaches. And if the predicate-term must have something to be "about" to be significant, then the class corresponding to it ("x is thin as a rake") must have members; that is, the set of all and only those things to which the description "thin-as-a-rake objects" applies. And yet it really seems possible to think and speak of things that do not exist, not simply with regard to fictional terms such as "Pegasus" or "Father Christmas", but terms that could have named real entities, such as "the queen of New York" or "Meroveus", and terms that could not have had real entities correspond to them, such as "round squares" and "married bachelors". I call this the "no-object" problem.

It might be thought that problems of this sort could be ignored consistently with retaining interest in accounting for intentionality, for in the great majority of situations, we experience, think and talk about things that exist, so it is tempting to suppose that we can focus on these occasions and ignore "no-object" situations as mere limiting cases, dealing with the latter by redeploying whatever solutions fit the former. But there are two reasons why this option will not work in the present case.

First, "no-object" situations may be peripheral to our everyday experience, but a variety of them is central to questions on which Putnam focused from early on: questions concerning the nature of scientific theorizing. Theories are constantly being supplanted by better theories, and among the items discarded or replaced are the terms in which those theories were formulated. In such cases, we decide that the postulates putatively referred to by those terms do not in fact exist. So the problem arises here also: nothing corresponds to the term "phlogiston", and yet it really seems possible to think and speak (truthfully) about it – to say, for example, "phlogiston does not exist".

Secondly, the problems that "no-object" situations reveal are not local and easily isolatable; they reveal gaps in our ability to account for intentionality in everyday cases. So we cannot simply ignore them or set them aside for subsequent solution. This fact was clearly recognized early on in the history of analytic philosophy by those who appreciated Bertrand Russell's "On Denoting". It is why his response is not restricted to problematic phrases such as "the queen of New York" or "the round square" alone, but invites us to regard all such definite descriptions and even perhaps names as conjunctions of existential statements. And it is a fact clearly appreciated by Putnam: it is why his work on reference is not limited to solving quaint puzzles about unusual terms with problematic referents.

For example, throughout the 1960s he was interested in the question of just *how* we can make statements about unobservables, and what such statements *mean*. And the no-object problem arises here in regard to names for *bona fide* theoretical but non-perceptible entities such as "set" and "function" (Putnam was committed to a realist interpretation of mathematics: "*something* answers to such mathematical notions"; Putnam 1975c: 60) and names for imperceptible entities, such as "particle" and "electric charge" (Putnam 1965b: 130–58; 1975c: 60–78). If some theories of physics are correct, there are no objects corresponding to the term "particle". Consider, for example, the *operationalism* associated with the American physicist P. W. Bridgman (1882–1962). On this view, statements containing theoretical terms such as "particle" are really statements about experiences resulting from specific scientific operations or about the results of measuring operations: the former are useful shorthand for the latter. (The popularity of this position, during the 1930s, owed to the widespread feeling that it was uniquely adequate to explain recent discoveries in theoretical physics, such as Einstein's recognition that, beyond what we can measure by signals of infinite velocity, no more could be meant by such terms as "infinite simultaneity".) Suppose this is the case. We nevertheless appear to be able to speak and think in these ways, just as we can talk and think using names for fictional objects and for items associated with discarded theories.

The problem of how this is possible survives the rejection of operationalism, as Putnam recognized (he often just assumed the falsity of that theory) (Putnam 1965b: 131). One difficulty is connected to the fact that we do not experience entities such as particles. Perhaps we do not need to in order to think and speak of unobservables in general: a strong dose of empiricism might be required to cause one to baulk at this point. But scientists often find it necessary to think and speak in terms of *that* particle as being some certain way. And it may be difficult to explain how, in the absence of direct or indirect perceptual information links to some particular object, they are justified in claiming to think or speak in this demonstrative way. How can it be said that this one particular item O_1 is the one that Adam is thinking or speaking about, the one with which he is cognitively and conceptually in touch, when it is unobservable? Without perceptual links, what justifies regarding O_1 as even *identifiable* (i.e. let alone actually identified) with O_2, the referent of his thoughts or words "that particle is F"?

Phrasing these questions in terms of identifiability may make it seem that they express a problem that is fundamentally epistemological in nature (how can one *know* "that particle is F"?), and Putnam occasionally treats them in that way (e.g. Putnam 1965b: 146ff.). But their roots lie in intentionality: how can one even *think* "that particle is F"? And intentionality is a different, if related, phenomenon, one that raises issues at least as basic as epistemology.[4] For we cannot explain what it is to know about something without accounting for what it is to think about it, but the converse is not the case. This is immediately obvious from the fact that we think about many things without knowing them. Thus I can believe something without knowing it, perhaps because it is false (and given the factive nature of knowledge, what is false cannot be known), or because I am not justified in what I think (so that even if it is true, I do not know it). Moreover, I can think something without believing it, let alone judging or knowing it, perhaps because I am still weighing it up as possibly true or possibly false (i.e. I have no such attitudes towards it), or because I think it is probably false (i.e. I have a doubting attitude towards it), or because I have decided it is definitely false (i.e. I reject it).

Finding suitable objects for individual words and referring terms to be "of" or "about" is one version of the "no-object" problem that any account of intentionality must face. Another is to find suitable objects for whole statements, propositions and thoughts. And it is characteristic of analytic philosophy in general and of Putnam's work in particular to treat this version of the "no-object" problem as of the greatest importance. For *holism* has been a dominating feature of the approach: wholes (thoughts, sentences, propositions) take priority over the individual parts (words, concepts) that compose them. Holism antedates analytic philosophy (it plays a role in Kant's argument for the judgement-dependent functioning of concepts; Kant 1933: B92–3); but it came to prominence with that approach, and particularly in the work of Frege, Russell and Wittgenstein.[5]

Holism comes in different versions depending on the nature of the priority claim. It can be strong: for example, that the meaning of the parts depends on the meaning of the whole. Or it can be weaker: for example, that elucidating the meaning of the parts depends on elucidating the meaning of the whole. These and other differences depend on differences in the force of the reasons for advancing the priority claim. Some go so far as to say that the meaning of a part *is* the contribution it makes to the meaning of the whole. Some adopt the weaker position that, if the part is to be meaningful, it must contribute to the whole's meaning. Others hold the still weaker sufficiency condition: if a part contributes to the whole's meaning, it is meaningful. But at whatever strength it is held, holism means that "no-object" problems at the level of parts are inherited at the deeper level of wholes. How is it that we can think, say and meaningfully ask for the truth-value of propositions such as "Sherlock Holmes could never hear the name *Reichenbach* without a shudder", given that there is nothing in the world for the names they contain to be about?

Putnam has focused on one such inheritance problem in particular: how it is that we can think, say and meaningfully ask for the truth-value of scientific theories containing concepts that either do not refer at all, or refer but are not strictly true of anything (Putnam puts the point this way in 1973a: 197). Niels Bohr had false beliefs about electrons in his theory of 1911, for example: he assumed that at every time there are two numbers such that the first corresponds to the one-dimensional position of a particle and the second to its one-dimensional momentum. So we have a choice. We can say that the same particles Bohr was referring to are now explained by present electron theory; the latter is an improvement on the former. Or we can say that "electron" and "particle" had a different meaning for Bohr; hence his theory and present theory refer to different things and evidence for the latter does not help falsify the former; indeed the latter is not even strictly comparable with the former, let alone an improvement on it. Putnam has favoured the first option (as advocates of the second, he identifies Paul Grice and Peter Strawson in their well-known response to Quine's attack on analyticity; Putnam 1975b: xiv–xvi; see also Putnam 1962b: 241; 1962c: 34–5), so he is obliged to account for intentionality in ways that accommodate it. Such an account must allow both Bohr and us to formulate theories out of propositions, and propositions out of constituent terms which refer to the same entities (particles; electrons), even though we have different beliefs about those entities, beliefs that include the scientific definition of the terms that refer to them. The main spur to Putnam's theorizing about the meaning of words and concepts has been to provide for such an account of intentionality.

The inheritance of problems with the parts of thoughts, propositions and statements is not the only cause of problems with these wholes. A new set arises when we consider the "no-object" problem just at the level of wholes. One puzzle in particular has a venerable heritage in philosophy, though it is only by exposing its roots in intentionality issues that we see it clearly: to explain how it is even possible to think or say what is false or not the case. Plato discussed a version in the *Theaetetus*:

> If someone judges, necessarily he judges some one thing. So in judging, he necessarily judges something that is; and in judging something that is not, he judges nothing, and hence is not judging at all. Thus it is not possible to judge something that is not.

> (189a)

Given Putnam's focus on explaining how false theories might give way to true theories of the same items, the puzzle is central to his concerns. If what one says or thinks is true, what one says must be meaningful, and if it is meaningful, it must be intentional: it must be "of" or "about" something; indeed, if what one says or thinks is true, it must be of or about what is the case. Now if what one says or thinks is false, what one says or thinks is nevertheless meaningful, and if it is meaningful, it must be no less intentional than a true statement or thought: it must be "of" or "about" something. But, being false, what one says or thinks cannot be about what is the case. We might say "it is 'about' what is not the case", but this just means there is nothing for what one says or thinks to be about. So someone who says or thinks what is false must actually be saying or thinking nothing, and hence must not actually be saying or thinking at all. Thus we seem driven to the conclusion that it is not in fact possible to say or think something that is in fact false or not the case.

Providing an account of intentionality which resists this conclusion is a deep task. One needs to show how propositions can be meaningful even if no fact corresponds to them. The problem is well rooted in the history of analytic philosophy, and was a principal stimulus for Wittgenstein in his early work. His solution, naturally enough, proceeded from his account of intentionality.[6] In his view, "the possibility of propositions", both true and false, "is based upon the principle of the representation of objects by signs" (Wittgenstein 1922: §4.0312); the account of propositional representation (*ibid.*: §§3–4.0641) is based on a prior account of representation in general (*ibid.*: §§2.1–2.225). So propositions are meaningful just in case they are about the world, and they are about the world by depicting it. Propositions depict in virtue of two kinds of relation: one that is internal and structural, combining its constituent names, and one that is external and representational, connecting each of those names with constituents of reality. This account of intentionality entails an elaborate atomistic ontology: in particular, there must be an object corresponding to each and every one of a proposition's constituent names.[7] But it does not require that there be a state of affairs corresponding to each and every proposition. So propositions can be meaningful even if no fact corresponds to them. Hence the possibility of false propositions is accounted for: we can think and say what is not the case.

Aboutness-gap problems

No-object problems are not the only cause of difficulty in accounting for intentionality. They occur when there is a breakdown in one of the terms of the relation: there is a thinking subject on the one side, but apparently no object to be thought of or spoken about on the other. Another set of problems arises from a breakdown in the relation itself: there is a thinking subject on one side and a set of putative objects on the other, but no means of connecting the two such that the activity of the one can genuinely be said to be "of" or "about" the existence, nature or behaviour of the other. Call these "aboutness-gap" problems.

A familiar way of motivating these difficulties is to argue for an error theory of experience and thought. We may suppose that what we think about or experience are the public entities out there and from which the world is composed. But what we are actually directed on are just private representations of those entities, items which exist in our minds alone and from which, at best, we are able to infer how things are in the world (for indications that John Locke held such a view, see his 1975: II.i.19, II.viii.15–18, II.ix.8, II.xi.17, II.xxiii.9, II.xxx.2, III.ii.2). Analytic philosophers such as Moore and Russell developed specific versions of this general argument, being particularly attentive to the private representations in the subject's consciousness on which perceptual and cognitive capacities were supposed to depend, labelling them "sense-data" (literally, what is given to the senses). The general account was widely adopted with local variations in the first half of the twentieth century, among others by the Vienna Circle and those of its associates who had a major influence on American philosophy in general and Putnam in particular.

The problems arising can appear to be epistemological – how can evidence about sense-data give us knowledge about material objects? But the underlying difficulty is intentional, an "aboutness-gap" problem – how can sense-data be said to be "of" or "about" material objects in the first place? The difficulty was usually expressed, and tackled, as a problem about knowledge (see in particular G. E. Moore, "A Defense of Common Sense" (1925) and "Proof of an External World" (1939) reprinted in Moore (1962)). We seem to know with some certainty *that* there are material objects, and something about *how* they are. Now material objects are not logically private (different people can perceive the same object), and their existence does not depend on being perceived (they can exist unperceived). But our knowledge of such objects is perceptual, or at least based on perceptual evidence. And perceiving is a matter of being impressed by sense-data, items that are logically private whose existence depends on their being perceived. So how *could* knowing about items of one sort give us any evidence *at all* – let alone knowledge – about items of so categorically different a sort? But two features of this knowledge problem should be noted. First, we cannot solve it unless we close the "aboutness gap"; that is, unless we show how sense-data comprise information that is of material objects. Secondly, if we close the "aboutness gap", we solve the knowledge problem; that is, our grounds for saying "subject A's sensory impression S is of or about material object O" are the very grounds required for saying "given A's knowledge of S, A has knowledge of O".

The aspects of intentionality illuminated (or darkened) by "aboutness-gap" problems came to be of special interest to Putnam in relation to his exploration of what William James called "the natural realism of the common man" (Putnam 1988b: 232–51; 1999 (i)). Since the seventeenth century, philosophy has been dominated by views of perception built on the premise that there is an "aboutness gap" that can be explored, accounted for and perhaps even contained by all related areas of the subject, but must at any rate be accommodated. To resist this history, deny that there is such a gap and overcome the problems accruing, it is not enough to assert that the (direct or indirect) objects of veridical perception are external things, aspects of an external reality. For, as the terminology suggests, it is consistent with that line of argument to regard one's thoughts and what they are about as belonging to two separate realms, an inner and an outer, related by causal connections. By contrast, Putnam has defended the "natural realism" he associates in particular with James, John Austin and John McDowell (1942–): "successful perception is a *sensing* of aspects of the reality 'out there' and not a mere affectation of a person's subjectivity by those aspects" (Putnam 1999 (i): 10).

Analyticity problems

Logical positivism of the kind influencing Putnam early in his career and setting the agenda for much of its course directed attention on another intentionality problem: how it is that we are able to think or meaningfully state the definition of any concept or word; the axioms, rules and theorems of logic; the axioms of arithmetic and other parts of pure mathematics, or indeed *any* proposition commonly regarded as analytic.

There are various ways to set up the problem, depending on one's account of what it is for a statement to be analytic. And that in turn depends on the way one interrelates such statements with others. The logical positivists agreed with the early Wittgenstein that three distinctions exactly coincided: the analytic–synthetic; the necessary–contingent; and the *a priori–a posteriori*. What coincidence means is that, if a statement is true in virtue of meaning alone (i.e. it is analytic), then it could not have a truth-value other than the one it has (i.e. it is necessary), and it can be known without any justification from the character of one's experience (i.e. it is *a priori*). Conversely, if a statement is true partly in virtue of the way the world is (i.e. it is synthetic), then it could have a truth-value other than the one it has (i.e. it is contingent), and it cannot be known without justification from the character of one's experience (i.e. it is *a posteriori*). So Wittgenstein and the logical positivists were agreed, for example, that Kant was wrong: there could not be statements which counted as necessary, *a priori* and synthetic. But there are subtle differences in the way they justified these interrelations that lead to differences in the way that intentionality problems arise.

In Wittgenstein's view, the crucial link is between the analytic and the necessary. For a sentence to say or mean something, it must provide information in the sense that its truth must exclude certain possible states that the world could be in. Now necessary truths exclude no such states. So not only do they say nothing, but the world can make no contribution to their being true. Hence their truth must be due to their meaning alone (i.e. necessary truths must be analytic statements) and must be knowable independently of experience (i.e. necessary truths must be knowable *a priori*). In the view of the logical positivists, it is the link between the analytic and the *a priori* which is crucial. They treated analyticity as conceptually prior to the other two characteristics: it could be used to elucidate necessity and the *a priori* because it did not itself stand in need of elucidation. (This largely explains why Quine's attack on analyticity was particularly devastating to their position.) All knowledge of the world is dependent on observation and experience. Necessary truths are true independently of observation and experience (i.e. necessary truths must be analytic statements) and knowable equally independently (i.e. necessary truths must be knowable *a priori*). Hence it cannot be the world that such statements are about. *A fortiori*, the world cannot play any role in determining that they are true. And hence their truth must be due to their meaning alone.

So the main analyticity problem for an account of intentionality is this. We cannot pursue rational endeavours, let alone scientific investigations, without appealing to propositions regarded as analytic: definitions of any term or concept, as well as propositions in logic and mathematics. And analytic statements are by definition meaningful, for it is in virtue of their meaning that such statements are true: it is in virtue of meaning *alone* that such statements are true. Neither the world as a whole nor any feature of it plays a part in determining what makes them true or knowable. *A fortiori*, it cannot be by being "about" the world, or any feature of it, that such statements are meaningful. So how is it that we are able to think about or meaningfully make analytic statements? Either there is something other than the world and its features which they are about or there is not. If there is, then we must posit the existence of entities inimical to positivist ontology. If there is not, we must give up the idea that statements need be about anything to be meaningful.

Putnam charted a path between three positions in addressing these problems, adopting certain of their features and rejecting others: positions represented by the logical positivists, by Quine and by Strawson and Grice. He disagreed with Quine on the question of whether there is an analytic–synthetic distinction.[8] His grounds were that the "open-list" argument advanced by Strawson and Grice was sound (Putnam 1962c: 35. Strawson & Grice 1956). The argument proceeds by inference to the best explanation. Consider certain lists of sentences: for example (a) "Bachelors are unmarried"; "Triangles have three sides"; "Either Abelard is dead or he is not"; (b) "The mug is on the table"; "It rains in Virginia"; "There are human beings in that room". There is widespread agreement not simply *that* these sentences fall into two different groups, but also *how* (i.e. (a) is one group, and (b) another). Moreover, the sentences assigned to the two classes form an "open list", in the sense that *different* people can go on classifying *different* sentences, ones they have not encountered before. How are we able to do this? Evidently not by using a small memorized list to which philosophers have assigned arbitrary labels. The best, most reasonable explanation is that there *is* a non-arbitrary analytic–synthetic distinction, and it is to that distinction we appeal (however unequal we are to the task of *formulating* it satisfactorily).[9]

Putnam nevertheless agreed with Quine at several points. He accomplished this by a subtle manoeuvre. The arguments that Quine used to attack the analytic–synthetic distinction had failed in that enterprise, but they could be redirected against the *a priori–a posteriori* distinction, at least as sometimes conceived, and win success (Putnam reflects on this reconstrual at 1975b: xvi).[10] On this conception, *a priori* truths are *absolutely a priori*: truths whose ability to be known is so wholly independent of the character of experience "that a rational man is *forbidden* to even doubt" them, as Putnam once glossed the phrase (*ibid.*).[11] And he denied that there are absolutely *a priori* truths (Putnam 1975a: vii–xiv; 1975b: vii–xvii; 1975c: 60–78).[12]

So Strawson and Grice were wrong to assume there are *a priori* truths. They were also wrong in the way they tried to rescue their position in the face of counter-evidence. Notoriously, statements once granted the status of being known to be true independently of the character of experience have been shown to be false, and precisely by appeal to experience. Of course, the claim that there are absolutely *a priori* truths might still be defended, and there are two obvious ways to do so. We might say, first, that the experience-based discoveries that apparently lead us to reject these statements actually just show that we should change the meaning and reference of their component terms. In which case, although we have little or no use for the old statements, they have not actually been falsified and certainly not by any experience-based discovery. Secondly, we might say that the *a priori* or *a posteriori* status of a proposition does not guarantee that that status be known at all, let alone known *a priori*. So a statement might be *a posteriori* and yet appear *a priori* until the requisite systematization of experience and observation (i.e. scientific investigation) reveals its true status. If so, then the claim that there are absolutely *a priori* truths will withstand the loss of any and all statements that are taken to be *a priori*.

Putnam developed a view from the early 1960s onwards that rejected both options by advancing particular interpretations of the analytic–synthetic distinction. "Interpretations" is in the plural because across time, and even in the same paper, Putnam interprets the distinction differently. So on the one hand he argues that the distinction is "a rather trivial one" that is easily made; on the other he argues that it can be a substantial distinction whose borderlines are sufficiently vague that it can be very difficult to draw: "virtually all the laws of natural science are statements with respect to which it is not happy to ask the question 'Analytic or synthetic? It must be one or the other, mustn't it?'" (Putnam 1962c: 36, 39). What is going on? Is the model itself inconsistent, or is it just that the terms are used somewhat ambiguously?

The latter, I believe. Putnam speaks of analytic statements in two ways: as those that are utterly immune to revision, and as those so central to the conceptual system of current science that they are immune to revision by experiment and observation alone; a rival theory has to become available. Putnam is explicitly in agreement with Quine here on the "monolithic character of our conceptual system": it is "a massive alliance of beliefs which face 'the tribunal of experience collectively and not independently'"; that "'when trouble strikes' revisions can, with a very few exceptions, come anywhere" (Putnam 1962c: 40).[13] There is good reason to think that "analyticity" unmodified applies to either conception; but to avoid confusion, call the first "absolute" and the second "relative". Depending on which is meant, we can make consistent sense of Putnam's conclusions about the triviality-ease and substance-difficulty of the analytic–synthetic distinction.

The analytic–synthetic distinction is essentially banal if we take an absolute conception of analyticity, according to which utterly unrevisable truths exist whose discovery requires no philosophical expertise. Constructing absolutely analytic truths is not difficult. For any noun ("red", "head", "lead"), there is a semantic category (colour; body-part; metal) such that we can produce truths of this sort by their concatenation: "red is a colour"; "a head is a body-part"; "lead is a metal" and so on. It is on instances of this conception of analyticity that Shakespeare has Mark Antony draw in his joking exchange with Lepidus:

> Lepidus: What manner o' thing is your crocodile?
> Antony: It is shaped, sir, like itself, and it is as broad as it hath breadth. It is just so high as it is, and moves with its own organs. It lives by that which nourisheth it.
> Lepidus: What colour is it of?
> Antony: Of its own colour too.
> Lepidus: 'Tis a strange serpent.
> Antony: 'Tis so, and the tears of it are wet.
> Caesar: (*to Antony*) Will this description satisfy him?
> (*Antony and Cleopatra*, Act II, Scene 7, 38–47)

The description might satisfy Lepidus, but only because he is presented as a fool; clearly the description should not satisfy. Far from needing the arcane arts of the philosopher, one does not even require the specialized knowledge of a lexicographer or linguist to construct statements expressing *a priori* truths of this sort and to appreciate what one has accomplished thereby.

The analytic–synthetic distinction only becomes interesting and troublesome if we endorse a non-absolute, relative conception of analyticity. On this conception, non-trivial statements such as "There is a past" and "All cats are animals" count as analytic truths (Putnam 1962c: 39; 1962b: 237–9). Statements of this sort are central to the web of beliefs composing our conceptual scheme; they are statements on which many others hinge and depend. This distinguishes them as a class from trivial statements such as "All bachelors are unmarried". There is one tell-tale sign of the substantive nature and importance of these cardinal statements: it can be a matter of considerable difficulty and philosophical–scientific–historical interest to say just which they are.

71

Consider, for example, what we should say about the statement that kinetic energy is equal to one half the product of mass and velocity squared (i.e. "$e = \frac{1}{2}mv^2$") in relation to the overall conceptual scheme obtaining in the period between Newton–Leibniz and Einstein. Scientists of the time might have advised us of the overwhelming systematic import of the statement. Historians might tell us that this was simply the definition of kinetic energy: any physicist would have described the statement in this way. Philosophers might tell us that, within any conceptual system taking pre-Einsteinian form, it would be quite impossible to conceive of replacing the equation with a power series whose first term is "$e = mc^2$". How much of this picture would change if it could be shown that, in this same period, "$e = \frac{1}{2}mv^2$" was consciously advanced over the alternative principle "e $= mv$"? Evidently we could no longer say that "$e = \frac{1}{2}mv^2$" was definitional, nor that an alternative principle was inconceivable. But the claims about overwhelming systematic import would still obtain. So we could modify the philosophical claim as follows: within any conceptual system taking pre-Einsteinian form, it would be quite impossible to conceive of an alternative to "$e = \frac{1}{2}mv^2$" as *preferable*. And this is perhaps sufficient to give the statement relative *a priori* status; it belongs to a group that "can be overthrown, but not by an isolated experiment. They can be overthrown only if someone incorporates principles incompatible with those statements in a successful conceptual system" (Putnam 1962c: 46).

Another kind of problem is concealed in Putnam's choice of "All cats are animals" as an example of a non-trivially analytic sentence. This might seem immediately odd: have we not just formed a trivial sentence in the approved manner, associating a noun with its semantic category? But in his view, such concatenations will only render trivially analytic truths when the noun in question is a "one-criterion word"; "cat" is not such a word because animality is not a necessary property of its referents, in Putnam's view. "It might not be the case that all cats are animals; they might be automata" (Putnam 1962b: 238). This claim itself might seem strange: surely on discovering that Sammy the Cat is an automaton, one of the things one would be inclined to withdraw from it, along with its daily food, would be the appellation "cat"? But the question is a good deal more complex than it first appears. For suppose scientific investigation reaches new heights in recognizing various sorts of possibility, and it turns out that – as we currently use these words – not just Sammy but every "cat" there is or has ever been is an automaton. Then at least we have a problem in deciding what we should say: (a) it has turned out that cats are not animals; (b) it has turned out that there are not, and never were, any cats; (c) it has turned out that some cats are automata. The question turns on whether, and under what circumstances, the meaning of the relevant words changes or has been changed. And Putnam agrees with Donnellan that there is a point – this may be it – where the question lacks a sufficiently clear sense (Donnellan 1962: 647–58; Putnam 1962b: 239).

We began this part of the chapter by establishing the main analyticity problem for accounts of intentionality, and have now examined Putnam's position on analyticity. We can end by putting the two together and asking what implications his view might have for intentionality.

It seems at first as if Putnam is heading in the direction of the same kind of problems as those facing early Wittgenstein and the logical positivists. For like theirs, his view makes appeal to analytic propositions necessary for scientific investigations and for other kinds of rational pursuit. Indeed, he elaborates on the theme. We must appeal to relatively analytic propositions in the form of the cardinal tenets of the conceptual scheme within which our empirical and quasi-empirical investigations take place. Secondly, as with early Wittgenstein and the logical positivists, there is no question but that Putnam regards these analytic propositions as meaningful. But at this point Putnam departs from his forbears, and in a way that has a direct bearing on issues of intentionality.

Early Wittgenstein and the logical positivists had supposed, first, that it was in virtue of their meaning that propositions should be accounted analytic; and, secondly, that it was in virtue of their meaning *alone* that such propositions were to be accounted true and knowable independently of the character of experience (i.e. *a priori*). These were the aspects of their view that caused problems for intentionality. For it cannot be by being "about" the world, or any feature of it, that such propositions are to be regarded as meaningful if their truth and knowability are wholly determined independently of the world. And as we have seen, Putnam denies each aspect of the position that brought his forbears into trouble.

Meaning alone cannot classify analytic propositions as such. The only propositions for whose analyticity this might appear a plausible account are trivial. Meaning alone cannot account for what makes analytic propositions true, for the set includes relatively analytic propositions, propositions whose analyticity depends on the cardinal position they take within some particular overall conceptual scheme. Finally, meaning alone cannot explain what makes analytic propositions knowable independently of the character of experience, for there is nothing here to explain: there are no such *a priori* propositions. Hence the world as a whole, or features of the world, play an essential role in determining what makes any substantial proposition true and what makes any proposition knowable. And thus this particular challenge to intentionality disappears. In order to explain how it is that we are able to think about or meaningfully make analytic statements, we need neither appeal to something other than the world and its features for them to be about, nor renounce the claim that propositions need be about something to be meaningful.

Part III

Content: earlier perspectives

Chapter 7

Mind

The Mind, that Ocean where each kind
Doth streight its own resemblance find . . .

Andrew Marvell, "The Garden"

The first half of Putnam's career was dominated in large part by tensions induced by his relationship to logical positivism and verificationism.[1] The results were felt principally in the philosophy of science, the philosophy of language, and the philosophy of mind.

In philosophy of science, the main components were a developing realism, a rejection of the idea that any truths are absolutely *a priori*, and an assertion of the quasi-empirical character of mathematics. Putnam's claims here required underpinning with a realist theory of meaning. So in the philosophy of language, his focus was on terms that are central to scientific investigations (so-called "natural kind" terms), and his perspective tended increasingly towards externalism or anti-individualism. In the philosophy of mind, Putnam was stimulated mainly to think and rethink functionalism, understood narrowly here as a particular set of claims concerning the nature of mental phenomena.

The present aim is to distil from the details of this work a sense of the developing point of view from which it was written, first introducing its component parts in relation to sub-areas of philosophy, and then reassembling the overall perspective. In keeping with the interpretative focus of this part of the book, equal attention will be given to lesser known early writings in which the roots and first sketches of views are to be found (Putnam 1962a; 1962b; 1963a; 1965c; 1967c; 1968; 1971) as to the handful of classic and regularly anthologized papers in which those views are fully worked out and receive their official form.

Points of view

Realism grew to be the focus of Putnam's attention in the mid-1970s; previously, it had been a dominating feature of his perspective. The transition from point of view to point of focus occurred for a number of reasons, but the most basic shed light on the earlier period.

Realism has been called, correctly enough, "a syndrome, a loose weave of separable presuppositions and attitudes" (Wright 1993: 3–4). It comes in different forms, of which an indefinite number are, or have been thought to be, viable. To depict each in relation to others would require a device with several dimensions: a simple two-dimensional spectrum might plot one kind of variation, with complete mind-independence at one end and the last form of qualified mind-independence before reaching a non-realist position at the other. But we would also need to plot variation in views about the kinds of entity regarded as mind-independent, the kinds of condition under which they can be so regarded, the kinds of feature giving reason to regard them in this way, and so on. A realist about mathematics may differ sharply from a realist about moral properties, not simply because each can deny that the other is correct to assert realism about their subject-matter, but because each can deny that the other asserts realism for the correct reasons. A defining claim of mathematical realists cuts directly against the core of most versions of moral realism, for example, that the existence and identity of the properties in question are quite independent of the natural and culturally acquired sensitivities and sensibilities that characterize us as a certain species of rational and social animal.

Putnam is a keen advocate of Ockham's razor: we should not multiply entities without necessity (e.g. Putnam 1959; 1965d: 130).[2] On one application of the maxim, we should resist delineating or emphasizing the different shades of realism unless the situation demands it. So compare two kinds of situation that might face a realist: one in which the chief call on their philosophical effort is external, to combat forms of anti-realism (i.e. any form of opposition to realism; it is the genus of which idealism, for example, is a species); and the other in which their main task is internal, to resist false forms of realism, or to define the most viable such form. The first situation does not demand delineation or emphasis of the differences internal to realism; the epicentre of conflict is external, so advocates can ignore their differences and pool their resources.

This was the situation in the first half of Putnam's career, at least as he perceived things to be. For verificationism in its various forms placed greatest demands on his attention, and verificationism is a form of anti-realism. Suppose we think that the meaningfulness of a statement implies its verifiability in principle; or, more strongly, that its meaning is given by its method of verification; or, more strongly still, that that method is limited to what is observable. Then we have a decisive reason to deny the realist's view: that the truth of the statement might forever transcend our ability to verify it at all, to know its truth; or at least that the truth might stretch beyond our ability to verify the statement by observation. For in so far as that statement is even intelligible, it must be meaningful. And its having any meaning at all, let alone its having the particular meaning it does, precisely depends on its being in principle verifiable, perhaps by observation alone. Hence, far from being possibly true, statements that exceed the observable, or that exceed all evidence we have or could have for them, are simply meaningless. This is why verificationism is a form of anti-realism. It explains why Putnam, while focused on verificationist ways of thinking, was concentrating on realism's external relations, its foreign policy. It was unnecessary for him to be overly concerned with internal affairs, with exact details of the shades of realism to be advocated.

This situation changed with the successes achieved by him and by other realists.[3] By the 1970s, a realist direction of thought was widely regarded as the dominant position on relevant questions. Hence its advocates felt free, for a time, to turn their attention inwards and to ask precisely which form of realism was correct. This was the situation for much of the second half of Putnam's career (or, again, as he perceived things to be). But this is a transition, not a point of abrupt change. In taking realism as his point of view, Putnam sowed the seeds for taking it as his point of focus. Or to put it differently, it is because of the successes he achieved in attending to philosophical subjects in a realist way that he had eventually to attend to realism itself.

Positivism

Putnam's challenge to verificationism started from, but was not restricted to, arguments against the principle on which it was based. The logical positivists had attempted to apply the principle to various problems in philosophy, and Putnam set about systematically attacking each of these applications.

Philosophy of mind was one of the first areas chosen for conflict, and within that broad area, particular questions relating to the mind–body debate and the problem of other minds. The central governing question in the mind–body debate is how mental phenomena are related to the physical aspects of our being. The corresponding question underpinning the problem of other minds is whether we can know (and if so how) *that* others lead mental lives, and *what* those lives consist of; what thoughts they are entertaining, what feelings they are subject to, what experiences they are enjoying, and so on. The first class of questions leads directly to questions about how to characterize the nature of minds and mental phenomena, and the second to questions about how to characterize the apparent asymmetry of access to mental phenomena as between the first-personal perspective persons have on their own mental lives and the third-personal perspectives they must take on the mental lives of others.

Putnam produced a steady flow of papers on these subjects from 1957 through the mid-1970s (see Putnam 1957c; 1960b; 1962d; 1963d; 1964b; 1967e,f; 1969; 1973b,c; 1975b,g. He continued to write on the topic after this point, but the main focus of his attack became views of the sort he himself had earlier advocated.) It is easier to appreciate the essential features of his own positive contributions if we approach them roughly in the manner by which they acquired their form: that is, in conflict with the alternatives.

Given their principle, it was natural for verificationists in the philosophy of mind to focus on the question of what might verify statements containing mental–psychological terms. There were various possibilities, allowing advocates quite considerable leeway. Some, for example, were phenomenalists on the issue: they claimed that it is subjective occurrences of a particular sort that verify statements such as "Abelard is in pain", namely one's own experiences, conceived of as logically private events. Others were objectivists: they claimed that the occurrences verifying such statements must be logically non-private; such events must be observable by those suitably placed with the capacity to recognize the evidence for what it is. Positions of the latter sort gradually acquired supremacy.

There was still room for more than one substantive view, however, for there are different ways in which the occurrences in question can be regarded as logically non-private. And depending on the view taken here, at least two quite starkly contrasting positions on mental phenomena are available. Thus some positivists who took the objective view insisted that the events verifying mental–psychological statements be publicly observable, recognizable as such without need of unusual experimental situations, or of developed and specific instrumentation, or of special training. Others claimed as vehemently that the events in question were of the type whose observability did require the methods, instruments and circumstances of full-blown scientific investigation.

This difference of opinion reflected a difference in the application of a background distinction, between "observational" and "theoretical" terms. Some were sufficiently impressed by the fact that mental–psychological terms and predicates such as "pain" have an ordinary everyday use that they concluded that such words must be ordinary observational terms (like "chair", "flame", "blue"). Hence the first option seemed obviously correct to them. Others were sufficiently impressed by the fact that scientific investigations reveal what our mental–psychological terms and predicates refer to that they concluded such words must be specialized theoretical terms (like "temperature" and "pressure"). From this perspective, it is the second option that seems correct.[4]

Advocates of the first option tended towards logical behaviourism (e.g. Hempel 1949). For if the events chosen to be verifiers of statements using psychological terms and predicates must be ordinarily observable features associated with psychological states, the whole complex of events constituting the everyday conduct of subjects is the obvious candidate. It is Abelard's crying out, his grimaces, his inability to attend to anything but the damaged part of him, together with other events that we naturally associate with someone's feeling the sharp sensations or throbbing aches resulting from bodily damage, that verify the statement "Abelard is in pain". And now the overall verificationist doctrine with its central principle can be brought to bear. Knowing what any sentence means is closely linked, if not identified, with knowing what verifies it. Hence knowing what the psychological subject-term "pain" or the predicate "is in pain" means must just be knowing what kinds of behaviour people in pain display, the events which show them to be in pain. Thus the set of events including wincing, crying out, grimacing and so on are fully part of the meaning of "pain", the concept expressed by the relevant terms and predicates. Indeed, propositions containing such concepts are equivalent to propositions about behaviour, and their inclusion in statements makes them translatable without loss of meaning into statements about behaviour. This is a matter of definitional fact which need not appeal beyond logical analysis for sufficient support.

Positivists who took the second option tended towards identity theory: the claim that mental–psychological terms and predicates refer to states that are identical with states of the brain and of the central nervous system (e.g. Feigl 1958). This conclusion was natural enough given the view that, for all their everyday use in ordinary sentences to report mundane events, psychological terms such as "pain" are actually theoretical terms, postulates for items in a theory that it is the role of science to assess. For our best such theory is that the items referred to by these theoretical terms are particular neurophysiological events: pains, for example, are to be identified with events taking place in regions such as the somato-sensory cortex, the thalamus and the limbic system. These brain-states are, of course, not objects of ordinary observation. Hence, on this view, seeing mental–psychological states for what they are requires dedicated instrumentation, experimental situations and specialist training.

This is not the only way in which identity theory differs from logical behaviourism. First, identity theory regards the fact that mental-psychological states are brain-states as contingent; behaviourism asserts that the facts about such states expressed by its conclusions could not have turned out to be different from the way they are. Secondly, the identity claim is regarded as true in virtue of the way the world is; behaviourism, on the other hand, appeals to meaning alone. Thirdly, the identity claim is only discoverable by appeal to the character of experience – specifically, the kinds of regimented experience constitutive of scientific investigation; behaviourism appeals to logical analysis. Hence, for all their common verificationist roots, positivists who advocated the identity theory drew a very different conclusion with a wholly different logical status from the conclusion to which behaviourist positivists were committed.

Responses

Putnam challenged each step of the paths taken by positivists in the philosophy of mind. The first few can be dealt with quickly. First, and as we have seen, he rejected the verification principle itself as false of the usual term "meaning". We can, of course, coin a new term, call it "V-meaning'", such that the V-meaning of a statement is its method of verification, and only those statements that have a method of verification are V-meaningful. But there are many statements whose meaning does not consist in their V-meaning, and we cannot infer that any statement lacks meaning if it is not V-meaningful. Secondly, Putnam rejected as contradictory the idea that verifiers of any statement might be identified with logically private events: nothing of that sort could count as a means of verification. So phenomenalist versions of positivism fell away. This left forms that made the verifiers of psychological statements objective, non-private entities. And here, as a third move, Putnam denied the validity of the distinction to which positivists appealed when they diverged towards either behaviourism or identity theory. The notions "theoretical term" and "observational term" are wholly misplaced in *any* application, let alone in the philosophy of mind. For they only exist as the converse of each other – "taking in each other's washing", as Austin (1962) would have said – in a dualism that is sustained solely by a false view of what it is to engage in scientific theorizing (Putnam 1962a: 215–27).

Against positivists who treated psychological terms as observational, and who therefore tended towards behaviourism, Putnam argued as follows. We can imagine possible situations in which a whole people is sufficiently like us that they feel pain, but sufficiently unlike us that they do not exhibit any associated behaviour at all, or whatever behaviour they do exhibit is wholly extraordinary (e.g. they giggle, laugh and slap their thighs in the manner of Bavarians). Moreover, such people might regard the behaviour we exhibit when in pain as similarly extraordinary in spite of – indeed *because of* – the fact that they have the same concept of pain (Putnam 1962d: 304–24; 1963d: 325–41). And the concept we share is a name for a sensation (Putnam 1975b: xii). So it cannot be that possessing the concept of pain is the same as knowing what connections in fact obtain between someone's being in pain and the particular events constituting their associated behaviour. There are indeed causal relations between mental states and behaviour, but the behaviouristic positivist describes them wrongly. We need to appeal to three terms here: (a) a neurophysiology which is causally related to (b) being in pain, which is causally related to (c) manifesting pain-behaviour. Behaviourism removes (b) from the picture. So the only answer it can give to the question "what causes that behaviour?" is "this neurophysiological state" when we should (or at least should also) appeal to "my being in pain". Finally, since the behaviouristic positivists have so completely misunderstood psychological terms and predicates, they have been wrong about their associated uses, and in particular about the venerable problem of other minds.

Against positivists who classified psychological terms as theoretical and hence tended towards identity theory, one of Putnam's most effective weapons was a simple *reductio* argument (Putnam 1969: 441–51). If identity theory were true, then it would be true contingently, synthetically and *a posteriori*. Hence any statement using psychological terms and predicates must have the status of a hypothesis. But the statements "I am in pain", "I am sore" and so on, are evidently not conjectures whose acceptability or justification requires further observation, experiment and argument. Hence the set of claims discussed is false. More particularly, if "I am in pain" is not a hypothesis, it cannot include an expression ("pain") which is actually a theoretical term and whose reference might turn out to be something like an ordinarily unobservable neuro-physiological brain-state. Indeed *any* theory of mental phenomena that treats this statement as a conjecture pending future experimental confirmation must be rejected – theories that claim that what the statement really means is that the subject has certain behavioural dispositions, or that the subject is in a state that obeys certain psychological laws, or that normally has certain causes, or normally has certain effects, or certain causes-and-effects.

Functionalism

In the course of setting out his arguments against logical positivism in the philosophy of mind, Putnam began to assemble his positive ideas so that they formed a position in their own right. The key idea in this process was that, in their essential nature and operation, minds have a good deal in common with computing machines of a certain type (see in particular Putnam 1960b; 1962d; 1963d; 1964b; 1967e; 1967f; 1969; 1973b).

The so-called "Turing machine" is an abstract computing device that can be partially physically realized in an indefinite number of ways. It must be capable of being in a finite number of states corresponding to a finite number of internal configurations, and able to scan information about itself and about other things. Putnam modified this notion to construct a series of thought-experiments involving rational agents, where "rational" and "agent" are to be understood in the senses adopted by standard inductive logic and economic theory (Putnam 1967e). So a modified Turing machine would conform to the basic model with the following additional specifications: it would be equipped to deal with the environment (sense organs would cause reports), able to estimate the probability of various relevant states of affairs, and completely determined in its behaviour by the utility rule (to maximize estimated utility).

Putnam began by arguing that a logical analogue of the mind–body debate arises for modified Turing machines – that the essential features of the other minds problem arise directly for such machines – and then asked what follows from this. To prove the premise conclusively would require going into each aspect of the complex of questions raised by each problem in the philosophy of mind and showing how it has its partner in a philosophy of Turing machines. But Putnam succeeded in convincing many by showing what could be done with some standard cases.

Thus a standard argument for dualism in the mind–body debate turns on the claim that our mental states are directly known to us in ways that our physical states are not. And Turing machines are devices of which it is true that they are in some state (e.g. computing) if and only if some component of their structure is a certain way (e.g. the main switch is set at position A, corresponding to "On"). So we should treat being in the state of computing as the logical analogue for being in some mental state, and having the main lever at position A as the logical analogue for being in some physical state. The machine knows directly it is in the computing state because that is the mode in which its scanning abilities give it information about itself; it only knows the main lever is in position A indirectly because to obtain that information, it must conjoin knowing it is in the computing state with knowing the relevant theoretical principle concerning its own structure, that is, that whenever it is in the computing state, the main lever is set at position A.

A standard argument for logical asymmetry in the other minds debate turns on the claim that our own mental states are directly known to us in ways that the mental states of other people are not. This asymmetry between first- and third-personal perspectives is reflected directly in the asymmetry of access experienced by Turing machines between gaining knowledge of their own states and gaining knowledge of the states of other such machines. For Machine 1 knows directly whenever it is in the state of computing for the reasons given above, whereas Machine 2 might only know that Machine 1 is in the state of computing indirectly, for example by conjoining observational knowledge that Machine 1 has its main lever in position A with theoretical knowledge that whenever Machine 1 has its main lever in this position, it is in the computing state.

Putnam's main purpose was to show what follows from the fact that problems in the philosophy of mind also arise for Turing machines. Much depends on what we take these classic problems to have been motivated by: the attempt to understand specifically human experience, or to understand what it would be for any being at all to count as having a mental life. If we take the first option, then it seems to follow from the fact that these classic problems are not unique to human experience that neither their existence nor their solution will tell us anything unique about human experience (Putnam 1960b: 362–85).

The thought is as follows. Suppose we are trying to explain why England and France were so often at war in the Middle Ages. We are assuming that this is a special case. Hence part of the explanation must involve features unique to these nations – the national character peculiar to each, for example. And so we expect that, in solving the question, we must have discovered something about the national character of England and France. But suppose it could be shown that essentially the same combative relations have arisen or would arise between any two nations at those levels of socioeconomic development at that degree of geographic proximity. We might then be encouraged to renounce the idea that medieval Anglo-French rivalry was a special case whose explanation appeals to unique features of their national character. Indeed, we might conclude something more radical: that this rivalry cannot really be about French or English character at all. For the same relations exist between other (actual or possible) nations, and those countries have nothing French or English about them.

In the same way, we might suppose that the mind–body debate and the problem of other minds cannot really be about minds at all: we share the problems with computing machines, entities that do not have minds. But this is where the distinction noted above comes into play. For suppose we take the view that these classic problems raise questions not about specifically human experience but about what it is to have a mental life at all. Then radically different conclusions become possible. The fact that we share these problems with machines certainly tells us nothing that is unique about *human* experience: machines are not human beings. But it might after all tell us something very significant about *minds*.

Two suggestions are in play here, one more radical than the other. The first is the founding idea of functionalism. In so far as the problems arise for Turing machines, and these machines are abstract devices that can be physically realized in an indefinite number of ways, then perhaps minds should be regarded in the same way: put simply, it is their functionality rather than what they are made of that makes them what they are (Putnam 1967e: 408–28). The second suggestion is a possible application of this founding idea. In so far as the problems arise for Turing machines, and they are problems about minds, then perhaps these machines should be regarded in the same way as minds: the definition of "mind" and the notion of what it is to lead a mental life should be extended to machines.[5]

Putnam explored these options, arguing for an interrelated set of claims that composed a functionalist "model" for mental phenomena. It is in terms of its standard causal relationships, its "functional role", that we understand the conditions for being in a computational state, rather than any features intrinsic to the item realizing that state. We should understand the conditions for being in a mental state in the same way, as functional and not (for example) physical. Different material structures can be mentally equivalent if they are different hardware implementations of the same computational program. The mind is such a program, and the brain is just one among an indeterminate number of different possible computer hardwares that can run it. So the functional role of a mental state is to be specified in terms of the states that standardly cause it and the states that it standardly causes. In the case of human minds, for example, this will often be a matter of perceptual inputs and behavioural outputs, where interactions with other intermediary states classed as "mental" also produce characteristic effects. So Adam, who desires to distract himself from a headache, is in a state that mediates causally between various other states: for example, on the one hand those states that give rise to the desire, such as states of the brain (being concussed) and intermediary/mental states produced by sensory input (being in pain, annoyed, distracted), and on the other hand states to which the desire in turn gives rise, such as behavioural states (clenching the teeth, nursing the head).

The functionalist model can be adopted by physicalists and non-physicalists alike, depending on what kinds of states they are willing to admit as eligible to serve in these causal mediations. Almost all functionalists have insisted that only physical states might serve. Even so, they are quite distinct from the most familiar type of physicalist: the identity theorist who identifies the mental with the physical in various ways – at the level of instantiation of a particular state, for example, or at the level of the particular state instantiated, or at the level of the kind of state instantiated. Since mental states are to be understood functionally and not in terms of contingent features of their implementation, they can be realized in any number of ways. We cannot identify among various different brands and models of computer *the* particular hardware that *is* a certain software program. And since the mind is such a program, mental states are similarly to be abstracted from the possibilities of their implementation. Quite different physical structures can be mentally equivalent because they can be causally equivalent. So even if we delimit the possible ways of realizing a particular mental state to physical ways, we cannot identify among them *the* state that *is* the mental state – the physical–biological state that *is* Adam's desiring, for example.

Putnam's focus on intentionality partly explains his extended interest in functionalism and his long advocacy of the position, for it is widely recognized that intentional states are, of all mental phenomena, the most susceptible to functionalist analysis.[6] Indeed, when Putnam later reviewed his work on functionalism, he focused exclusively on this one application: "According to this model, psychological states ('believing that *p*', 'desiring that *p*', 'considering whether *p*,' etc) are simply 'computational states' of the brain" (Putnam 1988a (v): 73)). And it was precisely when Putnam recognised that intentionality is one phenomenon that functionalism in fact *cannot* explain that he began to look for alternative models of the mental.

As we shall see, this realization about intentionality sprang from Putnam's examination of issues in the philosophy of language, and in particular what it is to mean something by using words. Some words are such that, being in the particular intentional state of meaning something by them cannot be just being in a particular computational state. Putnam's interest in what it is to mean something by using certain words was largely motivated by what first stimulated him to think about the philosophy of mind: the need to provide an alternative account of intentionality from that provided by the logical positivists. So we should first examine other aspects of the ways in which he distanced himself from his teachers. Then we may return to the problems raised by the philosophy of language for his functionalist account of mental phenomena.

Chapter 8

Science

Like the geometer who seeks attentively
But cannot grasp the axiom he needs
By thought on thought alone   Dante, *Paradiso*, XXXIII.133–5[1]

During his functionalist period, Putnam identified verificationism
with a particular form of anti-realism that he labelled "the idealist tendency": "even if it is not identical with the view that the 'hard facts'
are just actual and possible experiences, it makes little sense to anyone
who does not have some such metaphysical conviction lurking in his
heart" (Putnam 1969: 441). And by this time, a robust realism had
come to characterize his response to broadly verificationist ways of
thinking. But he developed towards this position, and it is one that is
actually antedated by his resistance to verificationism. So it is worth
tracing the various reasons for his finding a particular form of realism
increasingly attractive. And to do this effectively requires a return to
the roots of his anti-verificationism.

Trivalence

In 1957, Putnam published a paper containing various ideas
stimulated by the need to resolve problems posed by Reichenbach's
Philosophic Foundations of Quantum Mechanics (1944), and in
particular his description of various possible microcosmic physical
situations. These situations are such that it is impossible to verify or
show to be false certain statements describing them, and yet those
statements seem empirically meaningful in a straightforward way.
Putnam developed the problem by describing non-actual macrocosmic
situations with this same feature. For example, there may be a possible
world in which the statement "My car is between ten and eleven

kilometres from Berlin" is apparently meaningful but quite unverifiable; a world in which it is impossible to verify the position of a car at the moment of verifying its velocity using a speedometer. Now the robust realist response would be to claim that the statement may nevertheless be both meaningful and true, while the verificationist will deny that it is even meaningful (Putnam was particularly interested in the fact that the physicist Niels Bohr (1885–1962) had taken this latter position, calling it "complementarity"; Putnam 1957a: 171). But Putnam rejects both positions in favour of a third alternative: the statement is meaningful but neither true nor false; it has a third value, which he calls "middle". Whether or not a sentence is middle does not depend on whether we know or ever will know its truth, so it is not an epistemic value, although evidently it has epistemic implications (we will say of the statement above giving rise to the problem "I do not know whether it is true or not").

We should not underestimate the radical nature of this proposal, and hence the trouble Putnam takes to rebut verificationism in a way that offers an alternative to robust realism. For taking his option requires that we reject the assumption that meaningful statements are determinately either true or false (at least so long as they are not irredeemably vague). This principle (bivalence) is required for classical logic, but in Putnam's view, it is a prejudice characteristic of analytic philosophy and comparable with privileging Euclidean axioms. Like the geometric system built on those axioms, two-valued logic has a serious rival whose claims should not be dismissed for purely logical reasons (Putnam 1957a: 172). In rejecting bivalence, Putnam distances himself from a bias that is perhaps not simply distinctive of analytic philosophy as a whole but definitional of realism in particular. For some have argued that it is unrestricted acceptance of the bivalence principle that essentially distinguishes the realist from the anti-realist.[2] This characterization is deeply controversial when rigidly held (Wright 1993: 458–78; Blackburn 1993). But if there is a looser sense in which it is apt, then Putnam's position in this early paper is actually somewhat closer to verificationism (being a form of anti-realism) than to realism.

When justifying the addition of a third value, many appeal to phenomena of vagueness. (The world itself may be vague, or, alternatively, it may be that the concepts we use to describe the world are vague; in either case, sentences such as "This is a heap" used in reference to some particular collection of sand-grains may be meaningful and yet be neither determinately true nor determinately false.) But Putnam thought that what spoke most forcibly in favour of adding a third value were reasons provided by science. And here he was in strict accord with Reichenbach: both appealed to the fact that three-valued logic would allow one to preserve the laws of quantum mechanics in both its forms, wave mechanics and statistical particle mechanics, and consistently with the principle of no action at a distance as it is there formulated (that no causal signal travels with infinite speed) (Reichenbach 1944: 29–34).

This is not just a matter of convenience, both theoretical and practical. For in defending the claim that the mechanical laws are compatible with the principle in two-valued logic, its advocates are faced either with internal difficulties or significant counter-evidence. As regards the former, it would be quite inconsistent with the realist position for defenders of two-valued logic to rule out incompatibility between the mechanical laws and the principle on the grounds that it would be impossible to observe instances: for example, causal signals travelling faster than light. And as regards the latter, verificationist defenders of two-valued logic might appeal to the fact that no causal signals are ever observed, or otherwise detected, travelling faster than light. But Einstein and others have pointed out what the mathematics of quantum mechanics entails: in certain circumstances, such signals *must* have outstripped light (Einstein *et al.* 1935: 777–80).

Modifying conventionalism

In a privately circulated memorandum of 1959, justifying what he felt could be justified about conventionalism with respect to geometry, Putnam again made the nature and scope of empirical discovery the basis of his appeal (Putnam 1959: 206–14). Like Dante in the epigraph to this chapter, Putnam rejected the idea that geometers could arrive at the principles and axioms they seek without stepping beyond "thought on thought". And the specific object of his disagreement here was the claim that one could arrive at those principles without stepping beyond a certain kind of thinking, namely that circumscribed by whatever conventions we happen to adopt.

In Putnam's view, there is a sense in which the choice of which pure geometry or axiom system to employ in describing the spatial relations among bodies is indeed arbitrary, a matter of convention, and not in the merely trivial sense that it is up to us what meanings we assign to which noises or inscriptions – either because it is up to us whether to speak according to systems in which such entities have already been assigned meanings (i.e. established languages), or because it is up to us what new signs to introduce to those systems. There is a deeper level at which convention plays a role: there are at least two different ways of assigning meaning to the geometric terms (e.g. "length", "congruent", etc.) that go to make up the concept of a metrical field, and at some level the choice is up to us. In dealing with length, for example, we can choose whether to treat that magnitude in terms of the function of one argument or of two: of the physical object whose length is being spoken of alone, or of this argument together with the inertial system selected to be the rest system.

But this is not the unlimited freedom it may at first appear. It is certainly not freedom *from* physical facts about our world; if anything, it is a freedom gained *in virtue of* such empirical constraints. For the best available scientific theory – the dynamical geometry associated with the theory of relativity – tells us that, in order to describe the spatial relations among bodies, we need a metric whose magnitudes are a function of both arguments. Consistently with this theory, we can choose to fix the rest system by fiat. This would of course render the second argument inert. But a function with no "play" is still a function. So the claim above was specified carefully. It is up to us whether we treat length in terms of a function of one argument or two. But it is not up to us to mean by "length" a magnitude which is a function of one argument or two. We are free to construct situations in such a way that, in considering length, all we need consider is one argument. But we cannot choose whether length is a function of two arguments, nor whether we need consider both arguments in describing other situations.

So there is a sense in which the choice of a metric in our world is arbitrary. But this is a strictly limited freedom of choice, and one whose limits and constraints are set by physical facts about that world. And if this freedom makes choice of a metric sufficiently arbitrary to support a modified conventionalism, then that thesis is not a metaphysical or logical thesis, but a theory with empirical content. Indeed it is a *bona fide* scientific theory, one that introduces the concept of a metrical field (identical with the gravitational field) as a theoretical concept whose meaning is given by the overall account in which it is constructed or by which it is postulated and whose adequacy is tested in relation to physical facts about the world it aims to describe. The empirical content in conventionalism is not provided by the fact that it is a matter of convention which possible system we use; it is present in virtue of the empirical facts that make it possible to use some systems and not others.

If geometry has an empirical character of this sort, it might be assumed that it is always a conceptual possibility for the laws of geometry to be abandoned or overthrown. But this is not Putnam's view. Indeed, he stresses that an empirical theory can enjoy "privileged status" with respect to a particular body of knowledge. Before mathematicians had developed a non-Euclidean alternative, it was not a *real* conceptual possibility for the laws of Euclidean geometry to be abandoned by scientists:

> They could not have been overthrown by a finite set of experiments plus inductions of a simple kind (say, using Reichenbach's "straight rule"); nor even by a "crucial" experiment to decide between Euclidean geometry and any alternative theory of a *kind* known to the science of that time.   (Putnam 1963a: 96)

No empirical tests could have led to the overthrow of Euclidean laws. Suppose Carl Gauss's famous experiment (measuring the angular sum of a triangle formed by light rays emitted from far-off mountain peaks) had shown that there *was* an appreciable deviation from the value of 180 degrees. Without alternative axiom systems, this would not have been sufficient to disconfirm the Euclidean description of spatial relations. For instead of substituting a new geometry of higher-level laws by changing to a different axiom system, the phenomena could be explained by modifying the lower-level physical hypotheses associated with the old system. Deviations could be explained, for example, by claiming that the light rays used to make the sightings "bent". (This is, after all, consistent with the physics of relativity theory: that light has a mass and hence responds to gravity by bending in certain circumstances; for example, when light from a distant star passes a dense body such as the sun.)

What was required for the abandonment of Euclidean laws was instead the development of non-Euclidean geometries and their conjunction with a background of altered physical theory and empirical data. Various axiom systems were invented in the nineteenth century, each of which rejected Euclid's assumption that exactly one parallel line can be drawn through a point not on a given straight line. János Bolyai (1802–60) and N. I. Lobachevsky (1793–1856) made it their axiom that there are two lines parallel to a given straight line through a given point; Bernhard Riemann's (1826–66) axiom was that there are none. Either would be consistent with appreciable deviations from Euclidean value in a Gauss-like experiment. For with the first alternative axiom set, the interior angles of triangles are always less than 180 degrees and decrease as the area of triangles increases, while the reverse is true for the second alternative set: the value is always higher and increases with the area of triangles.

It would be similarly mistaken to assume from Putnam's stress on the empirical content of geometric statements that he does (or must) endorse the view that there is a discovery procedure for the correct system of geometry. For, again, that conclusion is not entailed and he resists the temptation to draw it. To claim that geometry has empirical character only requires that we should be able to justify choosing one geometric system over another if they are inductively inequivalent. This holds for systems of physics just as it does in geometry, where the paradigm example is trying to decide whether light is a vibratory phenomenon or a corpuscular process on the basis of experimental evidence. Given two or more high-level theories, each of which has acquired its form as an alternative explanation of the phenomena in question, and each of which leads to different predictions when combined with their acknowledged lower-level hypotheses, it is justifiable to prefer one. (Putnam's view here is in acknowledged accord with Ernest Nagel (1961: 258–9); see Putnam (1963a: 96).)

Reference

Putnam's argument for modifying conventionalism rests on a particular premise concerning the way words and concepts relate to reality: "The word 'length' has a fixed referent which did not change when the Einstein theory was adopted (although the nature of that referent became better understood)" (Putnam 1959: 208). It is with this claim that Putnam most directly challenges classic conventionalism of the kind associated with Poincaré, expressing a view of the way reference functions which is a central feature in the background account of intentionality on which he is tacitly dependent.

Consider the claim that the assignment of meanings to geometric terms (e.g. "length") is arbitrary. In one sense, this is true but trivial. It is certainly arbitrary that some particular assembly of marks or sounds should go to make up the linguistic expression assigned to things in reality – that "dog" refers to members of the class of dogs, for example; some other sign or vocable might have done just as well (though none of us had or has the choice, so long as we talk in English and abide by its rules). But if this were all the conventionalist claimed, their thesis would be of little interest and even less reach, for once a particular sign or vocable is chosen as a word in a language, represents a concept, is assigned a meaning, then it might be thought that it is no longer arbitrary, or not wholly up to us, which things it refers to. If we wish to use "dog" in English, for example, then we have a certain freedom as to whether or not to apply it to inanimate objects that look more or less like dogs (e.g. toys), but we cannot use it to denote green, happiness or a sunset.

And this is the point at which the conventionalist thesis becomes significant: it claims that the choice of a metric is arbitrary even *after* certain vocables have been assigned meanings and hence given roles as geometric terms. On this view, the meaning of geometric terms is stipulated by a convention associated with the system in which such words find their place. The details quickly become complex, depending in particular on what individual conventionalists decide to count as such a system; how strong the counter-influences must be before they consider the system replaced or defunct; exactly how far they regard the legitimate functioning of laws as determined by convention, and how far by empirical generalization; whether they regard fertile processes and successful applications in subsequent research as necessary or sufficient justification for introducing new conventions, and so on. So the conventionalist has room to play.[3] But for the purposes of exposition it is more helpful to tell a simplified story about the word "length" that is consistent with the overall approach and that contrasts starkly with Putnam's view.

Before Einstein's theory was adopted, the word "length" found its place in a particular system whose conventions stipulated a specific meaning for the term, one that entailed that part of what "length" *means* is a magnitude that is a function of just one argument (the physical object whose length is being talked about). So, by definition, any property of a physical body that could not be calculated by reference to data relating to that one function alone could not be length. In so far as they believed this, people before Einstein had perfectly correct beliefs about what the word "length" referred to, and they were right about the meaning assigned to the term. After Einstein, the system in which the word was used changed, and with it the conventions stipulating its meaning. Its meaning is now such that, by definition, any property of a physical body in a non-fixed rest system which *could* be calculated by reference to data relating to one function alone could not be length. And so long as they now use the term consistently with this new convention, people continue to have correct beliefs about what "length" refers to, and to be right about what meaning is assigned the term.[4]

So it should be clear how, and how deeply established, is the disagreement between the classical conventionalist and Putnam. The question turns on the intentional question of how words and concepts refer to reality. For suppose we agree with Putnam that the word "length", in English, has a fixed referent that did not change when the Einstein theory was adopted. Then this word must refer to a magnitude that is a function of two arguments. This was its referent even before Einstein's theory was adopted, when it was believed that length was a function of just one argument. So, before Einstein, people had incorrect beliefs about what the word "length" referred to; they were wrong about the meaning assigned to this geometric term. And, after Einstein, people changed in that they now knew (or knew more about) what that meaning was. But the meaning itself did not change. And that is because of a background view of reference, and hence of intentionality.

On this view, the nature of the connection between established words and reality is essentially and radically non-conventionalist. Far from its being up to us what meaning words such as "length" are given, the meaning of such terms is not even given by what is generally accepted as a rule for their use. The rules for use that are generally accepted are true or false, depending on whether they correspond to the rules actually determining the meaning of such terms. And the rules that actually do the determining are established by features of reality which it may require significant scientific investigation to discover or reveal. Since the rules that are generally accepted are answerable to the actual rules, and the actual rules are established by features of reality, it is to reality that generally accepted rules are answerable for their correctness. So if we characterize mastery of the use of an expression as use in accordance with the generally accepted practices of the relevant community, then mastery of use does not entail knowledge of meaning. Newton had mastered use of the word "length", but he did not know what it really meant.

This approach to reference explains why Putnam can only adopt a much modified conventionalism. The choice of what marks and sounds to assign to which meanings is arbitrary, but it is not up to us which meaningful terms refer to what entities. Indeed, this matter is fixed so thoroughly independently of us that we may be quite ignorant of the true meaning of terms we use regularly, and hence quite wrong about what their actual referents are, what their nature is, and so on. The choice of situation to which we apply geometric concepts such as "length" is up to us; and hence we may choose to use "length" in a context where we need take no notice of certain aspects of its meaning. But this is a modest freedom that amounts to little more than can be achieved by setting scope while quantifying over certain entities.

For example, the word "dog" refers to entities with various properties, one of which is that of being an animal. If we stipulate that the entity of which we are speaking is the set of animals, we can leave out the property of being an animal in giving an exhaustive list of dog-properties. But it is not up to us whether we can use the term consistently with the meaning assigned to it to refer to things that do not belong to the set at all. The same goes for the term "length". Neither the function specified by the second argument in relation to that magnitude nor the property of being an animal in relation to speaking of dogs is ever wholly inert. We can justify their absence from the set of things we focus on only because they are present in the set of things that constrain our perspective. Remove them from the latter and they must appear in the former. To clarify: suppose we make relevant changes to the set when speaking of dogs so that non-animals are no longer excluded. Then the property of being an animal must come back into focus. In the same way, we can adjust the situation when speaking of length so that the rest system is no longer fixed; and then the second argument must come back into play.

So realism about scientific theorizing requires a realist approach to reference. And that approach requires an overall account of meaning, a semantic theory in which the referential component finds its place. Putnam developed such an account over the course of several years, before presenting it in official form in the early 1970s; it is to that theory we now turn.

Chapter 9

Language

As far as the laws of mathematics refer to reality, they are not certain; and so far as they are certain, they do not refer to reality

Albert Einstein, *Sidelights on Relativity* (1922: 28)

Einstein's point draws attention to the complex interrelations among three topics: how it is possible to make statements in mathematics; how it is possible to know those statements; and how it is possible for those statements to be about what they are about. If we extend the question to the whole realm of scientific statements, then his remark captures Putnam's deepest concerns. Given the conclusions to which we have seen him come in his early work on scientific theorizing, it became evident that his background position on intentionality (and most particularly on the way words refer to reality) required support in two fundamental and related ways.

First, it was necessary to offer a consistent explanation of what occurs as a result of scientific investigations and discoveries. Only then might one accept his view of the situation we have just examined: that it is people's beliefs and knowledge which changed, not the reference of the words they used. Secondly, it was necessary to supply a consistent explanation of what and how words mean what they do. Only then might one endorse his radically non-conventionalist account of the connection between established words and reality. And in order to satisfy either requirement, it was necessary to take a position on the nature of mental phenomena.

Recognizing the urgent need for corroboration in these areas, Putnam spent much of the 1960s and early 1970s attempting to reinforce his overall approach with related accounts of science-induced change, of theories of meaning, and theories of mind.

Dualism of the theoretical and the observational

The effects of scientific investigation and discovery are partly determined by their aims and methods, or at least by their perceived aims and methods. Both these matters are often described in ways that stress uniformity. For example, the aim is held to be successful prediction and the method systematization of experimental data and observation sentences through forms of deductive and non-deductive reasoning. One troubling effect of taking this uniform approach to aim and method is that what counts as relevant evidence tends also to be rendered uniform and constricted thereby. In particular, there is a temptation to privilege what can be perceived by the human senses without extra instrumentation and to downgrade, marginalize or even exclude evidence gained through other means. If observed in practice, much of science – evidence relevant to genes, quarks, elementary particles, for example – would be devalued or left wholly out of the picture. Putnam treats this result as a *reductio* of the cause:

> The use of such expressions as "the aim of science", "the function of scientific theories", "the purpose of the terms and principles of a theory", is already extremely apt to be misleading. For there is no *one* "aim of science", no one "function of scientific theories", no one "purpose of the terms and general principles" of a scientific theory. Different scientists have different purposes. Some scientists are, indeed, primarily interested in prediction and control of human experience; but most scientists are interested in such objects as viruses and radio stars in their own right. Describing the behavior of viruses, radio stars, etc., may not be THE "aim of science", but it is certainly an aim of scientists.
>
> (Putnam 1965c: 233–4)

Given scientific practice, then, we have sufficient reason to regard terms such as "virus" and "quark" as intelligible and to postulate the entities to which they refer.

This argument connects several basic themes with which we are now familiar, two in particular. First, the function-based appeal to use of a particular sort (scientific practice) so as to support the meaningfulness of parts of language. Secondly, the intentionality-prioritizing appeal to what must be true if the referential relation between words and reality is to obtain so as to support a particular view of what it is to engage in theorizing in empirical science. This latter theme became increasingly important to Putnam through the 1960s, at first as a means of challenging logical positivism, particularly on the question of how to model scientific theorizing, and then as a source for his own positive account of meaning. Since he engaged point by point with the contrasting model and benefited from the opposition, it needs to be described in some detail.

Carnap and other logical positivists had embraced a form of logical reconstructionism that took understanding the language of science as a principal means of understanding science itself, its history, methods, role and purposes. One basic move was to identify as "theoretical terms" words such as "virus" and "quark", and to label the objects and properties to which they referred "theoretical entities" (see in particular Carnap 1936; 1955; 1956). The intent was partly classificatory and partly evaluative. The first goal was met by establishing a dualism of the theoretical and the observational (one whose application we have already noted, in relation to positivism in the philosophy of mind). So on the one hand there are publicly observable entities and properties such as rocks, water, the colour blue and (though some would not admit such things[1]) those observable with the aid of instruments such as temperature, pressure; on the other hand, there are unobservable postulates of scientific theories such as genes, viruses, quarks, radio stars, elementary particles, unconscious drives. The former are observational entities referred to by observational terms, while the latter are theoretical in those respects. A full-scale dualism of the theoretical and observational is then achieved by raising the distinction between terms and referents to the level of statements applicable in expressing scientific theories. Observational statements are those that contain observational terms and logical vocabulary alone; theoretical statements are those that contain any theoretical term.

The second, evaluative, aim was met by wedding this dualism to the verification principle under its more restrictive formulations. Suppose we limit the means by which statements are verified to two: the meaning/grammatical structure of the words involved, and foundational forms of sense-experience – perception of objects and properties, for example, either with or without the use of special instruments. Observational statements are directly verifiable in this way, using primary experimental data (e.g. the clicks of a counter; the readings of a registered pointer; the position of a meniscus). Theoretical statements are only indirectly verifiable, and in a way that is dependent on verifying the reference of the observational terms they contain and verifying the observational statements with which they are structurally associated. Hence the dualism of the observational and the theoretical marks a distinction between statements that are fully meaningful and intelligible, and those in the process of becoming so. This enables us to evaluate statements, rating them by their level of meaningfulness. And so we obtain a particular model of what it is to engage in theorizing in empirical science. Scientists start out with a system of axioms made up of theoretical statements. By observation and experiment, they gradually substantiate the empirical claims made by those statements. This specifies the particular meaning of whatever observation terms those statements contain. Moreover, it endows with a partial meaningfulness whatever theoretical terms are embedded within the system. This is in virtue of the structural relations and bridge-principles (operational definitions) obtaining between those theoretical terms and their meaning-specified observational associates.[2]

Logical reconstructionist positions of this sort came increasingly under attack in the first part of Putnam's career. One reason, developed from the late 1950s onwards, was that they incorporated a false assumption about dependence-relations. They assumed that observation terms and statements exist on a level that can endow theoretical terms with meaning and justify theoretical statements, and that can gain its own meaning and justification quite independently of the theoretical level. Whereas many began to deny that there is or can be a theory-independent observation language of this sort, either because the dependence-relation actually operates in the other direction, or because the relation can only be one of interdependence.[3] But the challenge of most relevance to Putnam's own view had been developed by Quine in the 1940s and published by him in 1950: not just that it is false to assume individual statements about the world might be tested individually by sense-experience, but that it is quite wrong to suppose in the first place that there are sufficient grounds for a dualism of the theoretical and the observational. The notion of meaning does not allow us to draw a sharp boundary between those statements whose truth-value is contingent on, and those whose truth-value is independent of, empirical evidence.

There are clear affinities between these challenges and that developed by Putnam: that we have no reason to suppose it is possible to give the meaning of theoretical terms using only observation terms (Putnam 1962a: 225–7). For this applies one general challenge to logical reconstructionism (that it incorporates a false assumption about dependence-relations) to the particular area chosen for another (that its dualism rests on specific false assumptions about meaning). But Putnam gives the strategy a deconstructive twist which is both original and far-reaching. The dualism of the theoretical and the observational underpins the standard account of the role theories play in empirical science. And the reason we adopt this dualism is to solve a particular problem: how it is possible for theoretical terms to acquire the meaning they require to carry out their assigned role, allowing justification in science to proceed from the top down, towards observational statements. But there is no such problem. For justification in science does *not* proceed from the top down but "in any direction that may be handy – more observational assertions sometimes being justified with the aid of more theoretical ones, and vice versa" (*ibid.*: 216). And if we have no such problem, we have no reason to adopt the dualism on which the standard account of scientific theorizing depends. So we should also abandon the dualism and the standard account along with it.

Meaning

But what of the original question: how are we to go about giving the meaning of terms such as "virus", "gene" and "quark"? Putnam sees no reason to follow Quine into scepticism about whether any such questions about meaning could be in good order (Putnam makes his departure explicit in 1965d: 126). Instead, he adopts a function-based approach, asking about the way such words are used and drawing support from the way they are learned. (See Putnam 1954a; 1960a; 1962a; 1965c,d; 1973a; 1975f.)

Terms are meaningful if they belong to the common language or have been explained by terms that so belong. We are introduced to them in a number of ways, but principally by a dynamic feedback process between lexical definitions and the imitation of other speakers (Putnam 1962a: 225; 1965c: 235; 1965d: 127). Roughly the same goes for so-called theoretical terms as for common-language words. We gradually sharpen our sense of the lexical boundaries of a word such as "mass", of what it does and does not refer to, by refining our sense of its functional boundaries, the variety of situations in which it can and cannot be used; and, conversely, we use imitation in use to refine our sense of the lexical definition. This process is made possible by the existence of syntactic and non-syntactic rules of which competent speakers have implicit knowledge: they use words correctly without being able to state the rules governing that use. For the meaning of specific words is a function of the rules governing their employment. And it is implicit knowledge of these rules that speakers gain when they acquire the ability to use new words: they pick up the ability to say "mass" in the correct circumstances and in ways that satisfy the need to communicate without acquiring the ability to state the rules making their usage correct.

This function-based approach to the theory of meaning can be made to join up with the claim examined earlier: that terms have fixed referents which do not change with changes in the theories used to explain those referents. By the mid-1960s, Putnam was arguing as follows:

> Suppose, for example, that one asks a typical native speaker of English for the meaning of the word "gold". He is likely to give one a mass of empirical information about gold (that it is precious, normally yellow, incorruptible, etc.), in addition to the essential linguistic information that "gold" is the name of a metal. Yet, if gold became as "cheap as dirt", or began to rust, or turned green, the meaning of the word "gold" would not change. Only if we stopped using "gold" as the name of a metal, or used it to name a different metal, would the primary meaning change.
>
> (Putnam 1965d: 128)

So the meaning of terms such as "gold" will survive changes not just to scientific theorizing but to other contingent circumstances. This claim is perhaps even more surprising since circumstances can change to such an extent that the features on which speakers depended for teaching and learning the meaning of the term (that "gold" refers to a precious, yellow, incorruptible substance, for example) are no longer features of its referent. So Putnam distinguishes here between the "primary meaning" of a word and its secondary connotations. The former is essential to the particular meaning of a word where the latter is not; only if the former changes will the meaning of the word change.

This has implications for what it is to know the meaning of words. Recall that, in Putnam's view, when it became clear that the word "length" refers to a function of two arguments, what changed was that people began having correct beliefs about the referent. Before Einstein, they did not know what length was. It does not follow, however, that they did not know the meaning of the word "length". Certainly, people who have false beliefs about the referent W of a given word "W" may not know how to tell whether or not a given thing is W. But, in Putnam's view, they may still know how to use the word "W". After Einstein, it is not that people know more about the meaning of the word "length"; they simply know more about *length*, the referent of the term (Putnam 1965d: 126–31).

There is a complication here; an intentionality problem. Putnam acknowledges that the referent of a word must be identifiable and actually identified as such; otherwise the word could not have the use it has. For identifying the referent means knowing what its essential properties are (i.e. those mentioned in the primary meaning of the word which refers to it) and that it has those properties. And unless someone is able to make that connection between the word and features of reality, the word cannot be used to refer to those features. For example, it must be possible to identify gold, to recognize that it is a metal, if the word "gold" is to be used as the name for that substance. Putnam reduces the scope of the problem by drawing another distinction: between knowing the meaning of a word and being able to identify its referent. The former depends on the latter, but in a restricted sense. As long as *someone* can identify the referent, it is possible for others who cannot identify it nevertheless to know the meaning of the word. So the set of people who count as knowing the meaning of a word extends beyond the set of people who are able to identify its referent. This is so even though the word's having the meaning it does depends on its referent being identified (Putnam 1965d: 128).

This reduces the problem rather than solving it altogether. For suppose no one has sufficient knowledge of the referent of a word to be able to identify it, to be able to know what its essential properties are and that it has them. Then that word cannot be used to refer on the strong view Putnam apparently endorses; there is no intentional relation in virtue of which it is "about" anything at all. But we can think of cases where this might seem incredible. Suppose that before 1066 and for some considerable time after, no one had any means of knowing which essential properties length has. Then there was no way of making the connection between the word "length" and any feature of reality; it was an empty name. And yet, so one would think, King Harold and his military advisers might surely have spoken meaningfully using the word "length" before engaging in battle with Duke William at Hastings.

The various distinctions Putnam draws between knowledge of meaning and knowledge of the object referred to enable him to preserve consistency between his basic view (that scientific discovery does not bring about a change in meaning) and a strong intuition shared by all: that mathematicians and physicists before Einstein were measuring and theorizing about the magnitude we all call (in English) "length"; that Galileo was studying what we call "temperature" before that particular magnitude was identified with mean kinetic energy of the molecules involved; that Newton was thinking about what we call "momentum" even though he defined it as mass times velocity when, if it is to be maintained as a conserved quantity, it must be rest mass times velocity. These scientists knew what these several words meant, and so were able to identify their enquiries as investigations into these properties. Their beliefs about the referent changed, but not their knowledge of the meaning of the term. Indeed, it might be supposed that it is only because their (implicit) beliefs about the meaning of "length" did not change that it was possible for their explicit beliefs about the referent to change. Otherwise, there would be nothing to prevent one supposing that it was information about a different word that one was acquiring rather than information about its referent; that there had been, in short, a change of subject rather than a change of beliefs.

Putnam's approach to these matters required refinement in three major areas:

(a) What precisely are the kind of words with whose meaning and reference we should be concerned in developing an account of scientific theorizing, and specifically of theory change?

(b) How are we to characterize precisely the difference in nature and role between the primary or essential meaning of words and their secondary connotations?

(c) How are we to characterize precisely the dependence-relations between those who can identify the referent of a word *as* its referent (by recognizing it as possessing the essential properties mentioned in the primary meaning of the word) and those who cannot?

Putnam developed his position by concentrating particularly hard on these questions from the late 1960s onwards, at the same time that Saul Kripke was working on complementary problems and solutions (Kripke 1972).[4] Their findings are sufficiently intertwined that they need to be treated together.

Natural kind words

> For if words are not THINGS, they are LIVING POWERS, by which the things of most importance to mankind are actuated, combined, and humanized.   Samuel Taylor Coleridge (1896: xvii)

Putnam was particularly interested in developing a theory about the meaning of so-called "natural kind words". This is the set of general names which includes "gold", "lemon", "tiger" and "acid" as members. Such words would provide Coleridge with the best example in support of his claim, for they are precisely names for the kinds of stuffs or species that we regard as having basic explanatory importance for human ways of living in the world. The essential nature of such kinds is not given by analysis of the words used to refer to them, but by systematic investigation into empirical facts of the sort made possible by scientific theorizing. These empirical facts concern the deep mechanisms that regulate and constitute items in the world. It is by appeal to these facts that we distinguish not just between the items denoted by different natural kind terms, but between the meaning of the terms themselves (Putnam 1970b: 139–44). So the essential nature of the stuff denoted by the natural kind term "lemon", for example, is a matter of its chromosome structure. It is this structure that distinguishes lemons from oranges, and the meaning of "lemon" from the meaning of "orange".

Working from this set of core claims, Putnam develops the following position. Being able to determine whether something is a natural kind of a certain sort cannot simply be a matter of applying tests to it to see whether it possesses the particular properties listed as essential to that item. For suppose one has a certain sort of fruit, a lemon say, together with a full description of its chromosomal properties: a list set out in the terms of particle physics. One may nevertheless have no notion of what a chromosome is. Or, having such a notion, one may nevertheless lack the theory according to which this particular set of physical features on the one hand is to be identified with those particular structural features definitive of chromosomes on the other. Or, having such a theory, one may nevertheless lack the knowledge (because one has not yet discovered) that having this particular chromosomal structure is the essential property of fruits of a certain sort. If any of these conditions obtain, then one will not be able to tell that this list of properties describes the essential characteristics of that sort of fruit (a lemon). Now this list of properties gives the primary meaning of the word "lemon"; it is the principle under which that sort of fruit is picked out or referred to; it is, in other words, the "intension" of the term. So knowing the intension of a term is not sufficient to know its "extension", the class of entities that the term is about or refers to (Putnam 1970b: 141–2). Moreover:

> Meaning does not determine extension, in the sense that given the meaning and a list of all the "properties" of a thing (in any

particular sense of "property") one can simply *read off* whether the thing is a lemon (or acid, or whatever). Even given the meaning, whether something is a lemon or not, is, or at least sometimes is, or at least sometimes may be, a matter of what is the best conceptual scheme, the best theory, the best scheme of "natural kinds".   (*Ibid.*: 142)

Now the premises of this argument concern what one may and may not know. And focusing on this fact suggests two causes for concern with its soundness. The first relates to the set of premises.

Putnam wants to claim that one may know the meaning of a word (or at least of the sort of words in question: natural kind words; take this caveat for granted in what follows) together with the list of properties an item must have to count as its referent on an occasion of use without knowing the extension of the word. There is a trivial sense in which this is true: the extension of the word "lemon" is the class of lemons and one obviously does not know every member of that class. But Putnam indicates that he has a more significant claim in mind: one may know the meaning of "lemon" and the list of its essential properties, and yet, on being presented with what is actually a lemon, not know that it is a lemon. This follows, in his view, from the fact that one may be ignorant in the ways listed above.

Now one may of course be ignorant of what a chromosome is, or of the theory in which it takes its place, and so on. That is not in dispute. What is less obviously possible is the situation Putnam needs for his argument: that one can be said to be ignorant of these things while still being said to know the list of properties which, it so turns out, lemons must have to count as such. There are various reasons to doubt that one can be said to know the property-list if one does not know what its various terms mean, and similarly to question whether one can be said to know what those terms mean without also knowing the overall theory in which they take their place. But perhaps the most powerful derive from the function-based approach Putnam himself adopts. On that account, it makes little sense to say that one knows the meaning of a word if one is ignorant in these ways and hence quite unable to use it.

The second disquieting feature of Putnam's argument relates to its validity, and specifically whether his conclusion extends beyond the evidence in its support. To see whether this is in fact the case, it is necessary to appreciate features of his developing overall position.

Putnam's premises focus on questions of knowledge (epistemology), and particularly what one may know and fail to know about the meaning and reference of particular words. The conclusion he draws is that the meaning of a term, its "intension", does not determine its extension, the set of objects which count as its referents. Now this is, on the face of it, a semantic issue, one that gives the logical character and referential function of the terms involved. And it is usually important to distinguish semantic from epistemic questions.

This is not to say that evidence relevant to one is not useful in elucidating the other. In one direction, this is obvious: knowing which object a particular use of the word "lemon" refers to requires awareness of the word's referential function. But it is less obvious that the semantic features of a term are to be elucidated by their epistemic features. Indeed Putnam himself exploits the gap: the fact that people believed the magnitude referred to by "length" to be a function of just one argument neither determines the reference of the term nor shows what does determine that reference. And in the present instance, there does appear to be a significant gap between the epistemic premises and the semantic conclusion. For there is no immediately obvious reason to discount the following possibility: that meaning *does* determine reference even though one might know the meaning and not know the reference. Indeed Putnam acknowledges this possibility elsewhere in the paper from which the troublesome quotation comes (Putnam 1970b: 151).[5] And if the possibility exists, then the conclusion is false while the premises are true.

So Putnam appears to be defending an inference that he himself has reason to recognize as invalid; to be ignoring a distinction he recognizes elsewhere between the semantic and epistemic features of referring terms; and to be denying what elsewhere he asserts: that meaning, at least on occasion, *does* determine reference. So what is going on? Here is one possibility. The phrasing in the quoted passage is a little misleading, but "in the sense that" is meant to indicate that Putnam's conclusion is strictly epistemological. Meaning does not determine reference *just* in the sense that one can know the meaning and not know the reference.

This interpretation saves the argument by reducing the scope of the conclusion to the area laid out by the premises. And it has the advantage of being consistent with the overall view Putnam was developing at this time which would achieve its fullest expression in "The Meaning of 'Meaning'", an essay that first appeared in 1975 but which was based on ideas that had been presented in various papers and unpublished lectures from 1968 onwards (Putnam 1975f: 229, n.†). These ideas will be the subject of extended discussion and criticism in

Part IV of this book; for the moment, it is sufficient to summarize points relevant to the preceding discussion.

Components of meaning

On the function-based approach, when enquiring into the meaning of a word, we ask about its use. This holds for the word "meaning" as it does for other words. And, so it turns out, our use reveals that we mean several different things by that word, or at least that what we mean by it has several different components any one of which would be sufficient in certain circumstances to count as the word's meaning.

Developing his earlier thoughts concerning the distinction between primary meanings and connotations, Putnam began differentiating between extensions, syntactic markers, semantic markers and stereo-types.[6] He uses these terms to answer the three questions (a)–(c) set out above, and in particular (a) to give substance to his account of natural kind words, (b) to characterize primary and non-primary meanings, and (c) to distinguish the roles of different speakers in a linguistic community. A set of examples will serve to introduce what he means by these terms and how he uses them.

So suppose we focus on the situation in which Adam tells Beth what he means by a natural kind word such as "lemon". (This is precisely the situation Putnam chooses for his most effective treatment of these issues in Putnam 1975f; see in particular pp. 229ff.) In perhaps the most straightforward instance, he can point to a paradigm belonging to the extension of the term, a particularly lemony lemon, and say "This is a lemon". Understanding what it is to define something by ostension in this way, and in particular understanding how to interpret pointing gestures in context, Beth may learn what is meant without further help.

Notice that she has been assisted to identify the substance in question by a feature of syntax and not just the pointing gesture and the context which helpfully provided a paradigm lemon and enabled her to identify it as the object meant by having it stand out from among other objects. Hearing that the object meant is "*a* lemon", Beth will assume that a count noun is being used, and so will think the chances are that an individual substance is meant. Contrast this situation with one in which Adam says "This is acid", or "This is water"; in these cases, Beth will assume that a mass noun is being used, and so will think it likely that some sample of an extended substance is meant. Putnam calls these components of meaning "syntactic markers".

Now consider the slightly different situation in which there are many individual substances before Adam and Beth and that his gesture alone would not pick out any one of them. Seeing that, of the several objects, there was only one fruit, he might say "This *fruit* is a lemon", and in that way have Beth learn what is meant. Or if there are many fruits but the colour of the lemon is unique, he might say "This *yellow fruit* is a lemon". Or if there are many yellow fruits but the position of the lemon is unique, he might say "This *yellow fruit on the plate* is a lemon". We can think of these various additions like the syntactic marker: they go along with the pointing gesture and help the hearer (so long as she knows *their* meaning) identify the object being referred to. They are features of the semantics of the language in use rather than its syntax, so Putnam calls these components of meaning "semantic markers".

Finally, consider the wholly different situation in which there is no paradigm instance of a lemon in front of Adam and Beth and hence no opportunity to use ostensive definition. In cases of this sort, Adam will fall back on description. He might say something like the following: "A lemon is an edible fruit which, when ripe, is yellow, shaped roughly like the ball used in American Football, with the size and general constitution of an orange (thick outer skin; juicy inside) although it tastes tart and sour." This way of giving the meaning of "lemon" resembles the ostensive definition method in some respects; most importantly, syntactic and semantic markers play a necessary role here too. But the ostensive definition itself has been replaced by collecting together easily perceptible features common to and distinctive of normal lemons, an assembly of characteristics whose central components are ways of telling (i.e. criteria) that something belongs to this particular natural kind. Not all lemons possess these properties. Unripe lemons are green, squeezed lemons are flat, candied lemons are sweet. Nor is it necessary and sufficient to speak of just those properties mentioned by Adam in describing what "lemon" means; different speakers will add or subtract features from his description. So the properties in question are "stereotypes" of lemons, and that is what Putnam calls these components of meaning.

Putnam puts these distinctions to immediate use in supporting the basic account introduced above. Science discovers the deep mechanisms that constitute the types of species and stuff known collectively as natural kinds. And what these investigations into inner constitution reveal are, in the primary sense of the term, the meanings of the names for these kinds. In that primary sense, "lemon" means an object with a certain sort of chromosomal structure, "water" means H_2O, "gold" means an element with the number 79, and so on. Moreover, in that primary sense, meaning determines reference; the entities to which uses of the word "lemon" refer are objects whose chromosomes are of a particular sort and arranged in a certain way, uses of the word "water" refer to H_2O, and so on. The meaning of a word in this primary sense (which incorporates its extension) is connected to the use made of that word by competent speakers. For part of what makes them competent is that they continue to use the word (e.g. "lemon") for the purposes for which it was introduced into the language, and that purpose was to refer to certain entities (i.e. lemons). But this is the only necessary point of connection between meaning in the primary sense and competent use. In other places, there need be no connection at all.

Consider the three most important. It is not necessary to know the inner constitution of a natural kind to introduce the word into language in the first place, for the word is introduced by ostensive definition: pointing at a paradigmatic instance of some entity (e.g. a lemon) and saying "That is a lemon". This is not a task for which one needs to know inner constitutions (think of unearthing what may be a hitherto-unknown element; one can give it a name before examining it).

Secondly, it is not necessary to know the inner constitution of a natural kind to acquire mastery in the use of the word assigned to it once it already has a place in language. For we have mastery if we continue to use the word for the kinds of entity to which it was first assigned. And we have other ways of accomplishing this task, recognizing the kinds in question, than by identifying their inner constitution. We can appeal instead to what Putnam calls "stereotypes": those easily perceptible features common to and distinctive of normal items of the sort. Before the discovery of chromosomal and molecular structuring, for example, people said "lemon" and "water" and succeeded in referring to lemons and water. This was because they used distinctive macroscopic features of those entities (a yellow football-shaped fruit; a colourless, tasteless, thirst-quenching liquid) to acquire, assimilate and pass on knowledge of which names were introduced to refer to which objects.

Thirdly, it is not necessary for acquiring mastery in the use of a natural kind term that each person be able to state explicitly what its uniquely identifying features are, either at the macroscopic/pre-theoretical level of stereotypes, or at the microscopic/theoretical level of deeper mechanisms. It is enough that one belong to a collective linguistic body whose members include people with the requisite abilities, and whose structure sustains cooperation between these experts and their fellow language users. The background to these final points is provided by what Putnam calls "the socio-linguistic hypothesis of the universality of the division of linguistic labor" (Putnam 1975f: 227–8). This hypothesis about language might appear too slender a support for the heavy weight Putnam intends for it; as he himself notes, the claim "seems, surprisingly, never to have been pointed out" (*ibid*.: 227). But if we see it not as a claim specific to language but as an instance of a general position on knowledge, it gains considerably in support. For it has long been noted that not all knowledge is personal; that the concept may be applied, for example, to the scientific or academic community as a whole rather than to the cognitive conditions of the individuals composing it; and that, when it is applied to the cognitive conditions of those individuals, it is in virtue of their membership of the community rather than of their abilities and states considered independently of that whole (see Williams 1972: 3).

The point is worth elaborating in the particular instance Putnam describes, since it arrives at a significant problem for the overall position. In his view, just as experts sustain ordinary speakers in their use of language, so natural kind words in their everyday use are held responsible to their use as technical terms, as components of theory. Ordinary speakers accept the judgement of chemists as to whether this colourless substance is water or ethanol. In the same way, and against a background theory of molecules (their structure, possibilities of combination, and so on), the meaning of "water" as any speaker uses it, expert or not, is in fact H_2O. The fact that experts know both the everyday use of natural kind words and the microscopic or theoretical details that give them their meaning is necessary if these two aspects of language use are to be connected. But it is not sufficient. Everyday speakers have to cooperate in a particular way with experts if their use of natural kind words is to count as such; that is, as actually referring to the entities this use of words purports to be about. Non-experts have to be willing to defer, to acknowledge that, in knowing both everyday use and meaning in the primary sense, experts have the authority to determine what non-experts mean when they use natural kind words.

So Putnam's overall position depends on a deference requirement that directly challenges a claim that would otherwise appear intuitively compelling. We non-experts may not know the chemical formula of water. But, so one might think, we are surely independently authoritative about what we mean when we use the term. The claim that we would be wrong to think this is not the only disturbing implication of Putnam's ideas about the meaning of natural kind terms, however. As we shall now see, when fully developed, they present a formidable challenge to his own function-based position on the nature of mental phenomena.

Chapter 10

Intentional states

I was often unable to think of external things as having external
existence, and I communed with all that I saw as something not apart
from, but inherent in, my own immaterial nature.

William Wordsworth, "Remarks on his 'Immortality Ode'"
(Ricks 1984: 131)

Wordsworth is not alone in feeling his thought and experience to be
constrained in this way. Descartes had come to a similar conclusion at
the point where his method of doubt gave way to reassertion of much
of what he had previously taken on trust. For it seems possible for the
meditator to sustain much if not all of his mental life whether or not
the world beyond his mind exists. So he may feel pressed to conclude
that the objects that his thoughts are about and that he had previously
assumed to be "external things" actually lack "external existence";
that the states of affairs that his experience enables him to "commune
with" are not objects and properties in the world itself, but
representations that are dependent on and "inherent in" his own
nature (conceived in the Cartesian way as immaterial); that the words
he uses, being dependent on thoughts for their meaning, are similarly
directed on and refer to representations belonging to himself alone,
rather than to worldly objects.

This is one way to interpret the Wordsworth passage. But very
different considerations might lead us to feel equally constrained in
the way he describes. For the option just described gives us one reason
to deny that what we think about and experience is external to us:
namely, that we consider such objects to be internal to us. But suppose
we deny what this option assumes: that it is correct to speak of two
disjoint and complete regions of logical space with an absolute
boundary between them: an inner realm consisting of things whose
nature and existence depend on their being thought about and
experienced, and an outer realm beyond, an external world consisting
of the things whose existence and nature are independent of our

mental lives. Relinquishing this assumption would give us another reason to deny that what we think about and experience is external to us: namely, that we can conceive of no such disjoint external world for their objects to exist in.

So the constraint under which Wordsworth feels himself placed is open to two strikingly different explanations. The first option denies that one does (or can) think about or experience the external world; the second denies that there is such an external world to be thought about or experienced. The first draws a boundary between our mental lives and the world, thus entirely restricting the reach of our intentional relations to what occurs within the former; the second erases that boundary, thus lifting any such restriction on our intentional relations. As we shall now see, these alternatives illuminate Putnam's position and its possibilities in the years around 1970; over the next three decades, his account of intentionality would move steadily away from the first option and centre on a version of the second.

Computational states

The first vital steps were made possible by results Putnam achieved in the philosophy of language, those we have just examined concerning what one means by using natural kind words. Philosophy of mind and theories of mental phenomena were the first philosophical sub-areas to feel the effects of change, for Putnam's functionalism came into direct conflict with his developing theory of meaning on the issue of intentional states.

As we have seen, the version of functionalism Putnam first advocated centred on modified Turing machines. Minded beings, like human beings, are modified Turing machines; the mind itself is the computer program associated with such machines; states of mind are states of such machines or disjunctions of them. Putnam later acknowledged that human beings and non-human animals present counter-examples to the claim that mental states are to be defined in terms of modified Turing machine states. They are minded creatures whose cognitive psychology is in various ways not representable by the modified Turing machine model. It is not just that no *single* machine state is a human psychological state, for that might simply mean that one's description via a machine table as a modified Turing machine applies at a different organization level from one's description via psychological theory as a human being. And this would leave open the possibility that any human psychological state is identical to a disjunction of a large number of machine states. The problem is that very many human psychological states are quite different from any machine state. The identity of human psychological states is dependent in part on learned and remembered facts and habits, for example. The identity of machine states, on the other hand, is determined wholly independently of learning and memory. So various human psychological states cannot be a disjunction of any number of machine states. *A fortiori*, mental states cannot be defined by reference to the states of modified Turing machines (Putnam 1973b).

But this admission leaves functionalism itself in place, for the functional role of a mental state may still be its essential defining feature. That role may still be defined in terms of the set of causal mediations that state makes in relation to various types of input, output and other intermediary states. Indeed, those causal mediations may still be understood as computational, the implementation of a certain kind of computer program. So the only change we are forced to make is to find a replacement computer program to serve as our model. States of the modified Turing machine may not set the pattern applicable to the states of any and all beings capable of leading mental lives. But *some* computational model may yet suffice for cognitive psychology and hence fulfil this role. And we have hints of where to look, given the foregoing discussion: a computational program that can accommodate the dependence of mental states on learning and memory for their existence and identity.

Putnam's account of the meaning of natural kind words, if correct, renders the search for such a program pointless; it leaves very little of his functionalism still in place. To see why, consider the following argument. Suppose that Putnam's version of functionalism is true, once shorn of its Turing machine modelling of the computational program in question. Then, by definition, mental states must be computational states. More particularly, for the case of human beings, mental states must be computational states of the brain and of the central nervous system.

Now, again by definition, computational states are to be defined solely in terms of the parameters that would enter into a software description of the machine or organism in question. So their identity as such is quite independent of other considerations. More particularly, and again for the case of human beings, an individual's computational states are to be defined and individuated independently of that individual's environment (whether that be its physical, non-human environment, or its socio-cultural and human environment) and of other individuals in similar states.

Intentionality enters at this point in the argument. Meaning something by a use of words – meaning that p – is an intentional state, a state which may partly be identified by the relations between the one using the words, the words themselves, and whatever the words refer to or are about. Moreover, being in the state of meaning something by using a set of words is to be in a mental state. In at least two fundamental respects, then, meaning that p is like thinking that p, believing that p, desiring that p, and considering whether p: these are all mental states which are also intentional states. So they are precisely the kind of mental phenomena for which Putnam's version of functionalism is supposedly in the best position to account. According to that theory, a human being's mental states are simply computational states of that individual. Hence that sub-category of a human being's mental states that consists of their intentional states – their meaning that p, for any value of p, for example – is to be defined and individuated without appeal to features of their socio-physical environment.

But this final claim is false for certain values of p, according to Putnam's own developing theory of meaning and intentionality. For suppose that p stands for a declarative sentence containing a natural kind word such as "water" or "gold" – "Water is good for the health"; "Gold is hard to come by", for example. Then what any individual means by these sentences depends partly on features of their socio-physical environment – the chemical structures of water and gold, for example. This is true *a fortiori* for those mental states that consist of an individual's meaning these sentences. Hence at least some of an individual's mental states cannot be defined and individuated without appeal to features of their socio-physical environment: namely, those that consist of their meaning a sentence containing a natural kind word.

So at least one of our premises must be false. The claims concerning the individuation of computational states and the mentality–intentionality of meaning that p are close to being true by definition. So this leaves us with a choice: reject either Putnam's version of functionalism, or his developing theory of meaning and intentionality. Either some mental states are not just computational states, or an individual's mental state of meaning that p for any value of p is individuable without appeal to features of their socio-physical environment. Putnam himself decided for the first option, regarding his arguments concerning natural kind terms as sound and his version of functionalism as flawed. So we should examine his arguments in favour of his developing theory of meaning and intentionality.

Environmental dependency

The most renowned argument turns on a thought-experiment involving Earth and its almost-identical double, so-called "Twin-Earth" (Putnam 1975f). The following states of affairs are possible, because actual. There is an Earth. On Earth there is a substance, water, with the chemical composition H_2O. There is a language whose words include natural kind words, such as the word "water". An individual human being called Oscar exists and lives on Earth in the year 1750.

We are to suppose that the following states of affairs are also possible (though presumably not actual). There is a Twin-Earth. An individual human being called Twin-Oscar lives on Twin-Earth in the year 1750. Twin-Earth is as similar as can be the case to Earth, and Twin-Oscar is as similar as can be the case to Oscar, while allowing for the following difference. On Twin-Earth, there is no substance with the chemical composition H_2O. There is, however, a substance which Oscar and the inhabitants of Twin-Earth call "water" and which has all the macroscopic and observable properties of H_2O on Earth. This substance (call it "twater" to avoid confusion) has the chemical composition XYZ. So XYZ on Twin-Earth looks, tastes and smells the same as H_2O on Earth; it is found in the same places and is used for the same purposes.

We are also to suppose that, on the dot of midnight, 1 January 1750, Oscar says "Water is good for the health". Being identical in every respect consistent with whatever differences proceed from the fact that there is one substance in their respective environments that has a different chemical composition, Twin-Oscar utters the same sentence at the moment.

Putnam claims that Oscar and Twin-Oscar mean something quite different by their words "Water is good for the health". The extent of the difference can be measured in the following way. What distinguishes their utterances is not simply that they have produced two different statements, but that they have used two entirely different sentences to do so. So this is not like the case in which two people produce the same statement using different sentences, for example, when I say "I am hot" and you say of me "You are hot". Nor is it like the case in which two people produce different statements using the same sentence, for example, when we both say "I am hot".[1] Rather, it is like the case in which I say "Water is hard to come by" and you say "Gold is hard to come by". For the two different sentences produced are used to express two different statements, and they do so for the same reason: although the predicates are identical, the constituent designators refer to two different things in the mouths of Oscar and Twin-Oscar. We might say, then, that Oscar's use of the word "water" is merely a homonym of the word Twin-Oscar uses, just as "bank$_{river}$" and "bank$_{money}$" are homonyms of each other. The fact that the signs have the same visual and acoustic form is not significant to the question of meaning. The cases are not entirely analogous, of course, since there is considerable overlap in role between Oscar's use of "water" and the word Twin-Oscar uses, whereas there is little or none between "bank$_{river}$" and "bank$_{money}$". But the essential point remains the same: whatever overlap exists in their role, the words themselves remain different.

Putnam's argument for this conclusion is simple, and may be reduced to two premises. First, he notes that "water" differs in its extension in the mouths of Oscar and Twin-Oscar. This is to say that the designated object for which "water" stands in Oscar's mouth differs from that for which "water" stands in Twin-Oscar's mouth. When Oscar used "water", it referred to the substance we refer to now on Earth as water, the stuff with the chemical composition H_2O. Twin-Oscar, on the other hand, used a word which referred to the substance with the chemical composition XYZ. And, by definition, the designated object for which a word or phrase stands is the extension of that word or phrase. Secondly, Putnam makes a natural assumption: that a difference in extension entails a difference in meaning. Or to express this differently, it cannot be the case that there are two different designated objects for which two words stand, and yet those two words mean the same thing. And Putnam's conclusion follows from these two premises: if there is a difference in the designated objects for which "water" stands in Oscar's and Twin-Oscar's mouths, then they mean different things by the word. And hence they mean something different by saying "Water is good for the health".

According to Putnam, this conclusion has the following implication: what any individual means by a sentence containing a natural kind word depends partly on features of their sociophysical environment. In the case of "Water is good for the health", for example, it depends on the chemical structure of water. Hence any mental states that consist of an individual's meaning sentences of this sort cannot be defined and individuated solely by appeal to their brain and central nervous system. And so functionalism, at least in the computation-state version he had held, must be false.

To complete the picture, Putnam used his Earth/Twin-Earth thought-experiment for a particular kind of diagnosis: to determine what is right and what is wrong concerning widely held assumptions among philosophers in the history of the subject who have dealt with language. It will be useful to define terms first. So distinguish between psychological states as they might narrowly be conceived, and such states under a broad conception. Conceived in narrow terms, being in a psychological state presupposes nothing about the existence of anything other than the individual to whom the state is ascribed. Conceived broadly, being in such a state does presuppose something other than that individual.

Putnam identified two common assumptions concerning what it is to mean something by the use of a word or phrase. The first is that meaning something of this sort is a matter of being in a psychological state as narrowly conceived; so call this the *narrow assumption*. The second is that the meaning of a word or phrase determines or fixes its reference. Or to express this position slightly differently: which object counts as the object designated by the use of a word or phrase on a particular occasion of use depends on the meaning of that word or phrase. Call this the *determination assumption*.

These two assumptions have determined much in the development of philosophy of language. But the first piece of information which the Earth/Twin-Earth scenario exposes is that, given the additional assumptions establishing the thought experiment (that there is an Earth and a Twin-Earth, etc.), the *narrow* and *determination assumptions* are not even consistent with one another. If the narrow assumption is true, then the fact that the two Oscars are as identical as can be shows that they must mean the same thing by using the word "water". So the determination assumption must be false, for if the extensions of the two uses of "water" differ even though the two Oscars mean the same by using the word, it cannot be the case that meaning determines reference. Conversely, if the determination assumption is true, then the fact that the extensions of "water" differ in the mouths of the two Oscars shows that they must mean different things by using the word. So the narrow assumption must be false; for if their meaning something by using the word were a matter of being in a state as narrowly conceived, and they are as identical as can be, what they mean must also be the same.

So the Earth/Twin-Earth thought-experiment reveals an inconsistency: it cannot be the case that the two assumptions are true together.

Moreover, in Putnam's view, wider considerations show that it is the narrow assumption we should reject and the determination assumption we should endorse. This is the second piece of information which the experiment makes clear.

In Putnam's view, we should regard the determination assumption as correct: the meaning of a word determines its reference. This assumption is not only consistent with the argument as rehearsed, it is deeply supportive of it, for it justifies and explains the second premise of that argument. It is precisely because meaning determines extension and because we readily accept this fact that we were ready to assume that any difference in extension entails a difference in meaning. The narrow assumption, on the other hand, should be regarded as false: meaning something by at least some kinds of words (i.e. natural kind words) must presuppose the obtaining of certain environmental conditions. Oscar and Twin-Oscar are, by hypothesis and considered as individuals, as identical as can be; Oscar is in some psychological state as narrowly conceived just in case Twin-Oscar is. So the fact that Oscar means water and Twin-Oscar means twater by their saying "water" is not something that can be explained by appeal to features of these individuals alone. If we are to explain why what they mean differs, we must appeal to those features of their environments relevant to the extension of the terms. Hence we must suppose that, at least in the case of some words, meaning what one does by using them is a matter of being in a psychological state as broadly conceived. In the particular case of meaning something by using the word "water", for example, the extra-individual features relevant to individuating that mental state are physical. For what explains the differences in what Oscar and Twin-Oscar mean are differences in the two physical environments of Earth and Twin-Earth, differences between substances composed of H_2O and XYZ. So the narrow assumption must be rejected.

And this is precisely why Putnam's version of functionalism should also be rejected; as one of a number of flawed positions in the philosophy of mind which entail the narrow assumption. Any account of intentionality that makes meaning something by using a natural kind word supervene on an individual's psychology, as narrowly conceived, must be rejected. Recall, for instance, the Wordsworth passage and the first interpretation of what gave rise to it. So long as an individual is capable of meaning something by the use of natural kind words, it must be false to claim or imply that their mental states might be the way they are, regardless of whether the world external to them exists, or regardless of what it is like; conversely, it must be true that there is a world external to an individual, and that it exists in some way, if they are to mean what they do by using natural kind words.

The relevant conclusion of Putnam's developing account of intentionality can be summarized in the following way, enabling its component parts to be clearly visible: (a) a subject S's meaning what he does (b) by using certain natural kind words (c) cannot be a psychological fact narrowly conceived (d) because it is partly determined by a physical fact about the world in which S lives (e), which is scientifically ascertainable.

Part (a) makes it clear that Putnam's focus here is on the implications for philosophy of language, and in particular for the theory of meaning. Part (b) notes that, within the scope of such a theory, Putnam's attention is directed more narrowly still on a certain class of words; namely, those used to denote kinds of stuffs or species that we regard as having basic explanatory significance. Part (c) reflects the view that meaning something by the words in question cannot be a fact about individuals that holds independently of the world external to them; *a fortiori*, it cannot be a fact about an individual's brain and central nervous system that holds independently of the external world. Part (d) notes that the meaning of natural kind terms determines their reference on physical facts about their extension. Putnam's "division of labour" thesis, which we examined previously, does not make the extension of such terms dependent on features of the socio-cultural environment in which speakers live; in whatever such environment and in whatever age, the extension of "water" still depends on its microphysical structure. The point is just that ordinary speakers can mean something that is hidden from them in virtue of experts from whom it is not hidden – speaking in 1750, for example, Oscar and Twin-Oscar have no reason to know that they are referring to H_2O and XYZ respectively, even though they are; nor even that what they mean by using the word "water" differs, even though it does. In short, socio-cultural phenomena can play a role in explaining how meaning is transferred or mediated, but not how it is determined. Finally, (e) records Putnam's view that the relevant facts *are* scientifically ascertainable in his examples. It is unclear whether they must be. A familiar sort of realist would assert that the relevant physical facts in virtue of which a speaker means what he does by a natural kind word might forever transcend our knowledge, and perhaps even our ability to know them.

Opposing strategies

There are two broad ways in which to challenge Putnam's position: that it is unfounded because the arguments in its support fail, or that it is undeveloped because the arguments in its support can be extended. In one direction, critics claim that Putnam goes too far; in the other, they claim that he does not go far enough. We shall examine both strategies in what follows.

Consider first those who claim Putnam does not go far enough. Strategies of this sort may be appreciated most easily if we focus on those elements of his main claim that we have already isolated and individuated. So, as regards (a), we should perhaps extend the conclusions beyond the philosophy of language to the philosophy of mind and to an account of intentionality as conceived quite generally. On this view, it is not simply meaning something by using natural kind words which is to be broadly conceived, but entertaining any propositional attitude which is expressible using them – thinking about water, for example; having beliefs about it; desiring it; and so on (see McGinn 1977). The argument would be simple enough. Intentional states are individuated by their truth-conditions; that is, where x and y are intentional states, x is the same state as y just in case x has the same truth-conditions as y. And the truth-conditions of Oscar's intentional states differ from Twin-Oscar's when they have water-thoughts. For if Oscar and Twin-Oscar believe that "Water is refreshing", what they believe is true if and only if, in one case, H_2O is refreshing, and, in the other, case, XYZ is refreshing. Hence Oscar and Twin-Oscar must believe something different which they express by their words "Water is refreshing"; indeed, they must be in different intentional states.

We might extend the other components of Putnam's developing theory of intentionality also. In brief, and in relation to (b), we might widen the focus from natural kind terms to others, and in particular to those words with a similarly basic explanatory role: for example, other general terms, demonstrative expressions ("This F"; "That F"), and predicate-expressions. As regards (c), we might challenge the assumption that psychological facts and states must be conceived narrowly, so that the "broad" state of meaning something by a natural kind word must be some kind of composite: a narrow psychological state, combined with relations between the subject of that state and the world. Putnam seems to make this assumption when he says that meaning something by a natural kind word can be decomposed into several factors, and in particular what is common to Oscar and Twin-Oscar (the "stereotype" or set of descriptions used to identify samples of the extension) and what is distinctive about them (the extension or truth-conditions of the sentences they utter). So instead of claiming that a psychological state as narrowly conceived cannot be *all* there is to meaning something by using certain words, perhaps we should say that there is *nothing* about such meaning that is intrinsic to the individual. This would be to revise the dominant conception of what it is to be in a state of mind, making it broad or world-involving by regarding the notions of a psychological fact and state as denoting the kinds of entity that could themselves incorporate relations to the world. This would be to accommodate Putnam's findings by extending the mind itself, rather than attaching non-mental environmental relations to it. As regards (d), we might want to allow for the determination of meaning by socio-cultural facts, rather than delimiting it to the physical features of the subject's environment. And finally, in relation to (e), we might extend the relevant facts to what is macroscopically ascertainable, and perhaps even ascertainable without appeal to the special sciences.

Those who wish to adopt the opposite strategy, of claiming that Putnam goes too far, might begin by pointing to weaknesses, or apparent weaknesses, in his Earth/Twin-Earth thought-experiment. It might be said, for example, that the difference in meaning between Earth and Twin-Earth depends on the fact that scientists in each environment can tell that H_2O is not XYZ. This is an example of an apparent weakness, however, for the thought-experiment takes place in 1750, before modern chemistry, when scientists could not have told this difference. Yet the reference of "water" still differs, at least on the realist view we have seen Putnam defend from the start of his interest in matters of reference under the impact of scientific change. It is not plausible – indeed, perhaps, the development of science requires that it is not consistent – to say that the reference changed when the scientists discovered more about water.

An alternative strategy would pose a kind of constructive dilemma for Putnam. His argument requires that Oscar and Twin-Oscar should not differ in their intrinsic properties; all that should differ is certain features of their environment. The problem is that most of our bodies are composed of water. So either there is water on Twin-Earth after all or there is not. If there is, Twin-Oscar does have the resources to mean and think about H_2O, so there is no difference in what he means or thinks. If there is not, Twin-Oscar must be mostly composed of a substance entirely different from Oscar, so there is a major difference between them, one that we might suppose carries over into their psychology, as narrowly conceived. This is an example of a genuine weakness with Putnam's thought-experiment, but one that can be remedied by minor modifications to the original case. For the cause of the problem indicates the strategy for response: choose another natural kind, one out of which the bodies of Oscar and Twin-Oscar are not constituted. Suppose then that what these individuals say is "Topaz is beautiful to look at" (see Segal 2000: 25–6); the rest of the argument goes through in the original way.

Modifying matters in this way has the additional benefit of evading several other objections of a similar type, objections that focus on weaknesses with the original case but do not trouble the underlying argument. First, for example, it motivates Putnam's claims without the need to posit Twin-Earth. For it so happens that, on Earth, topaz is macroscopically indistinguishable from citrine, although their chemical composition is quite different: $Al_2SiO_4(OH, F)_2$ and SiO_2, respectively. Secondly, the topaz–citrine example is not simply conceptually possible but nomologically possible. Although nothing with a significantly different structure from H_2O could be macroscopically very like water, something (i.e. citrine) is macroscopically identical to topaz and yet has a significantly different structure. Thirdly, this example focuses on a concept with sufficiently sharp boundaries. There is no danger that "topaz" might refer to such a spread of substances beyond $Al_2SiO_4(OH, F)_2$ that it might equally be said to refer to SiO_2. Putnam's own case seems to fail in this respect. For his argument requires that the truth-conditions of "Water is good for the health" differ between Earth and Twin-Earth. But the word "water" is used in an imprecise way on Earth, covering substances with similar macrophysical properties to H_2O but wholly different chemical structures; consider tap water with its various additives and impurities, or the hydrogen isotope heavy water (D_2O). Given this referential generosity, there may be no principled reason to disallow the claim that "water" covers XYZ also, in which case, of course, the truth-conditions of the sentence in question would remain the same across Earth and Twin-Earth.

Perhaps the strongest set of objections to Putnam's developing theory of meaning and intentionality picks up from those noted at the end of Chapter 9. It is plausible to suppose that, in the main, we know what we are thinking; that believing we are having a certain thought is enough to justify that belief; that knowing what we think does not depend on appeal to the evidence of our own behaviour or experts. Yet

Putnam's position seems to challenge these general kinds of so-called "first-personal authority". Moreover, it challenges that specific kind of authority expressed by Wittgenstein in his remark "The meaning of a word is what the explanation of meaning explains" (Wittgenstein 1958: §560). For in 1750, before the advent of modern chemistry, the twins would give the same explanation of what they mean by using the word. But, so it turns out, they are in certain respects wrong about what they believe they think, and in certain respects they are just under-informed and need to appeal to experts to know what they think. They are wrong because they think there is no difference in what they mean; they are under-informed because it takes experts to tell them what in fact they do mean.

At this point, appeal might be made to Putnam's notion of the "linguistic division of labour". Suppose that what one means by using an expression is something that can be known by all speakers who have learned its use in virtue of the fact that some speakers (members of the special expert-class) have a way of recognizing what the expression refers to and picks out. Then it seems we can resist the worst implication of Putnam's arguments. Scientific experts do not *tell* us what we know; we do not need to appeal to them. What we know we already know as a result (via dependence on the expertise of scientists) of what they know. But this response raises various questions in its turn, and in particular concerning the world at a time when the experts did not know about the chemical composition of water (or, what comes to the same thing, when there were no water-experts). Did no one *at that time* know what they meant when using the word "water"? If so, then our claims to first-personal authority are still challenged. For it seems that what authority we have over what we think does not derive from us but has been acquired through results obtained by others. If Oscar and Twin-Oscar live long enough, then apparently they *will* be in a position to be told what they think, at least to the extent of being told what they mean by using the word "water".

Part IV

Content: later perspectives

Chapter 11

Reality

I begin to draw a figure and the world is looped in it, and I myself am
outside the loop; which I now join – so – and seal up, and make entire.
The world is entire, and I am outside of it, crying, "Oh save me, from
being blown for ever outside the loop of time!"

Virginia Woolf, *The Waves* (1931: 21–2)

What Woolf describes here as the plight of novelists with certain kinds
of realist or naturalist programme, Putnam recognized as the predicament foisted on certain kinds of philosopher, and, specifically, on those
who would espouse the kinds of view endorsed by Putnam himself in
the first half of his career.[1]

Suppose one is setting out to describe everything that is, "the
world", whether as an artist or as a philosopher or as a scientist.[2]
There are ways of doing so that inevitably leave one's own self, or significant aspects of oneself, out of the picture. Recognizing that one is
outside one's own representation of the world can be a terrifying experience for anyone who has a hand in it: the human being who thinks of
the world in a certain way, for example, or the artist who portrays it in
writing, in painting, in music. For it can seem that this really is the
way of things; that the world, in so far as one can recognize it as such,
is indeed removed, lost, uncontactable. And it is that feeling to which
Woolf gives memorable expression, an emotional response to the anxiety that one's experiences, thoughts and uses of language are not
"about" the world at all; or, worse, that they are not about anything at
all; worse still, that there is nothing for them to be about.

But anxiety and terror are not the only responses to the possibility
of this "aboutness gap" (as it was labelled in Chapter 6), for the experience of this variety of intentionality problem can also be plain
galling. This is especially the case for philosophers committed to finding ways in which the world should be represented. They are more susceptible than most to the charge that their efforts are simply
self-defeating. Yet this is precisely the upshot of attempts to describe

everything that is in ways that leave out aspects of the one doing the describing, for in choosing this approach, the philosopher has left out a part of the world, and hence has not described all that is. And the problems now arising are responsible for a deeper unease than mere professional embarrassment, for if the world is indeed lost and uncontactable, given the "aboutness gap", then at best any representation that did accurately capture it could mean nothing to us. It would be a kind of fluke that we could not even recognize as such. At worst, the world would be wholly unrepresentable. Hence, in leaving out aspects of the one doing the describing, the attempt to describe is itself rendered wholly incoherent. It is not simply that the descriptive enterprise will be unable to achieve *all* the ends it sets for itself, it will be incapable of achieving *any* of its own ends.

How might the philosopher sabotage his own endeavours in this way – in Austin's fine phrase, "dribbling briskly into position in front of his own goal, squaring up to encompass his own destruction"?[3] Hints are to be found in the passage from Woolf and the kinds of artistry to which she is alluding. Writing in a way that conforms to the tenets of realism or naturalism directs not only one's choice of subject-matter (the ordinary and trivial, for example) and technique (procedures to resist idealization, romanticism, ennoblement so as to ensure that the representation retain the "shape" of what is represented), but also one's perspective. The world to be described is perceptible and thinkable to all; hence it must be independent of any. So if one's representation is to be true of and to the world, it must similarly be independent of what is particular to one's perspective on it. And it can seem that the only way to accomplish such objectivity is to remove oneself from the representation altogether, as both point of focus and point of view.[4]

It is because Putnam perceived in his earlier views an underlying tendency to conceive of the philosophical and scientific task in this way that his position underwent significant development from the mid-1970s on. Indeed, the second half of his career has been dominated in large part by tensions induced by his relationship to his own earlier views. These views were developed, as we have seen, in conscious and conscientious revolt from the logical positivism and verificationism advocated by his teachers. So we might expect that the results would principally be felt in the same areas as the results of his earlier work. In fact, the story is considerably more complicated, because his interests have extended beyond philosophy of science, philosophy of language and philosophy of mind to issues in the history of philosophy, to ethics and aesthetics, and in particular to the proper methods and goals of philosophizing. But his continuing focus on intentionality issues underpins these developments. And it is by appeal to his stable concern with these deep problems that we best understand the significant changes made in these years to aspects of his views that lie closer to the surface.

Epistemic features

Putnam's evolving relationship with verificationism offers the most immediate way to appreciate the significance of these changes, for it might have seemed that his earlier attacks on that position were sufficiently comprehensive to make evolution of this sort impossible. But by the mid-1980s, Putnam was able to look back over his work in the previous decade and describe it as having developed predominantly due to the appeal, and hence under the influence, of notions whose ancestry was clearly verificationist. (See Putnam 1976a (i)–(vi); 1976b: 95–119; 1976c: 121–40; 1983a: vii–xviii).

This is primarily because he came to believe that verificationism had identified precisely those aspects of the one describing the world that could not be left out of the picture if the portrayal itself was to be possible, let alone complete. For verificationism had stressed the extent to which the representational enterprise was dependent on the knowledge of the one doing the representing: "I have come to see that one cannot come to grips with the real problems in philosophy without being more sensitive to the epistemological position of the philosopher than I was willing to be" (Putnam 1983a: vii). Putnam is here emphasizing two respects in which knowledge came to exercise a more central role in his thinking, one more immediate and one more reflective.

In the more immediate sense, greater sensitivity to epistemology is required of philosophers when they address perennial philosophical problems. Putnam advanced this view most forthrightly in relation to central problems in the theory of meaning. For reasons entailed by his developing account of intentionality, he looked in the mid-1970s to Michael Dummett's verificationist semantics for "inspiration" (Putnam 1983a: xvi).[5] On this view, we cannot divorce the questions of whether or not a proposition has meaning, or what particular meaning it has, from the conditions on understanding that proposition, on knowing what it means. A "realist" semantics based on truth-conditions that might never be known by us (because they forever transcend our ability to grasp them) is now accounted unintelligible.

Truth cannot be so radically unconstrained by conditions on knowledge. Properly conceived of, it is itself an epistemic notion.

Equally unintelligible is the kind of realism that claims there might be a theory that is "ideal" from every point of view (its coherence, plausibility, simplicity, conservatism, utility) and yet still be false. The notion that the truly "ideal" theory must underlie these epistemic signs of ideality is unintelligible. Verificationism was right to stress that we cannot make sense of realism in this guise, although the precise positions formerly advocated by its major representatives need to be modified in quite major ways. Verificationism was right about the fact that, and about why, the conditions on understanding propositions should be made central to the elucidation of their meaning, but appeal to understanding alone is not sufficient to account for meaning: elucidating meaning presupposes elucidating intentionality, and particularly the kinds of intentionality manifest in reference – "reference is what the problem is all about" (Putnam 1976c: 129; also *ibid.*: 127–30; 1983a: xvi–xviii). Finally, verificationism was right to make epistemic notions such as verification and falsification central in accounting for the meaning and meaningfulness of propositions (Putnam, 1976c: 127). But it went wrong here in identifying sense-data with the "hard facts" that make verification and falsification possible; indeed, it is a matter for debate whether those procedures depend on "hard facts" at all, however conceived (*ibid.*: 127–8). We have the option here of calling the overall position a form of "non-" or "anti-realist semantics". But Putnam prefers to call it "verificationist semantics"; it is, after all, quite consistent with certain versions of realism (for example, the "internal realism" he advocated for a time; see *ibid.*: 128).

In the more reflective sense, philosophers need to become more sensitive to epistemology when they address philosophy itself, asking which the real problems are and what methods are most appropriate in dealing with them. In Putnam's view, reflection on the epistemological situation of philosophers reveals not only the fact that rationality evolves, but the importance of that fact. It leads him to make various claims specific to analytic philosophy, each of which proceeds from the observation that "as philosophers, we seem caught between our desire for integration and our recognition of the difficulty" (Putnam 1981e: 303). Here, his view of verificationism is less positive, at least as that position was formerly represented.

His first reflection is that analytic philosophy is self-deceiving when it portrays itself as a mode of reasoning set rigorously apart from ideology and other non-rational associations to the culture in which it finds itself. During the period in which analytic philosophy retained a fairly precise and recognizable shape as a set of specific modes of philosophizing, it was intensely ideological. With the demise of logical positivism and its verificationist programme, it has become less ideological; but it has also lost much of its definitive shape. Putnam's second claim is that analytical philosophy is self-deceiving when it describes itself as attacking philosophical problems in a piecemeal, small-scale kind of way.[6] The intention, of course, is to contrast it with the integrated, system-building style of so-called "continental" philosophy. Again, however, the defining movements in analytic philosophy – logical positivism; a more generalized verificationism; the Quinean programme which succeeded them – have been thoroughly large-scale and integrated. Finally, Putnam claims there is a fairly specific and time-bound cultural situation in which analytic philosophy finds its home. It is best understood as a form of modernism, sharing with other forms much the same internal strains and external conflicts (Putnam 1981d: 170–83; 1981e: 287–303).

Terms of reference: speakers

At the heart of Putnam's argument with his own earlier views is an intentionality issue. He came to see that conceiving of the referential relation between uses of language and the world in his old way led directly to the kinds of self-defeating predicament sketched above. Conceived in the old manner, reference could not hope to achieve its ends; either the world is forever beyond referential contact, or there is nothing for our uses of language to be about.

Now any attempt to represent the world is dependent on maintaining referential contact with it, from the mundane efforts of everyday thought to the grandest endeavours of scientific theorizing. So failures in accounting for reference spell doom for any attempts to account for the world. As a consequence, Putnam put all aspects of his former conception of reference under close scrutiny: what precisely the terms of this relation are, and what relates them, under what circumstances and under what conditions.

There is a temptation to see language itself as one term of the referential relation: it is statements made up of referring terms concatenated with predicates and other linguistic devices that bear the intentionality of this relation; it is these entities that are "of" or about the world. Putnam argued, instead, that the intentionality of this relation is dependent on users of the language ("speakers", as he says, meaning the description to apply to those employing other modes also, such as writers) (Putnam 1976c: 123). This is in accordance with a view that Peter Strawson famously argued for as part of his attack on Russell's theory of descriptions and the presuppositions on which that theory rested (Strawson 2004: 1–20). It is speakers who form the group of possible terms in the referential relation, not the words they use; so it is speakers who bear the intentionality of this relation. We often say that certain linguistic terms such as names refer. But, strictly speaking, it is the *user* of such terms who refers. We need not get rid of the phrase "referring term" altogether, nor condemn the usage with which it is associated. But we do need to regard this particular transferred epithet and its dependent usage with greater caution than most. When a friend says "my heart is sick for love" we look to the friend, not to his heart. Similarly, when a philosopher points out that names such as "Pegasus" fail to refer, it is not to this word that we should look in the first instance but to speakers and to the sets of conditions under which they might try to use it.

The significance of this move may not be immediately apparent, but it reflects and supports Putnam's rehabilitation of the epistemological perspective within the theory of meaning. Suppose we take the opposing view and ascribe the referential function to linguistic entities such as statements and the subject-terms and predicates composing them. Then we will be predisposed to deny that epistemic issues could have a direct role to play in explaining how reference works: the entities we would then regard as basic to the referential function evidently lack the means to engage epistemically with anything. If, on the other hand, we regard users of language as the basic term in the referential relation, we will be equally predisposed to treat the semantic issues arising as partly epistemic in nature. For example, it is by knowing which individual their use of a name refers to that users of language are able to express and communicate their thoughts using the term. And since knowledge is thus central to their use of the term, it is essential to the means by which the entities regarded as basic terms in the referential relation achieve their ends.

Terms of reference: the world

Putnam expended similar efforts in revising his view of the other term of the referential relation, that assembly of objects, properties, states of affairs and so on forming a speaker's environment and signified collectively by the term "world". There is a temptation to regard this term of the referential relation as wholly independent of any particular representation we have of it. But there are even stronger views available. It is consistent with the independence claim just made that there must nevertheless be *some* representation of the world, possible or actual, which is true to it. So a stronger view would hold that what the phrase "the world" refers to would count as such even if it were incapable of accurate representation by us human beings at any time. And an even stronger view would hold that the world's status is such that it might forever transcend attempts on the part of anyone at any time to represent it accurately.

One consequence of regarding the referent of "the world" in this way is that it becomes impossible to describe it, as a matter either of the highest probability or of certainty (Putnam 1976c: 130–33). It becomes impossible with high probability if the world admits only one correct representation, and with certainty if it admits several different equivalent representations. Consider attempts to describe the physical properties of the world in terms of space–time points and fields. Some theories construe space–time points as objects, some as properties; some construe fields as objects, some as particles acting at a distance. Some theories deny what is here presupposed by both: lines and their parts all have extension and there are no points. Some theories modify this rejection: there are points but they are mere logical constructions out of line segments. So we have the possibility of several different theories constructed out of statements expressing propositions that are internally consistent with other propositions in the same theory but that contradict propositions about the same objects in the other theories.

Now one response would be to claim that the world admits only one correct representation; hence only one of these theories can be true, and there are facts of the matter determining which. But there is high probability that these facts will forever transcend our ability to know them; what, after all, would facts of this sort be like? How would they be identifiable as such? Hence adopting this attitude towards attempts to describe the world sets the threshold on description so high as to make its achievement all but impossible.

The alternative response would be to allow that the world admits of more than one correct representation; this is a position Putnam identifies with the "sophisticated realist". On this view, internally consistent theories that match the world, however much they may contradict each other, are to be regarded as equivalent (Putnam draws here on notions of equivalence described by Reichenbach and Quine; see Putnam 1976c: 133–4; 1983c: 26–45). But now a different problem arises.[7] Statements containing terms such as "point" or "object" that express propositions basic to the construction of one theory must change in truth-value when considered in the light of other theories: one, for example, that denies points exist at all, or another that regards points as properties rather than objects. This will be so even though propositions in the first theory form an integral part of an overall description that is equivalent to the overall description provided by propositions in the alternative theories. So we are pressed to say that the truth-value of the statements expressing the various propositions depends on whichever theory is in question. Hence properties ascribed to the world as part of what makes it what it is – the property of being an object, for example, or of being a point, or a property – are themselves theory-relative.[8]

Now the cause of divergence here is the use of terms that are fundamental to each theory, so the space of contradiction will not be localized or isolatable, but must ramify and extend throughout the subsidiary propositions giving form to each. Hence the truth-value of almost any statement purporting to describe the world will be dependent on whichever theory is in question. And almost any property ascribed to the world as part of what makes it what it is will be theory-relative. So the world itself ends up being theory-relative: we cannot say, independently of theory, how the world is. And this fact is recognizably disastrous to the overall enterprise once we recall its defining aim. Our task was to find a way of describing the world where the referent of the term "world" is to be conceived of as something wholly and necessarily independent of any particular representation we have of it (and this is only the weakest form of the conception at issue). Thus a representation cannot intelligibly be said to "describe" the world, so conceived, if we cannot say how the one is independent of the other. In particular, it is only if we can say how the world is, independently of any theory, that we can make sense of the claim that some theory describes the world correctly. We have now found that this cannot be done. Hence, so conceived, it is equally impossible to describe the world.

What should we conclude?[9] One implication is obvious given the *reductio* form of the foregoing argument. We have seen what is entailed by conceiving of the world in such a way that it is wholly independent of any particular representation we have of it. So we should renounce that conception. The referent of "the world" should be regarded, in a way still to be determined, as dependent on the representations we have of it.

So Putnam has effected changes to both terms of the referential relation – a sub-set of intentionality. Instead of regarding reference as a matter of language relating to the world conceived of as independent of particular representations, we should think of it as language users relating to a world conceived dependently on the representations they have of it. And these changes to the terms of the relation force us to make changes to the relation itself. First, it must be the kind of relation that takes language users as a term. And, as we have seen, that introduces epistemic features to the relation that could afford to be absent when it was conceived of as relating mere pieces of language to the world. Secondly, it must be the kind of relation that takes representation-dependent items as a term, for on the rejected view, "the world" had a determinate reference independently of whatever means were at our disposal for representing it – the totality of concepts and the rules for their combination that together make up our conceptual scheme, for example. So the referential relation itself had to be conceived of in a way that maintained this independence from the world; its existence and identity had to be insulated from changes in the world, so that changes in the one could not affect what was essential to the other. Now this position has been rejected: determinate reference for "the world" has been made to depend on our means of representing the world to ourselves. And so the referential relation itself must now be conceived of in a way that is consistent with these dependency relations. How is this to be achieved? In Chapter 12 we shall examine Putnam's response to the questions arising.

Chapter 12

Reference

"What are you thinking of so earnestly?" said he.
Catherine coloured, and said, "I was not thinking of any thing."
"That is artful and deep, to be sure; but I had rather be told at once that you will not tell me."
"Well then, I will not".   Jane Austen, *Northanger Abbey* (1990: 15)

Catherine's interlocutor is teasing her, of course. She is not being deep; her artfulness is quite conventional. But there is depth to the joke. Given the intentionality of thought, either there is something of which she is thinking, or she is not thinking at all. So she is being artful in pretending that there is some third possibility: thinking without an object of thought. This is a standard tactic to preserve a generally desirable fiction: one rarely likes to be caught not thinking. And her conversation partner is being playful in pretending to allow her that possibility. In calling it deep, however, his irony shows what he really thinks. It is unthinking of her to suppose she can disguise her non-thinking in this way. This is an instance of the higher nonsense (and her rather wild response shows she knows it); it is also the kind of pseudo-problem which, if we are not careful, leads to fruitless philosophizing.

If there is no third possibility, no thinking without an object of thought, then we are pressed in giving an account of thought to say what kinds of thing we might be thinking of. We have seen how Putnam revised his views about these matters, and in particular of the "thing" of which one is thinking and speaking when one refers to "the world". This term of the referential relation is dependent on our means of representing it to ourselves, and in a strong sense. Our (visual) experience only presents its objects to us in relation to our theories of (visual) perception, however simple and implicit those theories are; it is only in relation to our (equally simple and implicit) theories of language use, of meaning and of truth, that we can use language to refer to things. It remains to examine the implications for experience, thought and talk as a whole. If that of which we are thinking–experiencing–talking is dependent in this way on our total conceptual system (comprising our theories of perception, of language, of meaning, of truth and so on), then we must account for what it is to think of, experience and talk about entities from within that conceptual system. We know what that entails for one term of the intentionality relation; what should we say about the relation itself?

Referential relations

Putnam's response to this question was framed in a way that reflected the immediate stimulus to rethink the issues involved. Strongly physicalist approaches to reference began to appear in the early 1970s, heralded by an article he later described as "extraordinarily brilliant and provocative" (Putnam 1978a: 4): "Tarski's Theory of Truth" by Hartry Field (1972, reprinted with postscript in Field 2001: 3–29). To establish the contrast, consider the essential features of the position Putnam had been developing since the late 1950s. (Putnam (1978a: 1–6) helpfully clarifies the essential features of his earlier views, particularly as expressed in his Oxford talk (1960a: 70–84).)

Users of language construct symbolic representations of the world, their environment. Such constructions require interaction of a causal kind between the language user and the world. Properly managed, there is a kind of dynamic feedback process in operation here, for the success or otherwise of a language user's efforts to deal with their environment will help determine their ability to represent it accurately, while the accuracy or inaccuracy of their representations will affect the viability or success of their efforts in dealing with the environment. So we should regard the relation between the world and users of language (or language; recall that Putnam moved only latterly to focusing on users) as part of "a causal model of human behaviour" (Putnam 1978a: 4). One of the advantages Putnam claimed for this model is that it helps make sense of the notion of truth to which he was committed: namely, that truth depends on the existence of a specifiable correspondence relation of a certain sort (call it relation R). This relation has three terms: it takes the whole of a linguistic system as one term; particular uses of that system – for example, statements – as another; and, as the third, those particular extra-linguistic facts relevant to the statement, facts of the kind whose totality helps make up reality.

On this view, a sentence is true if and only if it is by the triadic relation R that it stands to reality; true assertions are those that correspond in this way to extra-linguistic facts. And it is Putnam's approach to reference as part of the causal interactions between speakers and reality (the causal model of human behaviour) that enables him to conceive of truth in this way. It explains how extra-linguistic entities can be related to our uses of language in such a way that the truth of the latter can be made to depend on correspondence with the former. Semantical conceptions of truth which appeal to purely intra-linguistic aspects of the use of the word "true" cannot make sense of the correspondence to reality in virtue of which assertions count as true.[1] Moreover, it is difficult to see how such conceptions could account for assertions that are neither true nor false. This is a significant issue for Putnam, as we have seen, given his fundamental interest in scientific theorizing: possible microcosmic physical situations and non-actual macrocosmic physical situations may give rise to assertions that are neither true nor false. The correspondence theorist can appeal to the specifiable correspondence relation R to answer the question; such assertions do not bear the appropriate relation to the extra-linguistic facts.

What, then, are we to make of relation R; and, in particular, how is the causal interaction between speakers and their environment to be understood? This is the main issue to which Putnam's views of reference bring us, and it is the issue on which Field's article caused him to focus. Field proposed a radical answer to this question which might at first have been thought to accord with Putnam's own views and purposes. It was apparently consistent with Putnam's position because it accounted for reference in terms of causal relations and extra-linguistic facts. It was radical because the proposal amounted to a physicalist reduction of the notion of truth (or of truth-conditions) to non-semantic terms.[2]

In Field's view, a speaker successfully uses a term a to refer to some object O just in case a definite causal relation obtains between his use of a and O, or between a and objects of the kind to which O belongs. The possibilities of a physicalist reduction here are entailed by the way the referential relation is understood: just another entity in the natural-causal order and to be studied as any other relation between physical objects is studied. Knowing about reference therefore depends on the results of empirical investigation just as much as knowing the things that relation enables us to refer to. On Field's view, then, reference belongs to the same basic class of relations as "x is the cause of y", or "x is chemically bonded to y", or "x is positioned at point y at time *z*", and so on. Now Field conceives of the relation as between uses of language and the world: so one small peculiarity is introduced here (and even this could be avoided if only it were *users* that were taken to be in question). Unlike "*x* is chemically bonded to *y*" and other such common scientifically investigable relations, "*x* refers to *y*" *can* take words (considered as just another kind of worldly thing) as its first term; moreover, unlike these other relations, it *must* take words in this position.

So the relationship between Field's views and Putnam's earlier perspectives is close at key points. Both emphasize the importance of reference in determining meaning; both argue that reference is a matter of causal connections. Moreover, Field's account of the definition of the referential relation is relevantly similar to Putnam's account of the definition of magnitudes such as "length" and natural kind terms such as "water". As a result of scientific investigations, it turned out that what one means by talking of "the length of a physical object" is the function of two arguments rather than one: properties of the object in question, together with properties of the inertial system selected to be the rest system. As a result of scientific discoveries, it turned out that what one means by "water" is H_2O. It is similarly up to empirical investigation to discover for us the nature of the referential relation, in both the general and the particular case.

Argument from convergence

Putnam began to modify his position in such a way as to make equations with strongly physicalist views like Field's impossible. One way to begin charting the divergence is to note his growing appreciation of a particular overarching claim, one that seems at first not merely consistent with, but supportive of, the views just sketched; namely, that realism is itself an empirical hypothesis. This position implies much about philosophy's external relations to science. In particular, a realist of this sort:

> argues that science should be taken at "face value" – without philosophical reinterpretation – in the light of the failure of all serious programmes of philosophical reinterpretation of science, and that science taken at 'face value' *implies* realism. (Realism is, so to speak, "science's philosophy of science").
>
> (Putnam 1976a (iii): 37)

Treating realism as an empirical hypothesis also has major implications for philosophy's internal relations, its conception of itself and the issues in relation to which it defines itself. Reference is one such issue. On this view of realism, it is not just that which words relate to what things by way of reference is an empirical matter to be secured by empirical enquiry; the claim that this is so is *itself* an empirical proposition and therefore similarly subject to appropriate empirical means of testing. Of course, this is a meta-enquiry, at one remove from ordinary observations and the systematic acquisition of evidence through experimentation; its primary points of focus are entities existing on a different level from physical objects in the macroscopic world. But we determine whether realism captures the notions of truth and reference that we employ by examining what theories of the world we use, and how we use them, in much the same way that we arrive at those theories: by examining the world.

So, for example, it is characteristic of realism to claim that statements can be false even though they follow from our theories, together with sentences expressing the sets of observations supporting hypotheses derived from those theories. Thus a realist will accept statements such as "Venus might not have had carbon dioxide in its atmosphere even though it follows from our theory that it does" (Putnam 1976a (iii): 34). Now we might ask whether what the realist thus accepts accords with the role that concepts such as reference and truth play in our overall scheme. And if we consider realism to be an empirical hypothesis, we will answer this question by empirical means: for example, by testing for whether acceptance of such statements accords with speakers' collective behaviour. Putnam offered several examples of confirmation in the form of behaviour, both specific to scientific theorizing and generally applicable to language users. Since in each case realism alone (or realism best) accounts for an aspect of behaviour, it is supported by inference to the best explanation.

One kind of case relates to progress achieved within the history of science, and in particular the steady increase (in both number and scope) of its predictive triumphs. With an improved success rate, the behaviour of scientists exhibits a well-known phenomenon: they tend to develop theories that converge more and more on each other, steadily postulating newer theories with greater generality on the basis of the predictive success enjoyed by older theories in more restricted domains. One interpretation of this phenomenon settles the matter in favour of realism: it is the manifestation of an increasingly adequate approximation to the truth, where the truth about the subject-matter in question is thus understood as (to an extent that different versions will specify differently) independent of our theorizing. Putnam thought this the best explanation because the only alternatives would appeal to the miraculous (Putnam 1975h: 177–94). His interpretation is controversial, however, and for two different kinds of reason.

First, the notion of "approximating to the truth" or of "progressing towards the truth" needs careful clarification. Criteria have to be offered for determining proximity of this sort, for assessing it, and in such a way as to avoid rehearsing the conclusion in the premise-set. This may be difficult to achieve, for the obvious way to think of such approximation is on the analogy of spatial relations between two distinct objects, at least one of which is movable. As objects of the one sort (i.e. theories) progress from earlier to later, their greater predictive success is a mark of the fact that they are moving closer to an object of another sort (i.e. the truth). But this model begs the question against the non- or anti-realist, for the realist notion of what it takes for something to count as the truth about some subject-matter has to be assumed for the model to work: that the truth is relevantly independent of our theorizing; that the notion of verisimilitude is to be understood in a way that requires a distinction between what is true and what holds according to an ideal theory. And if this is what is being built into the empirical "fact" that requires explanation (i.e. that theories tend to progress towards the truth), then the opponent has an easy way of resisting the conclusion: there is no such fact and hence no need for such an explanation.

A second challenge to Putnam's argument points out that successful prediction may not be a reliable indicator of truth at all, let alone of the claim that truth plays the role realism assigns to it in our conceptual scheme. The realist interpretation is certainly not the only possible interpretation, and perhaps neither the only plausible one nor even the best. Adding ever more complex epicycles to the movements of the planets secured greater predictive success for the Ptolemaic model of planetary motion, for example. But we do not take this as evidence that the various component theories within that model were convergent on the truth, that the later theories were getting any closer to the truth by treating earlier theories as limiting cases. And this recipe seems applicable in a significant number and range of cases: that false theories can be made to attain to increasing predictive success by the invention of extra rules and constraints, modifications that account for apparent anomalies as special cases, or as ordinary cases in special circumstances, to be treated according to special laws (these complicating factors are discussed at length by Larry Laudan (1977; 1984)).

Argument from fixity of reference

Putnam offered a second set of arguments in support of realism that was related to the first by the link of predictive success. These arguments also used phenomena associated with scientific theorizing; they also depended on inference to the best explanation. But these arguments differed from the first set in a number of ways. The evidence to which they appealed concerned the issue of referential relations directly. Moreover, they employed as a premise a distinctive claim about those relations, one that we have already examined at some length: that certain kinds of term should be regarded as preserving their reference over many different kinds of change in theory. So these arguments had a narrower appeal than those just discussed which could be endorsed by supporters of various different accounts of reference.

Arguments of this second type begin by pointing out that later theories make different claims from the earlier theories on which they improve; that is precisely what makes them *distinct*. But later theories make claims deploying the same central theoretical and explanatory terms as earlier theories; that is precisely what makes them *improvements*. So theories formulated using terms for magnitudes (e.g. length, temperature, pressure) and theoretical postulates (e.g. genes, viruses, quarks and, depending on one's view of such things, pains) make advances on each other by making claims about the same referents, predicting the behaviour of those objects with ever greater precision or generality. Hence the existence of these objects must be as the realist construes it, no less than the meaning of the terms used to refer to them, independent of any particular theorizing about them.

Now this argument is a hypothesis concerning an empirical claim: that there is a particular set of facts about progress in science, and we cannot explain those facts unless we suppose that the central theoretical and explanatory terms employed by scientific theories to express their claims succeed in referring throughout the transition from earlier to later versions. But unless this kind of argument is applied in a quite strict and limited way to certain kinds of theorizing about certain kinds of subject-matter, it is open to challenge. The history of science contains several examples of cases in which theories have achieved increasing predictive success even though their central theoretical and explanatory terms have failed to refer. Often-quoted examples include the caloric theory of heat, and theories that employed empty terms such as "phlogiston" and "electromagnetic ether".

So it seems that, unless we narrow the argument's scope so that it does not appear to cover these cases also, we have a choice. Either the empirical claim is false: the facts concerning progress in science are not as the realist supposes them to be. Or the explanation fails: although these facts are consistent with realism, they are also consistent with some form of non- or anti-realism. For progressive predictive success over changes in theory is compatible with the emptiness of the central theoretical terms used to formulate those theories.

Argument from correspondence

A third set of reasons offered by Putnam in support of realism also appealed to the explanation of empirical data and also concerned referential relations (Putnam 1976b: 95–119; 1976c: 121–6). The main features of this alternative argument are as follows. The best explanation of certain empirically discoverable and testable facts calls on a particular model of correspondence between words and sets of things in the world. These facts concern the collective behaviour of speakers. And this particular correspondence model, correctly construed, implies realism about the relevant subject-matter. We need to examine each claim in some detail, beginning with the first.

Putnam employed a model associated with the Polish mathematician and logician Alfred Tarski to account for the kind of correspondence he perceived as obtaining between words and sets of worldly things. So we need to be aware of some fundamental features of this model if we are to appreciate his argument. The basic feature to which Putnam appealed is this: we can describe the correspondence between two items (in this case, between formal languages and their interpretations) in terms of the satisfaction relations existing between them (Tarski 1983; originally published in 1935).

Tarski proposed that we distinguish between a purely formalized language (call it L) and an *interpretation* of L (call it I). So suppose that L is a very simple language: it consists of a small number of names (a, b, c) and of predicate-expressions (F, G, H) which, when appropriately conjoined, form a finite number of sentences. What counts as appropriate depends on the syntax of L, the structural and combinatory rules whose totality gives definition to the language. These syntactic rules determine, for example, which putative sentences count as such (they are "well-formed formulae") and which do not. So the syntactic rules might tell us that the result of placing a predicate-expression F next to a name a, so that the whole has the form "Fa", is a sentence, correctly concatenated. What these rules alone do not tell us about is what the components of L actually *do*, what their role or purpose might be; we would naturally answer that question by saying names "refer" to things (persons, for example), that predicate-expressions "apply" to things (properties, for example). But we have no means of offering such a response as yet, not without a set of such things and a set of rules specifying which of them the names a, b, c refer to, and which of them the predicate-expressions F, G, H apply to. In other words, we need a structure consisting of things, and a set of rules establishing and constraining the correspondence between those things and the words of L, if the latter are to be ascribed their proper function of referring to the former.

And that is precisely the role of I, the interpretation of L. I is a structure that consists of various domains of individuals, together with the classes and relations defined in those domains. So suppose I contains three persons (Abelard, Bernard and Heloise) and three properties (the properties of being funny, grim and hairy). Then we can use I to add some semantic rules to the syntax of L, rules that correlate the variables of L with the individuals of I and thus supply them with values. For example, "a in L refers to Abelard"; "b in L refers to Bernard"; "c in L refers to Heloise"; "F in L applies to funny things"; "G in L applies to grim things"; "H in L applies to hairy things".

These correlations allow us to accomplish a number of different tasks. For example, we can now assess the sentences of L for their truth. So consider the sentence "Fa". Using the structure I and the rules corresponding to it, we can work out whether that sentence is true on a particular occasion of use. Among the individuals provided for L by I is the person Abelard and the semantic rules correlate that person with the name a so that Abelard may be said to satisfy a in L. Among the properties provided for L by I is that of being funny, and the semantic rules correlate that property with the predicate-expression F so that being funny may be said to satisfy F in L. So if Abelard is funny, we can say that the sentence "Fa" is satisfied in L, given I, and hence true on this occasion of use.

Of course, we can move immediately to a deeper, more general level and specify what must be the case if that sentence is to be true on *any* occasion of use: it is true if and only if Abelard is funny. And we may continue to go deeper: to work out, for example, what must be the case if any sentence of *L* is to be true on any occasion. (Tarski argued, controversially, that in accomplishing this task we would have defined truth itself for that particular language, that we would know what true-in-*L* meant.) Given the syntactic and semantic rules established above, for example, "true as a sentence of *L*" should entail that "*Fa*" is true as a sentence of *L* if and only if Abelard is funny. And this is so because the sentence "*Fa*" is satisfied in *L*, given *I*, if and only if Abelard is funny. And this is so in turn because of that correspondence between words and sets of things that the rules associating *I* with *L* express.

In sum, we may obtain a number of useful results, including a formal notion of true as a sentence of a language, by appealing to satisfaction relations. We may even use this formal notion of satisfaction to shed light on the correspondence relations between words and things. And this was what Putnam attempted, using facts about this correspondence to explain in turn the collective behaviour of speakers, in particular what he called "the success of the language-using program" (Putnam 1976b: 100):

> What "succeeds" or "fails" is not, in general, linguistic behaviour by itself but total behaviour. E.g. we say certain things, conduct certain reasonings with each other, manipulate materials in a certain way, and finally we have a bridge that enables us to cross a river that we couldn't cross before. And our reasoning and discussion is as much a part of the total organized behaviour-complex as is our lifting of steel girders with a crane. So what I should really speak of is not the success or failure of our linguistic behaviour, but rather the *contribution* of our linguistic behaviour to the success of our total behaviour.   (*Ibid.*: 100–1)[3]

There is widespread agreement (or at least agreement is possible over a wide range of different metaphysical positions) about one form of explanation, which comes in three parts. People have a tendency to achieve certain kinds of aims; linguistic behaviour contributes to this success-rate in total behaviour because people generally behave in such a way that their aims will be achieved if their beliefs are true; and many instances of many of the kinds of beliefs they hold do tend to be true. Such beliefs fall into various categories: personal propositional beliefs (e.g. about which individual we are, where we are, what we are doing); personal practical beliefs (e.g. about how to do basic things, such as eating, talking and moving); and even perhaps impersonal beliefs (e.g. about certain fundamental elements of the thinking and behaviour of members of one's society or culture or generation or e.g. academic; religious community). And in Putnam's view, what this explanation of success in our total behaviour ultimately depends on is an appeal to the role that learning plays in our total behaviour. "Learning" here is taken to mean not only the acquisition of new beliefs, but of reliable means of belief-formation: the means to acquire an ever greater number of true beliefs.

If we reject the idea that the reliability of our learning methods can be justified *a priori*, then we must appeal instead to the idea that this reliability is a fact of nature, and one to be accounted for as we account for other facts of nature (Putnam 1976b: 103–4). And it is at this point that the third claim in Putnam's argument comes into play. On his view, the correspondence between words and sets of things (understood on the Tarskian satisfaction model) *can* explain these facts of nature; and it can *only* do so if that correspondence is construed in ways that imply realism about the relevant facts. Hence we infer realism as the best explanation of the empirically discoverable and testable facts in question: the collective behaviour of speakers, motivated to engage in linguistic interchange by their appreciation of the various kinds of success that reliability in such behaviour brings them.

The argument is as follows. When we describe a normal speaker as reliable in saying "That cat is hungry" or "That cat has had enough to eat" on seeing Sammy slinking or waddling by, as the case may be, we are claiming that they probably accept whichever statement is true. Now we might be able to use a causal account of visual experience to explain why, if Sammy is hungry, the speaker probably accepts "That cat is hungry"; and why, if Sammy has had enough to eat, the speaker probably accepts "That cat has had enough to eat". But this is not quite sufficient to explain why the speaker is to be accounted reliable, for the adjective is only applicable if we can characterize the speaker's acceptance of these statements as an endorsement; as an "accepting-as-true" of the claims made by the statements in question. And it is notoriously difficult to account for and explain what such endorsing behaviour comes to. In Putnam's view, the realist is uniquely able to do so by appeal to the Tarskian model of correspondence and satisfaction relations.

Consider an English sentence, "That cat is hungry". The subject-term correlates with a contextually salient animal of the feline species so described; the predicate correlates with the set of hungry things; sentences of the form "That *a* is *F*" are true if and only if the object referred to by "That *a*" has the property of being *F*. This implication of an acceptable truth-definition for English allows us to supplement the causal account of visual experience, for we can now say what it is for speakers to accept-as-true sentences of the form "That *a* is *F*" when such sentences are used to issue statements. And we can explain why reliable speakers are to be accounted as such by appeal to this notion. If Sammy is hungry, the reliable speaker probably accepts-as-true the statement that is true: namely, "That cat is hungry"; and if Sammy has had enough to eat, the reliable speaker probably accepts-as-true the statement that is true: namely, "That cat has had enough to eat". So we obtain the following picture. A causal theory of visual perception tells us that when a certain state of affairs visibly obtains (e.g. that cat's being hungry) and the speaker is appropriately related to appreciate it, he may utter and would certainly endorse the relevant statement (e.g. "that cat is hungry").[4] This theory appeals to a correspondence between words in a certain language (i.e. English) and entities in extra-linguistic reality. And this correspondence is taken up into another theory: a semantics of truth that tells us that the statement is true if and only if the state of affairs obtains. Hence "We can be viewed as systems that reliably produce true sentences when a certain variety of states of affairs obtain" (Putnam 1976b: 105).

This explanation of the contribution of our linguistic behaviour to the success of our total behaviour is realist. "That cat is hungry" corresponds to that cat's being hungry. It is not that a non-realist cannot appeal to notions of correspondence; they can. For example, they might say that the sentence corresponds to some fixed set of expectations about the future, such as certain behavioural consequences. But it is not open to the non-realist to appeal to that direct correspondence between words and extra-linguistic reality which Putnam finds at the heart of the Tarskian truth-definition. Moreover, Putnam's explanation of reliability conforms explicitly to his rethinking of realism, for it is a realism intimately related to the various relevant views and theories that partly constitute our total conceptual system. For example, when we say that a speaker probably accepts-as-true statements that are true by appeal to their visual experience, we are also saying that this way of learning about the world is reliable. This claim rests in turn on our theories of visual experience and of the semantics of truth.

So the realist account of reliability proceeds from within the conceptual system in which those theories take their place.

Putnam acknowledged that this realist account provided no more than a sketch of reliability in relation to one relatively simple case of learning. But since in his view it is the *only* explanation of the relevant natural facts, it is certainly the best ("unless we want to jettison or ignore our entire body of natural science and scientific explanation, no alternative account is even in the field today" (Putnam 1976b: 105)). This is Putnam's third argument for realism, treating that position as an empirical hypothesis to be inferred as the best explanation of certain empirical facts. It is the strongest of the three, and in what follows we shall examine the ideas to which it leads. For the moment, it is sufficient to note that the argument depends directly on features of Putnam's developing approach to intentionality.

Chapter 13

Truth

> "We have got to the deductions and the inferences," said Lestrade, winking at me. "I find it hard enough to tackle facts, Holmes, without flying away after theories and fancies."
>
> "You are right," said Holmes demurely; "you do find it very hard to tackle the facts."
>
> Arthur Conan Doyle, "The Boscombe Valley Mystery" (1981: 89)

The laugh is on the policeman, Lestrade, as is customary in detective stories. But it might be wise to side with him and cultivate a proper diffidence. The notion of a fact gives rise to a number of problems that are "very hard to tackle"; in particular, one that is dependent on an issue we have already addressed: how it is even possible to think or say what is false or not the case. As noted at the time, this general issue concerning negativity has an eminent history and a deep connection to background problems of intentionality. And those particular instances of the negativity issue that turn on the notion of "fact" and on the relations between facts and theories might have given even Holmes pause, offering Lestrade the last laugh. Putnam's own approach to these questions has been dictated by the general fallout from his arguments for realism as an empirical hypothesis. So we need first to examine those wider implications.

Strong physicalism

Putnam's third argument for realism as an empirical hypothesis rested on evidence concerning the behaviour of whole statements. But his modified version of realism also has significant implications for the noun-phrases and referring terms out of which those statements are partly composed. Together, these implications for statements and for the parts of statements contrast directly with the strongly physicalist account of reference, associated with Hartry Field and others, which we reviewed in Chapter 12. On that approach, recall, a speaker refers to an item O when he issues a statement containing a referring term a if and only if this use of a is causally related to O in some definite way (that way being discoverable by empirical investigation and substantiated by scientific theorizing).

One problem with strong physicalism, in Putnam's view, is that it answers a basic question with the resources necessary for answering a subsidiary question. As we have seen, he gives a vital role to causal relations of a certain kind in explaining how speakers pick out referents for the use of terms. These are the relations in virtue of which the practices of current speakers in using a certain word are to be regarded as linked to the situation in which that word was first assigned a referent, and linked in such a way as to justify the claim that current usage of the word is consistent with the conditions under which it entered meaningful discourse. So we need to appeal to causal relations to answer the question "How are we to specify the reference of a term for the sake of the speakers using it?" But the question strong physicalism claims to answer is "What *is* reference?" Of the two questions, this is the more basic: since we need to know what reference is before we can say how it is to be specified for the sake of speakers, even being able to ask the latter question presupposes an answer to the former.

The second problem with strong physicalism is related to the first: it ignores the dependence of reference on conceptual schemes. Suppose we overlook the fact that strong phsyicalism attempts to answer the basic question "What is reference?" and suppose that it addresses the subsidiary question "How should reference be specified?" It is on stronger ground here because causal relations play a clear role. But on Putnam's view, as we have seen, specifying the reference of terms for the sake of speakers using them requires appeal not just to causal relations between a and O, but to social cooperation among the users of a, and (at least where natural kind terms are in question) to background scientific theories about the nature of O. Putnam sums up this position in the following way: "there is a real world but we can only describe it in terms of our own conceptual system", adding with characteristic dash "Well? We should use someone else's conceptual system?" (Putnam 1976a (ii): 32).

The referential relations between terms and elements of the world need to be described and accounted for in terms of the conceptual scheme of the people doing the referring. This claim about statement-parts is strongly related to the foregoing claims about whole statements. As we have seen, the correspondence relations between whole statements and reality that explain the reliability of language users (in particular, those aspects of the overall scheme relating to perceptual and semantic theories) themselves need to be described and accounted for in terms of our own conceptual system. And this has implications for the referring terms out of which those statements are partly composed. We are to say that the term "electron", for example, refers to electrons. This is in accord with the criterion established by Tarskian satisfaction-relations: that "*x* is an electron" is satisfied by an extra-linguistic object, *O*, if and only if *O* is an electron. Putnam adds: "*how else* should we say what 'Electron' refers to from *within* a conceptual system in which 'electron' is a *primitive* term?" (*ibid.*).

Now this statement may seem quite trivial, but the appearance is deceptive. It is informative and a matter of some interest (to philosophers of language, for example) that the kind of correspondence existing between words and extra-linguistic objects in the primitive reference of one to another is such as to be representable by formulae of this simple sort. This is not to deny that we could add to the original statement and make it more complex. On the basis of subsequent empirical investigations and a background theory, for example, we might be able to show that electrons are particles with a certain mass and a negative unit charge. This would enable us to supplant the original statement with the following: "'electron' refers to particles of such-and-such a mass and a negative unit charge." And this statement may appear less trivial than the original. But, again, this appearance is deceptive, for, on investigation, we discover that the very same features which made the original statement seem trivial occur here also. So the primitive terms in which the second statement is formulated (for example, "charge") still accord with Tarskian satisfaction-relations (e.g. "*x* has a negative unit charge" is satisfied by an extra-linguistic magnitude *N* if and only if *N* is a magnitude with a negative unit charge). And the description and justification of these referential relations still depend on background theories and the conceptual system on which they rely, together with "that vast fund of unformalized and unformalizable knowledge of man upon which we depend and with which we live and breathe and have our being every day of our lives" (Putnam 1976a (vi): 76).

The nested structure of allusions in this quotation is worth a passing note since the phenomenon reflects the equally complex allusive structure characteristic of Putnam's modes of thought and expression, and since this is one of the few places in his writing where the phenomenon is sufficiently condensed to be illustrated. Putnam is half-quoting from Paul's speech in the Acts of the Apostles describing God (17:28); Paul himself is half-quoting the Greek poet Epimenides describing the nature of divinity (or the divinity of nature); and the underlying claim for which this ancient and biblical terminology is pressed into service obtains its most familiar expression in philosophy in Peter Strawson's description of the subject-matter of descriptive metaphysics:

> there is a massive central core of human thinking which has no history – or none recorded in histories of thought; there are categories and concepts which, in their most fundamental character, change not at all. Obviously these are not the specialities of the most refined thinking. They are the commonplaces of the least refined thinking; and are yet the indispensable core of the conceptual equipment of the most sophisticated human beings.
>
> (Strawson 1959: 10)

Interest relativity

Putnam's treatment of the dependence of reference on conceptual schemes becomes more precise with his account of one subsidiary area: explanation, and its relativity to the interests of the relevant parties.

Putnam developed a view here because he was interested in the question of how we might be justified in claiming that words in a language other than our own are "about" extra-linguistic objects. This is, of course, just a special case of the intentionality problem now familiar to us: of how we are justified in claiming that *any* words are about such objects. But the problem inherits additional complexities when we step outside our own language, for there we do not even know what words *purport* to be about. The problems arising are difficult enough when we consider languages that are foreign to us in the usual sense: languages that count as such merely in virtue of being "second" languages to us; languages other than that in which we were taught language use itself.[1] But Putnam was prompted by Quine's work on radical translation to consider second languages that are fundamentally foreign to us: languages concerning which there are no dictionaries or bilingual persons to whom we can appeal, no pre-existing linguistic knowledge on which we can draw.

In order to justify believing that there is indeed reference in these radically different languages, to give substance to the claim that they contain words that are "about" extra-linguistic items, we need to know *whether* those words purport to be about anything, and *what* they purport to be about. So we need to find ways and means of working out what is being referred to. And using the famous example of a radically foreign community who say "gavagai" when confronted by a rabbit, Quine himself denied that this is possible.

Consider advancing the claim: "'Gavagai' refers to an object O, if and only if O is a rabbit." The supposition might be supported by various sorts of experience; but those same experiences might match a number of other hypotheses equally well, alternatives that contradict the first. For example, those who say "gavagai" may do so in circumstances and with the appropriate accompanying behaviour where reference to rabbit behaviour might be inferred, or reference to rabbithood, or to undetached rabbit parts, or to the rabbit (the general term), or to any other set of rabbit-related features. Hence any preference we might feel for one translation over another would reflect a pragmatic resolution on our part to choose *some* option. It would have to be an arbitrary decision of this sort, for there is no "fact of the matter" corresponding to the preference which would justify it independently of our pragmatic resolve. And if we tried to construct whole translation manuals for the language, the problem would replicate itself for all the various subject-terms and predicates of which they consisted. This would occur directly for words such as "gavagai" whose various possible meanings are given directly (by ostensive definition, for example). For those words whose meaning is given indirectly, being determined in part by the meaning of other words, the problem would arise indirectly; it would be inherited from the words on which they depended.

In all cases, then, incompatible hypotheses with contradictory implications about meaning would be supported equally well by experience. From this, Quine inferred that there are no facts of the matter about whether any given translation manual for any given language is correct. And he drew the radical conclusion that there are no facts of the matter about the meaning of any given sentence in any given language, our own first language included.[2] The implications for intentionality are grave. On a plausible view, we require acquaintance with such facts about meaning to be able to say not just what the words of a language refer to, but whether they refer at all. And if there are no such facts to be acquainted with, even in our own language, then we might be unable to justify or give substance to the claim that there is any such thing as genuine reference.

Putnam resists Quine's conclusions, agreeing with those who claim that Quine's argument is unjustifiably parsimonious with the resources available to translators. There are two main ways of making this point. Either Quine works with too limited a notion of experience (i.e. whatever else translators may have to rely on), or he ignores resources in addition to experience (i.e. however experience itself is conceived). Those who take the first route can claim that experience alone, if properly conceived of, should enable translators to regard one hypothesis about the meaning of sub-sentential expressions such as "gavagai" as more appropriate than another.[3] Putnam takes the second route. He starts by pointing out features of the practice of translators when confronted with *non*-radical second languages: they do not rely on experience alone, but on gauging the interests of the people whose language they are translating. Suppose we take the main point of translation to be rationalization of the behaviour of those using the foreign language (Putnam 1976a (iii): 44). Human nature is not thoroughly modifiable or arbitrary – it is "not all that plastic", in Putnam's phrase (1976a (v): 56). What is characteristic of and salient about human interests and cognitive processes has a structure that is heavily determined by innate or constitutional factors. Hence we can use behaviour and various models of rationality to hypothesize about which interpretation is the most probable out of the indefinite number of alternative possibilities. We should approach the reference of sub-sentential expressions in the radical case in the same way.

Putnam's idea develops as follows. Technically, a range of possible options exists for the reference of "gavagai". But once we take on the interested point of view of the person using the term, we recognize that it must mean "rabbit" (for example), and not "rabbithood", or "rabbit behaviour", "undetached rabbit-part", "the rabbit" or any of the other supposedly viable options. For taking on interests in this way enables us to structure a certain space of explanations. Suppose we do so in such a way that the hunter's actions reflect concurrent thoughts expressible throughout using the term "gavagai". Given this structure, the translation of "gavagai" that is consistent with the simplest explanation of a hunter's rational behaviour in saying the word, shooting a rabbit, taking it home and cooking it, might be "a rabbit". For it is indeed rational for him to be thinking thoughts expressible by the sentences "Ah, I see a rabbit; I want a rabbit to eat; let me shoot, cook and then eat a rabbit." And alternative translations such as "rabbithood" or "rabbit behaviour" would not match thoughts and action rationally within this space of explanation. If we ascribed to the hunter thoughts expressible by the sentences "Ah, I see rabbit behaviour; I want rabbit behaviour to eat; let me shoot, cook and then eat rabbit behaviour", we would suppose him absurd or worse.[4]

On Putnam's view, then, ascribing reference to a term depends on using the conceptual resources available to us to construct a space of explanations, one that acts like a theoretical posit in relation to the persons and their behaviour whose attempts at reference we want to understand. This may involve taking on someone else's interests as our own, and, from within that perspective, marrying up how they would be likely to behave with how in fact they do behave. Engaging in this imaginative project will afford clues as to why they behave as they do (why, for example, they say what they do), which in turn helps us determine what they must mean by the words they use.

Putnam gives substance to his claims concerning the interest-relativity of explanation by drawing on an example used by others for similar purposes (e.g. Garfinkel). A notorious bank robber was asked "Why do you rob banks?", to which he replied "That's where the money is". Now, according to the argument, "why"-questions of the form prompting this response always presuppose a certain space of explanation, one that determines which possible answers are indeed explanations and which are not. And this space is relative to the interests of the relevant parties. So if a would-be criminal asked the question, with an interest in gaining advice about his chosen profession, the robber's comment would be a genuine answer, one that provided a (partial) explanation of his activities. But others might ask that same question with different interests in mind. And this enables us to construct cases supporting the interest-relativity of the situation from the opposing direction. Suppose the question were asked by someone who had an interest in why the robber engaged in the profession in the first place, rather than in his *modus operandi*: a social worker, for instance. Then evidently his response is not an explanation, not even a partial one; indeed, it should perhaps be regarded as no answer at all, but rather a (witty) avoidance of the question. This appeal to "why"-questions is designed to show that explanation is interest-relative: until we know the various interests of the relevant parties, what would count as an explanation will be left undetermined.

Now this conclusion is perhaps too strong for the evidence in its support, for we might hold that the original question ("Why do you rob banks?") is simply ambiguous. What would count as a responsive explanation can be sufficiently determined by knowing which of (at least two) *bona fide* "why"-questions is being asked: "Why is it *banks* you rob?", or "Why is it *robbing* you do in banks?". So we need not appeal to the interests of the relevant parties once we know which question is at issue. Of course, knowing which question is at issue may depend on knowing the interests of the person asking it. But that is a different and non-controversial matter; it is generally acknowledged that disambiguating sentences is in practice usually interest-relative. The question is whether *explanation* is similarly dependent. If it is, then we would expect appeal to interest to be necessary even *after* the sense of the original sentence had been identified. And that is controversial. Consider the bank-robbing case again. If we know that what the questioner means by his utterance is "Why is it *banks* you rob?", we would know which possible replies would, and which would not, count as the kinds of explanation sought. We would not need to know either that the questioner is himself a bank robber, or what interests he brings to the conversation.

Facts and theories

Putnam emphasized the interest-relativity of explanation in order to account for the reference of sub-sentential expressions, itself a sub-set of that perspective on intentionality that required conceiving of realism as an empirical hypothesis. Turning from this comparatively limited range of interest, we can now widen the focus to encompass a larger field of enquiry. This is to follow Putnam's own lead, for his own emerging perspective on the intentionality of thought and language required a reconceiving of the notions of truth and of fact, together with a revised view of their relations with theorizing and the background organization made possible by schemes of concepts.[5] And we can begin appreciating his renewed investigation of these issues by linking up with a basic intentionality problem that he reviewed earlier in his career and that we have already examined: how it is possible to think or say what is false.

Facts are often taken to be worldly entities like states of affairs which are correlated with propositions in such a way that the obtaining of the former makes the latter true. Among the problems that then arise is what we are to say about so-called "negative" facts. Consider Lizzie Borden, since Putnam encourages us to; she who killed her parents with "forty whacks" of an axe (Putnam 1999 (iii): 52). We might say that what makes the proposition "Lizzie Borden killed her parents" true is the obtaining of a certain state of affairs: for example, a state in which three objects (Lizzie Borden and her parents) stand to each other in a certain relation (that of killing). The order of the relation turns out to be important, for that relation is non-symmetric. Mutual slaughter is of course possible: someone might be killed by the person they kill; so the relation of killing is not asymmetric. But it is not symmetric either (unlike the state of affairs in virtue of which "Lizzie Borden is the same height as her mother" is true). The truth of the proposition "Lizzie Borden killed her parents" does not entail the truth of "Lizzie Borden was killed by her parents". And now the offshoot of the basic puzzle arises: how is it even possible that the corresponding "negative" proposition ("Lizzie Borden was not killed by her parents") is true?

On the one hand, we might say "the fact that Lizzie Borden was not killed by her parents". This would be to explain the truth of the "negative proposition" by appeal to the existence of a certain sort of fact: call it a "negative fact". But then we will have the difficulty of saying just what kind of thing such a fact is, for we will seem to be claiming that what makes the proposition true is the obtaining of the state of affairs in which her parents did not kill Lizzie Borden. So we are committed to the idea that, for every possible description of a state in which the world is not, there is nevertheless a state of affairs which makes that description true. And we might justifiably baulk at allowing for the existence of such states of affairs, especially if that means admitting the existence (if only in a subordinate sense) of the objects and relations of which they are composed. Now our ontology begins to take on a baroque aspect. Why should we not also include round squares and unicorns? They are presumably objects in the states of affairs composing negative facts whose obtaining makes negative propositions such as "round squares and unicorns do not exist" true.

On the other hand, we might say "What makes the proposition 'Lizzie Borden was not killed by her parents' true is the non-obtaining of the state of affairs in which her parents killed Lizzie Borden". This would be to explain the truth of the negative proposition by appeal to the absence or non-existence of a certain fact: the fact that, in certain counterfactual situations, would have made the same proposition false. But then we will have the difficulty of saying what makes any proposition true. For we will have allowed that there are propositions whose truth is not simply consistent with, but dependent on, the absence or non-existence of any corresponding fact. And once we allow this analysis for certain cases, the general picture of explanatory correlations between facts and propositions begins to seem unmotivated: if the truth of the latter is not dependent on the existence of the former in every case, why should we suppose that dependence obtains in *any* case, let alone dependence of an explanatory sort? So perhaps the truth of corresponding positive propositions ("Lizzie Borden killed her parents") is not to be explained by the obtaining of states of affairs with which they are correlated. Perhaps consistency with whatever is the correct explanation requires that we deny such correlations, or that we reject the particular conception of states of affairs that is necessary for expressing such correlations.

The problems rehearsed by examining these alternatives make two features salient: on the one hand, what is required of any realist account of facts; on the other, how difficult it is to meet those requirements. And both features find their roots in the intentionality problem. To account for the truth of propositions, we need to say what they are about; explanatory correlations between propositions and facts give us one kind of answer; but that answer will be quite unacceptable if the only ontology able to support it is too baroque. These issues become more complex still when we consider the kind of hypothetical propositions necessary for expressing the kind of realism Putnam endorsed in the first half of his career. On this view, as we have seen, propositions must be allowed to be false even though they follow from our best body of current theories, together with that collection of statements about the world supporting those theories whose truth is itself supported by our observations of the world. So realism of this sort is defined around its acceptance of propositions such as the following:

> (V) Venus might not have carbon monoxide in its atmosphere even though it follows from our ideal theory that it has.
>
> (Putnam 1976a (iii): 34)[6]

And propositions of the sort typified by (V) raise a specific instance of the kind of problem-case just noted. How is it even possible that propositions referring to scientific theories and observation data, including hypothetical negative propositions such as (V), are true?

On the one hand, we may be tempted towards an answer that requires the existence of situations in which the antecedents of propositions such as (V) are actually true: situations composed of objects and relations whose existence must be posited, and whose totality in turn composes whole worlds which must themselves be posited. But this may be thought to extend our ontology too far into the baroque.

So we may be drawn in the opposite direction, claiming that there need be no such situations for propositions such as (V) to be about in order for them to be true. But this is explicitly to renounce any attempt to explain the intentionality involved in such propositions, and implicitly to threaten any account we may have of the intentionality involved in straightforward instances. So we appear to be caught in an impasse; neither route offers an escape.

Correspondence

This predicament is typical of situations in which two contending "solutions" actually share a common fault, and Putnam's developing approach to intentionality provided him with the resources for just such a diagnosis. Particularly significant here are the views we have examined concerning the nature of reference and the role of conceptual schemes.

Both problematic options assume that there must be a single kind of determinate reference between our words and objects in the world – a "correspondence" that is independent of conceptual scheme – if the one is to be about the other (Putnam 1983a: viii). Given this assumption about intentionality and cases such as (V)-type propositions, it is inevitable that we should be drawn to one or other option: either accept that such propositions are intentional and hence commit ourselves to the existence of as many objects and relations as they purport to be about, or deny that such items exist and hence commit ourselves to denying that such propositions are intentional.

The solution is to give up the assumption, a move for which Putnam's emerging intentionality provides further, independent justification. Once we become "even a little bit psychologically sophisticated", we should relinquish the notion of scheme-independent and uniquely determinate correspondence relations between what we think or say and reality (Putnam 1983a: viii).[7]

It is not enough to give up one half of this notion; for example, to retain the notion of scheme-independent correspondence between what we think or say and reality, while denying that such relations could form a single fixed set. For suppose there is no unique determinate correspondence but several (as envisaged for example by Quine's preferential option for ontological relativity; Quine 1969), while the actual world itself is nevertheless conceived of in a unique and determinate way. Then, Putnam argues, the term to which correspondence relates what we think and say cannot be the actual world of which we have experience, but something else altogether. And we should resist positing a world which we do not experience, a noumenal world of some sort, for our thoughts and words to be about (Putnam 1983a: xii–xiii). There may be a way to resist this argument, however. Just as there can be many ways to relate to an object while the object itself is one (there are, for example, many ways to give, grasp, present or represent a single object), so it is not obvious why the existence of a plurality of possible correspondence relations entails a plurality in both terms of those relations. In the present instance, for example, we might explain the possibility of different possible correspondence relations to a term that is nevertheless one by distinguishing the different possible ways it is open to us to represent the uniquely determinate world of our experience, both mentally (in what we think) and linguistically (in what we say).

Relinquishing the old realist model of scheme-independent and uniquely determinate correspondence relations comes at a price, of course. In particular, it seems to undercut the ways in which some externalists about content have been sketching out the intentional relations between reality and semantic contents, encouraged in large part by Putnam's own earlier views. As he expresses one implication of the current position, "the idea that the 'non-psychological' fixes reference – i.e. that *nature itself* determines what our words stand for – is totally unintelligible" (Putnam 1983a: xii). This view should be discarded along with the notion that theories are "descriptions of the world": the idea is quite empty if we cannot say how the world is independently of theory.

I say that Putnam "seems" here to undercut content externalism because it is possible from the context that he has only a restricted conception of mental representations in mind, one which he associated with what we have called "narrow content". If this is so, then his point is consistent with two-component versions of externalism about content: namely, those that (a) accept that there is such a thing as content narrowly conceived, but (b) deny that content of this sort exhausts the ways in which minds represent the world, because they (c) affirm that there must be such a thing as content widely conceived if our thought and talk about the world is to be possible. Advocates of such a view may then offer the following motivation for the passages just quoted. In so far as mental representations can be conceived narrowly, it is senseless to compare them with worldly objects and relations whose totality composes states of affairs. In so far as mental representations can be conceived widely (for example, if we suppose their existence and identity to depend on the existence and identity of worldly objects and relations whose totality composes states of affairs), then such comparisons become intelligible. Indeed, it is at least coherent and may be definitional to suppose that there is sufficient correspondence between such representations and the world as to enable the latter to determine the former.

Putnam offers two further reasons for renouncing the old realist model. First, it is false to claim that there must be a single determinate reference between our words and reality, between what we think or say and the world. There are always indefinitely many distinct relations of this sort that satisfy whatever theoretical or operational constraints our practices may impose on our use of a language. To suppose otherwise is to imply, among other things, that there must be a unique reference-preserving translation between any two languages. And this we have found to be false, even if interest-relativity supports our pragmatic resolution to go with one translation rather than another.

Putnam characteristically extended this Quinean point to cover scientific theorizing. Just as there are inequivalent relations between words and objects across different languages, so there are inequivalent relative interpretations of one theory within the schema set by another. There is no difficulty here, no impasse, so long as we detach ourselves from the assumption that the programmes and procedures in terms of which we understand uses of language must themselves be modelled independently of those uses and of any description or schema within which they find their place. Putnam puts the point fancifully, alluding to the fashion world by anthropomorphizing the central concept: "Models are not lost noumenal waifs looking for someone to name them; they are constructions within our theory itself, and they have names from birth" (Putnam 1980: 25).

His second reason for relinquishing the old model of scheme-independent and uniquely determinate correspondence relations is more significant still: it is unintelligible to suppose that an ideal theory might really be false, a theory, that is, whose contents are endorsed by ideal investigators of an ideal investigation pursued through ideal circumstances to an ideal end. To claim this is to suppose that such a theory might still really fall short of the truth, that there is something it lacks. But there is no intelligible account available of quite what such a theory lacks, of what maintains this gap between ideal theory and truth, of what this gap consists of, or of what might close it. This is the deepest point of attack and the one with the most significant implications, for it directly relates the problem of intentionality to questions about truth, as Putnam recognized. If it is unintelligible to say that an ideal theory might really be false, then that must partly be due to the nature of truth and to the way in which it should be conceived. It would be senseless, for example, if truth could not be conceived as forever exceeding verification or falsification by experience.

These issues raise deeper questions than those concerning the mere meaning of the denoting term or its logic. As Putnam emphasized at the time, "realism depends on a way of understanding truth, not just a way of *defining* the word 'true'" (Putnam 1976a (iii): 37). And his attempts to elucidate our conception of truth led to a thorough overhaul of his own realism about the concept.

Chapter 14

Experience

> This is typical of the release from metaphysical terrors: they leave little behind them when they disappear, because we can see, after they have gone, that what they threatened is not only unreal but unintelligible.
>
> Bernard Williams, *Shame and Necessity* (1993: 152)

Putnam's emerging account of intentionality brought him, as we have seen, to revise his conception of truth. He made surface changes of formulation and changes of emphasis over this period, but the deep idea remained constant. Truth is not correspondence with states of affairs whose nature and existence are independent of minds. More specifically, it is constrained by those mental phenomena involved in conditions on knowing things. This is the exemplary instance of Putnam's awareness of his overall redirection in this period: "I have come to see that one cannot come to grips with the real problems in philosophy without being more sensitive to the epistemological position of the philosopher" (Putnam 1983a: vii).

Epistemic constraints

The claim that we need to accommodate various ways in which our conception of truth is epistemically constrained follows from definitions like the following, which Putnam endorsed for a time: "Truth . . . is some sort of (idealized) rational acceptability – some sort of ideal coherence of our beliefs with each other and with our experiences *as those experiences are themselves represented in our belief system*" (Putnam 1981a (iii): 49–50).[1] On this view, a belief that is rationally acceptable in epistemically satisfactory circumstances is true: there is nothing more to be added to it, no gap to close before truth itself is reached (Putnam 1979b: 167; 1983a: xviii; 1983d: 85).

A position of this sort puts a great deal of pressure on the notions of satisfactory circumstance and acceptability, features that are themselves conditioned in Putnam's view by the overall conceptual system in which they are located. And this may seem to open the door to relativism of a certain familiar sort. Since every internally coherent conceptual system is as good as every other, and beliefs are made true in relation to such systems, any belief that can be made to cohere with any system must be as good as any other belief with this same property, even if the beliefs in question, and even the systems to which they are related, are wholly incompatible with each other. Putnam resists this conclusion by denying part of the antecedent. It is false to say that every conceptual system is as good as every other: judging between such systems is made possible by external relations to the world. Putnam is free to make this claim because his approach "does not deny that there are experiential inputs to knowledge; knowledge is not a story with no constraints except internal coherence; but it does deny that there are any inputs which are not themselves to some extent shaped by our concepts" (Putnam 1981a (iii): 54). The argument works quite hard the spatial metaphor of an inner and an outer ("internal–external coherence"; "inputs–outputs"), and needs to be unpacked accordingly. The main idea seems to be as follows.

Truth is a matter of rational acceptability. The rational acceptability of a theory or conceptual scheme, like the rational acceptability of the single statements or beliefs composing them, is largely a matter of coherence, of fit. But this does not entail that theories or conceptual systems are freewheeling, quite detached from the need to be consistent with the way the world is. As Putnam notes, theories and systems that are inconsistent with perceptual experience (for example, those supporting beliefs such as "human beings can survive underwater unaided for days") are open to being judged as poor. This is because theories and systems include statements and beliefs of several different kinds, some heavily dependent on "inputs" from experience and some not. All such statements and beliefs are judged by their coherence with each other: "coherence of 'theoretical' or less experiential beliefs with one another and with more experiential beliefs, and also coherence of experiential beliefs with theoretical beliefs" (Putnam 1981a (iii): 55). And given that systems incorporate statements and beliefs that are heavily dependent on experiential input, they incorporate external constraints into the overall requirements on internal coherence. "Experiential" beliefs are judged in part by their fit or lack of fit with the way the world is, while "non-experiential" beliefs are judged in part by their fit or lack of fit with experiential beliefs. Hence all beliefs are in the end, and directly or indirectly, judged in part by the way the world is. And so, to resist relativism, we need not appeal at bottom to any other notion than rational acceptability, understood in large part in terms of internal coherence. Some theories or conceptual schemes are better than others because some are rationally acceptable and some are not. Those that are not internally coherent fail to be rationally acceptable. Those that contain experiential beliefs that are inconsistent with the way the world is (or at least with the way it is represented as being through the inputs of experience) fail to be internally coherent to some degree.[2] The internal coherence of schemes and theories incorporates all the external constraint we need to judge between them.

One query about this picture arises from Putnam's own claim, as quoted above: that the "inputs" represented by experience are to some extent shaped by concepts.[3] It might be said that, if experience is constrained by concepts in this way, it can hardly exercise in return the kind of constraint over concepts necessary for resisting relativism. But the assumption that power can only be exercised one way is false in the general case and may be rejected here in a number of different ways that accord with a large spectrum of different positions.

So from a more rationalist direction we might still think of experience as at least equally shaped by relations to the world as it is by concepts. And we might support that view with considerations such as either of the following: because experiential "input" just is that conceptual engagement with the world that consists of such external relations to the world, or because such relations provide the content of experiential inputs that it is the role of concepts to "shape" or organize ("conceptualize"). Alternatively, and from a more empiricist direction, we might consider concepts themselves as at least equally shaped by the external relations made possible by experiential inputs as such inputs are shaped by concepts. We need not suppose that this is true of any but a few concepts (for example, those actuated in certain simple and direct perceptual engagements with the world), so long as those concepts have a sufficiently significant role within the overall scheme to which they belong to make that scheme itself dependent on external relations. On any of these approaches or those like them, external relations and concepts are to be conceived as exercising constraints and shaping powers reciprocally on each other. Hence the fact that experiences are shaped by concepts need not render experience itself inert with respect to conceptual systems. Systems of this sort may be constrained in various ways; for example, the requirements of internal coherence may incorporate the need for consistency in external relations to the world. And the main support for such relations may be the experiential inputs which conceptual systems themselves make possible.

External constraints

Two more problems arise in relation to Putnam's account; they are more troublesome, related at a deep level, and perhaps partly responsible for significant modifications that he made later on to his approach (Putnam 1999). The first grows from a worry about how seriously we are to take the adoption of inner-outer language, of experiential "inputs" to internal coherence, and of the phrase "shaped" to describe the effect that concepts have on experience, as if experiences exist alone and entire of themselves and only need "conceptualizing" to suit some specific extra purpose.[4]

As we have seen, Putnam regards experiential inputs as providing vital rational (reason-sensitive) support for what we think and say, both in terms of particular justifications for particular beliefs and statements, and combinatorially in helping to justify the theories and conceptual systems composed of such beliefs and statements. These claims form a crucial part of his resistance to relativism. But it is difficult to see how rational relations of this sort could be consistent with the picture to which Putnam's language seems to be tending: one in which the world and conceptual systems are separated by a divide that it is the purpose of experience to bridge; where experience itself is conceived of as a mere "input" to the internal coherence of conceptual systems from outside the conceptual; in which experiential engagement with the world is not regarded as a proper set of various forms of conceptual activity; indeed, in which the ways that experience represents the world as being are entirely non-conceptual, and only need "shaping" by concepts when they are to become the contents of exercises of genuine conceptual activity, such as believing and judging.[5]

This picture is not at all uncommon. One way to arrive at it is to endorse views commonly held by the British empiricists and bequeathed by them (particularly through the advocacy of Russell and C. I. Lewis) as a standard position in mid-century analytic philosophy. But by placing experience and its contents (the way it represents the world as being) outside the scope of the conceptual, this standard picture risks placing it also outside the scope of the epistemic, and

hence ineligible as a term in genuinely rational relations. We make
such relations intelligible to ourselves by thinking about what it is to
make claims, and to be entitled to make them; to draw inferences, and
recognize entailments; to bind ourselves to commitments, and have
them endorsed; to offer justifications, and to be supported by evidence
in so doing. These are all conceptual activities as various philosophers
have emphasized (Kant, Frege and Wittgenstein in particular).
Indeed, they are so thoroughly dependent on the structures that concepts make possible that it may seem quite unintelligible to suppose
that anything could be rationally significant independently of conceptual engagement on the part of the one for whom it has that significance. But this is precisely what the standard position requires, if held
in conjunction with the view that experience gives rational support,
whether to beliefs and judgements, or to whole theories and conceptual systems. So suppose we agree with Lewis that "There are in our
cognitive experience two elements, the immediate data such as those
of sense, which are presented or given to the mind, and a form,
construction, or interpretation, which represents the activity of
thought" (Lewis 1956: 38).[6] To resist relativism in the way Putnam
requires, we have to suppose that the impact of this "given" might
have sufficient rational and epistemic significance for those to whom it
is given that it grounds forms of knowing, serving as a justifier for
their beliefs and judgements. And it is not readily intelligible how
something without any "form" or "construction" or "interpretation"
whatever, let alone the conceptual form required for making claims,
drawing inferences, endorsing commitments or offering justifications,
could have such significance or take on this role.

The second and related problem with Putnam's position grows from
queries about how distant it really is from the views with which he
contrasts it. The notion that truth is a matter of some kind of rational
acceptability was designed, as we have seen, not simply to advance the
claim that truth is in some sense epistemically constrained; it was
meant to undermine the view that truth "involves some sort of correspondence relation between words or thought-signs and external
things and sets of things" (Putnam 1981a (iii): 49). Now this view
might be rejected for a number of reasons: because there is no match
between what we think and say and the world; or because, although
there is such a match, it does not explain or justify intentionality, the
fact that what we think or say can be about the world.[7] But these are
not the reasons for which Putnam rejects it. Indeed, he is keen to point
out how regarding truth as a matter of rational acceptability in

relation to a conceptual system is not only consistent with, but explains, how words and thoughts match reality, and hence how intentionality is made possible:

> "Objects" do not exist independently of conceptual schemes. *We cut up the world into objects when we introduce one or another scheme of description.* Since the objects *and* the signs are alike *internal* to the scheme of description, it is possible to say what matches what. (Putnam 1981a: 52)

As the emphasis and careful phrasing make salient, what is crucially different about the views in contention is this: the view Putnam wishes to discard matches what we think and say with what is *external* to a conceptual scheme, while the view he wishes to retain matches what we think and say with what is *internal*. He has not renounced the attempt to explain intentionality in terms of a certain kind of correspondence, still less a representational relation, between words, thoughts and reality. But he now locates both terms of the relation within the conceptual, where the alternative is to make that relation amphibious, able to connect terms that exist within and without that scheme. Hence the real difference between the contrasting views is made to depend on a feature with which we are now familiar: the language of inner–outer and of relations that cross the divide. And this is the main reason why a deep connection links the two problems under discussion.

There is a problem with Putnam's "internalist" picture, and one that becomes clear when we recall the way Putnam resists relativism.[8] Conceptual systems are supposed to determine the notions of satisfactory circumstance and rational acceptability on which truth depends. They are dependent on the way the world is for their internal coherence, a constraint, crucially, that is regarded as operating from outside the system. It is experience that relates the system to what is outside it, experience that must then itself be regarded as an "input", an impact on the conceptual from what is not conceptual. And it is by appeal to the external constraints provided by experiential input, together with the relations they establish between a conceptual system and the non-conceptual world, that we are able to judge that system. Hence, by appeal to the criterion that Putnam makes crucial to his contrast between two different accounts of intentionality – whether both terms of the representational relation are depicted as within the sphere of the conceptual or not – his present position actually counts as "externalist". The rational constraint that experiential inputs exercise over conceptual schemes from outside them could only be rendered possible if those inputs related the conceptual with the non-conceptual; experience would have to enable one to match beliefs, judgements and statements regarded as internal to the scheme with objects, properties and states of affairs regarded as external to it in such a way that the veracity of the former might depend on and be checked by its correspondence with the latter. So whatever faults Putnam found with "externalism" that made him seek an alternative, the proposed substitute turns out to be quite as "externalist" and hence heir to those same faults.

Concept-dependence

As we have seen, the two problems with Putnam's account are related. Both may most readily be formulated in the way that they are generated: by appeal to certain uses of inner–outer language. So it is no particular surprise that they are also related in their resolution.

The alleged externality of experience is the key issue. Both of the problems we have rehearsed may be made to disappear with a single significant modification to the model which the inner-outer language denotes: to replace the notion that experience is a mere "input" to the internal coherence of conceptual systems from outside the conceptual with the conceptualist idea that "all perception . . . involves the application of concepts"; that experiential engagement with the world is itself a proper sub-set of the conceptual; and hence that experience does not mark a boundary between the "inside" of conceptual systems whose business it is for minds to organize, and the "outside" of objects and states of affairs whose totality makes up the world (Putnam 2002 (vi): 109); see also 2000a (i)–(iii)).

Putnam worked intensively on these ideas throughout the 1980s, prompted by the root puzzle to which we have seen him brought by his work on the relations between the nature of truth and the role of conceptual schemes: that "the notion of comparing our system of beliefs with unconceptualized reality to see if they match makes no sense" (Putnam 1981a (vi): 130). It took a while longer for Putnam to recognize and advocate the solution to this puzzle: to regard experience itself as conceptual. He continued to cling for a time to a version of functionalism that blocked this possibility (*ibid.*: 79). As he later recognized, this version implied that experience does not put us in touch with worldly objects and states of affairs at all, but only (and at best) with the sensations that those objects and states cause in us (Putnam 1999 (i): 18–20). Relinquishing this view in favour of concept-dependence about experience produced a new outlook on intentionality that Putnam made public in a set of lectures in 1994 (eventually published in book form in 1999).[9] The result undermined "a disastrous idea that has haunted Western philosophy since the seventeenth century, the idea that perception involves an interface between the mind and the 'external' objects we perceive" (1999 (iii): 43). It is worth commenting on this spatial metaphor of an "interface" between experiencing subject and world experienced, since Putnam makes extensive use of it (1999 (i)–(iii)).[10] The basic idea seems to be this. Minds and the world inhabit two distinct logical spaces that are at best contiguous: what enables the one to be affected by the other is that experience acts as an intermediary; experience exploits the contiguity between minds and the world, transferring information about the one in a form that the other can assimilate. This idea is disastrous, in Putnam's view, because it undermines our hopes of accounting for intentionality. Representing minds as separated from the world by a gulf that only experience can hope to bridge is a major obstacle to "seeing how our minds can be in genuine contact with the 'external' world" (1999 (iii): 44).

Putnam identifies the basic idea here as "Cartesian". But, as he acknowledges, it survives rejection of substance dualism, the trademark claim made by Descartes in his account of mental phenomena. As this claim affects our subject, intentionality, it is the idea that there are two fundamental kinds of substance involved in intentional relations, immaterial mental phenomena and material worldly phenomena. We can then describe the intentional directedness of the former variously: as a matter of their being "ideas" of the latter, or "impressions" or "sensations". In what we might call this *fully* Cartesian picture, experience has to interpose itself between the material and the immaterial and thus provide whatever contiguity is possible between minds and the world.

Suppose we renounce Descartes's dualism in favour of a monist materialism about intentionality: the mental phenomena directed on worldly objects are as material as those objects. The disastrous idea survives because experience may nevertheless still be regarded as interposing itself between two different separate kinds of item (though both now material), providing whatever contiguity is possible between minds and the world. In this *semi*-Cartesian picture, the contiguity in question is between one sort of material item (brain processes) and another (objects). As Putnam acknowledged, this is the picture adopted by his own earlier functionalist identification of mental properties with computational properties of the brain (Putnam 1999 (i): 18ff.; referring back to his 1981a (iv): 79). The intentional directedness of brain processes is then understood as a matter of the causal impacts made on them by the material objects they are about. Thus to say we perceive external objects, that a particular subjective experience *E* is "about" an object *O*, is to say that *O* causes us to have *E*. Hence Putnam's resistance to the semi-Cartesian model can be traced back to his rejection of "strong physicalism" about reference. For the semi-Cartesian is charged with a task that Putnam had deemed hopeless ever since that position on reference had claimed to achieve it: of showing how "the referential directedness of our thinking about the objects we think about can be constituted out of or in some way 'reduced to' the *causal* impacts of those objects upon us" (1999 (iii): 43–4).[11] The fully Cartesian and semi-Cartesian views differ radically in all sorts of ways, of course. But they share the same basic idea: that the experiencing subject and the world experienced are sufficiently divided from each other that whatever contact exists between them can only be made possible by the interposition of an intermediary. Experience is then conceived of as that intermediary. Hence we reject both views by conceiving of experience of the world as not merely causal but cognitive and conceptual (1999 (i): 10). For then we are free (at least in veridical situations, if not also in certain situations where we hold false beliefs) to regard subjects and the world as undivided from each other; we are not blocked from thinking of subjects as *in* the world they experience, rather than set over against it; indeed, we are encouraged to view subjects as *open* to the world in their experience of it.

This is no *ad hoc* claim, one that we have no independent reason for asserting other than that it provides a solution to an embarrassing problem. In Putnam's view, this claim is the only way of insisting that it is really worldly objects that are experienced. For on both the fully Cartesian and semi-Cartesian picture "it has to seem magical that we can have access to anything outside our own 'inputs'" (*ibid.*: 19). On these views, we might *say* that we experience worldly objects; but this could only be so in a "Pickwickian" sense, for the most that we could commit ourselves to is that our experiences are caused by such objects. And so we must admit that what we *really* experience are just the inputs themselves, those "affectations of our sensibility" that have been variously labelled "ideas", "impressions", "sensations", "sense-data", "qualia" and so on.

In Putnam's view, the way in which subjects represent the world to themselves in experience is cognitive–conceptual and not merely causal. This does not mean that experiencing the world as being a certain way necessarily entails believing or judging that it is that way. This is just as well, since we may sometimes seem to see things that we do not believe exist (mirages, for example), and seem to see things as behaving in a certain way even though we do not judge that they are actually behaving in that way (for example, wheels represented on film that seem to turn backwards). Experiencing the world is, of course, vitally different from other cognitive ways of engaging with it, even from other conceptual ways: forming beliefs, or doubts, or judgements. But just as believing, doubting and judging are all essentially different from each other and yet still count as forms of conceptual engagement with the world, so experience may be regarded as both a unique and a conceptual form of engagement.[12]

The first of our problems is then resolved. By drawing experience into the scope of the conceptual, there is no impediment to regarding it as rationally significant. The claims made on its behalf, to providing reason-sensitive support for beliefs and statements, theories and systems, become intelligible. For concepts have the role of making reason-sensitive relations possible – the making of claims, drawing of inferences, recognizing of entailments, endorsing of commitments, offering of justifications and so on. And in so far as experiences determine and help articulate those relations, they are themselves determined and articulated by the concepts that form their contents.

The second problem is also resolved. By making experience a conceptual engagement with the world, the two requirements are immediately satisfied: to constrain conceptual systems rationally in such a way that their internal coherence resists relativism, and to do so in the "internalist" manner, without appealing to external correspondence relations with external items. Being conceptual, the contents of experience are eligible to being counted as providing rational support for the beliefs and statements whose totality composes a theory or system. And, by being about the world, the contents of experience enable us to judge beliefs about reality – in particular, to compare the way in which "experiential beliefs" represent the world as being, on the one hand, with the way experience itself represents it as being on the other. Since non-experiential beliefs are judged in part by their fit or lack of fit with experiential beliefs, and experiential beliefs are judged in part by their fit or lack of fit with experience, the whole conceptual scheme is to be judged, directly or indirectly, by the way the world is represented as being.

Hence much of Putnam's original response to the charge of relativism survives his proposal of a single basic revision: to regard the contents of experience as conceptual. Some theories and conceptual schemes are rationally acceptable and some are not; we need not appeal to a more fundamental notion than internal coherence in accounting for rational acceptability; those theories and schemes that contain experiential beliefs that are inconsistent with the way the world is represented as being are not internally coherent. But the revised view neither provides, nor accepts the need for, an external constraint. Given the conceptual nature of experience, all the constraint we need to judge between schemes and theories is provided for from within: it is still a matter of internal coherence. In brief: if we retain the notion that experience is an input from outside the sphere of concepts, we are forced to retain the old correspondence theory; if we can reject that theory, it is because we can reject the notion that experience operates externally; if we can conceive of experience as both reason-supporting and internal, it is because we can conceive of it as conceptual; and if we can coherently represent experience as conceptual, we can coherently represent the experiencing subject as within – undivided from, open to – the world experienced.

Facts and values

As we have seen, one crucial move in Putnam's progress towards this openness view was dependent on a conclusion to which he was led in the 1970s by his researches into the nature of truth and the role of conceptual schemes: his recognition that "it makes no sense" to compare our systems of beliefs with unconceptualized reality (1981a (vi): 130). The idea played an equally crucial role in his approach to facts and values, and the relations between them. So we may complete our account of the contents of Putnam's later thought by examining this second major off-shoot of the earlier conclusion.

A common view holds that a complete dichotomy exists between facts and values. Putnam has recently recorded and examined the substantial history of this outlook (2002a (i)–(iii)). It has been particularly influential in moral theory, being strongly associated with the emotivism of A. J. Ayer and C. L. Stevenson. Since this was the moral theory that the logical positivists found most congenial, and since that theory required the notion of a complete fact–value dichotomy, we can regard Putnam's interest in the question as a final reflection of his abiding concern with the problems and solutions that defined philosophy in his youth.

Various ways have been found to separate facts from values and to treat each as belonging to wholly different logical spaces. One method appeals to differences in the uses of language: it posits that there are two kinds of statement in operation, one "descriptive" and one "evaluative", for example; or again, one declarative and one a special kind of imperative. Another way to mark the distinction is by appeal to differences in what uses of language express: for example, that there are two kinds of entity being talked about (states of the world on one side, and the feelings or attitudes of subjects on the other), or that there are two kinds of justification or warrant for what is being talked about (those statements that may, and those that may not, be regarded as objectively true or as supported by reason). There are also various ways to maintain the integrity of these two realms. One appeals to the analysis of language use: although some utterances may be partly factual and partly evaluative (and even some single words, for example, so-called "thick" ethical terms, such as "cruel", "generous", "rude"; Putnam 2002a (ii): 34–43), this is a matter of surface grammar only; analysis will expose the two separable elements and identify the manner of their combination. Another way to mark the difference appeals to logic: factual and evaluative statements are governed by different inferential rules; the relations obtaining between them differ. This view is entailed by (but does not itself entail) the well-known Humean view that no evaluative statement may be deduced from a factual statement (the so-called "is–ought gap").

In Putnam's view, there is no such complete dichotomy between facts and values. The notion that they belong to two "totally disjoint realms" lacks rational foundation (Putnam 1981a (vi): 127). The various attempts to separate them, such as those just rehearsed, rest on untenable arguments and over-inflated truisms (Putnam 2002a: 1–2). Moreover, the historical and justificatory roots of the distinction lie in another false dichotomy: the attempt to divide statements and judgements into "analytic" and "synthetic". If we reject this distinction, as we should, we should reject the fact–value dichotomy also. This will have deeply beneficial effects on our philosophical outlook. For these two dichotomies have "corrupted our thinking about both ethical reasoning and description of the world". Once we have renounced them, we will be free to see "how evaluation and description are interwoven and interdependent" (Putnam 2002a: 3).

One immediate form of resistance to the notion of a fact–value dichotomy springs from the recognition that there are certain facts we value. But this is not yet sufficiently forceful as a response to undermine the dichotomy. For suppose we held that facts were things we could recognize as facts and that we could recognize as valuable, but where neither form of recognition was dependent on the other (or at least where the former was not dependent on the latter), then the dichotomy would remain: we would merely have noticed that it is possible to take two fundamentally different perspectives on the same state of affairs, one descriptive and factual, the other evaluative.

Putnam undermines the dichotomy by pursuing the original recognition. It is not just that we value certain facts; that we value them is a condition for the possibility of our recognizing them as facts. And he chooses the hardest example for making this case: "factual statements themselves, and the very practices of scientific inquiry upon which we rely to decide what is and what is not a fact, presuppose values" (1981a (vi): 128). Putnam's argument for this rests on the basic recognition noted above, together with connected conclusions from his 1970s investigations. Since the notion of comparing our belief systems with unconceptualized reality is nonsensical, "the claim that science seeks to discover the truth can mean no more than that science seeks to construct a world picture which, in the ideal limit, satisfies certain criteria of rational acceptability" (*ibid.*: 130). And this truth-centred link between the aims of scientific enquiry and the notion of rational acceptability provides a ready account of just why such enquiries presuppose value:

> The fact is that, if we consider the ideal of rational acceptability which is revealed by looking at what theories scientists and ordinary people consider rational to accept, then we see that what we are trying to do in science is to construct a representation of the world which has the characteristics of being instrumentally efficacious, coherent, comprehensive, and functionally simple.
>
> (*Ibid.*: 134)

These characteristics are values, of course. Hence our ability to recognize facts presupposes our ability to recognize values, and this is so in the strongest sense: recognizing facts depends on our having a representation of the world; it is the purpose of science to construct such a representation; that representation is formed according to our criteria of rational acceptability; and those criteria are in turn determined by what we value – the simple, the comprehensive, the coherent, the instrumentally efficacious. So the condition for the possibility of our recognizing facts as such is that we have certain values. The dependence works in the opposite direction also: "we need no better ground for treating 'value judgements' as capable of truth and falsity than the fact that we can and do treat them as capable of warranted assertibility and warranted deniability" (Putnam 2002a (vi): 110). And this conclusion undermines the fact–value dichotomy. Our evaluative thinking determines our descriptive thinking, and is in turn determined by it. Hence we cannot treat facts and values as belonging to two independent and disjoint logical spaces or "realms". Reflecting on this result and how it was arrived at enables us to draw attention one final time to the two major themes covered in the first parts of this critical interpretation: those determinants of Putnam's thought represented on the one hand by the context created by his philosophical ancestry, and on the other by the intentionality-centred character of philosophical quest. For the demise of the fact–value distinction, following on from the collapse of the analytic–synthetic dichotomy, represent the deepest possible attacks on logical positivism. And the arguments that enabled Putnam to draw these conclusions followed from claims that Putnam used to motivate his concept-dependence about experience, the position that most completely captures his mature outlook on intentionality.

Chapter 15

Conclusion: an integrated vision

> I believe that the unfortunate division of contemporary philosophy
> into separate 'fields' often conceals the way in which the
> very same arguments and issues arise in field after field. We
> can only regain the integrated vision which philosophy has always
> aspired to if at least some of the time we allow ourselves to ignore
> the idea that a philosophical position or argument must
> deal with one and only one of these specific 'fields'.
>
> Putnam, Ethics Without Ontology (2004a: 1)

Previous chapters have described the settings and circumstances into
which Hilary Putnam's philosophical thought fitted during his formative years; they have defined the character of that thinking over the
whole course of his development, depicting its contours in relation to
alternative perspectives on core issues; and they have examined the
content of his major contributions to philosophy, narrating the most
significant movements in his thought across the span of a long career.
This final chapter is retrospective and stimulated by the passage
quoted above. Given what we now know of Putnam, what sense can we
make of what is suggested here: that his contributions to philosophy
do in fact reflect his vision of it as a unified field; that these contributions are themselves to be regarded in a unified way?

Unpredictability

It has been said of John Austin, a philosopher Putnam greatly
admires:

> There are good philosophers whose next book or paper or remark,
> however good, is more or less extrapolable from the last two or
> three; sometimes even one may find oneself feeling, presumptu-
> ously no doubt, that one could almost have written or said it for

them, by a bit of induction on the basis of what came before. Austin was not in the least like that.   (Warnock 1973: 45)

Putnam is not in the least like that either, and it may be helpful to begin by saying why.

There are predictable ways of rendering oneself unpredictable. Some philosophers make a habit of refusing to advance positive doctrines of their own, instead devoting themselves to puncturing the constructions of others. That is perhaps the most common way to be unexpected: to campaign destructively in territory others have mapped out, for the measure of one's success is the waste left behind, an absence without trace, without clues to one's next move.

Putnam does not belong to this group. He has advocated or imparted doctrines concerning all the major philosophical issues, from metaphysical questions about the nature of the world and the mind, and epistemological questions about scientific explanation and the *a priori*, through methodological problems about the proper means and aims of philosophizing, to ethical and political questions about the possibility of living with others. He can be a belligerent controversialist, aiming to destroy one or another position. But this seems always to have been in the interests of establishing a suitable alternative.

Thinkers who offer positive answers can do so unpredictably in various ways. Some offer answers in a piecemeal way, solving problems as they arise rather than as part of a systematic exposition. Putnam has not courted mystery of this sort either. Throughout much of his career, he has addressed problems about our relations with the world in thought, experience and language as issuing from the most fundamental question for philosophy, the question of intentionality. Dating the precise moments of transition from one approach to another is a matter of debate, but that a larger scheme has always encompassed even his most narrow contributions is not.

Putnam belongs in that small class of thinkers: the positive, unified and yet unpredictable. There is no reason to suppose that at any time he knew of or followed the unified plan we are now able to set down, any more than a wanderer necessarily knows of or follows a map of the territory through which he ranges. We might track his movements through the wilderness and note them down as the route traced, but that is after the event. Putnam, we may be confident, had no overall plan to follow, no route to observe, when confronting the problems that stirred him to write.

Over the course of his career, he has maintained a series of different settled philosophical positions, has imparted several doctrines; but at no time have his views been inhibited by absolute fidelity to a particular convention or intellectual tradition. Indeed, he seems to have taken pleasure in putting forward arguments that appear sound or at least plausible, even though they inflict great damage on favoured systems. This is especially true in the areas of epistemology and theory of meaning. He has evidently been concerned to develop a coherent doctrine of philosophical method. But his lasting impact has been the exercise of a rare technique that is probably not teachable: to press questions so that they seem asked precisely for the first time; to pose problems urgently so that they appear fresh, vital, unresolved.

Realism

William Hazlitt said of Coleridge: "There is no subject on which he has not touched, none on which he has rested" (Hazlitt 1991: 55). This tart observation would fit Putnam also if we were obliged to privilege his own occasional remarks and the trajectory laid out for his career by commentators. In particular, undue significance has been given to the question of which form of realism to adopt, prompted in part by the persistent recurrence of that question in his own later self-reflections. This tendency should be resisted, as a more cautious reading of that same source indicates. In the "Introduction" to his first retrospective collection, Putnam commented that his interest "has not been in beating my breast about the correctness of realism, but has rather been in dealing with specific questions in the philosophy of science from a realist point of view" (Putnam 1975a: vii). In other words, realism has been his point of view, not his point of focus. Confusing the two has proved hard to avoid. Realism is simply the most important of the many issues investigated by Putnam where the opportunity to mistake point of view with point of focus arises. But the temptation to confuse the two lures one on to deep mistakes, for the character of one's attention and what one attends to are quite different things. This is so even when, as is peculiarly characteristic of philosophy, we attend to the ways we attend (indeed, maintaining the distinction seems to be a precondition of such self-reflection). And the confusion is fatal if not avoided, particularly to the enterprise of critical interpretation.

For example, assessing Putnam's writings with the assumption that realism is their focal point has conferred on his output an exaggerated impression of irregularity, changeability and unpredictability. It has led commentators to treat his stance on which brand of realism to adopt at any one time as the main, sometimes even the sole, index to his development. And the result is indeed a story of radical discontinuity, even if it is restricted to registering the peak intensities of Putnam's realist commitments. We are first introduced to Putnam the Scientific Realist, whose long-term passionate advocacy of that position was shockingly renounced in the 1970s; then Putnam the Internal Realist, who spent a good decade refining public perception of quite what that position amounted to; then a kind of Interim Putnam, as various features central to internal realism were allowed to wither away; then Putnam the Commonsense Realist, with who knows quite what to follow. This is a false impression, as I have argued over the course of this book. From the standpoint of the work itself, rather than from his occasional remarks about it, there are clearly subjects on which Putnam has lingered sufficiently long to put down roots. And of these, the problem of intentionality stands out as most salient.

Representing integrity

There are many ways to find or reflect integrity in a body of work, and it will help avert misunderstanding of my interpretative claims if we focus on this issue for a moment. We may start from some general impressions. I believe anyone who has made a close study of Putnam's writings and then stood back would agree to something like the following. We could not easily identify these writings as the work of one person if they were not directly associated with one name. They cannot be described in terms of any single group of features, except in so vague or loose a way as to be unhelpful. Yet they do have an integrated character, a mode that belongs to the body of the work, a consistency across the series.

Of course, it is possible to gain an impression of consistency from writings of poor quality. This will usually be due to the mechanical repetition of ideas, or the grip of conventional methods that the writer ought to escape. These forms of consistency are forced on the writer rather than chosen by him. But the more items produced, the easier it is to spot failures of this kind. And this enforced consistency is precisely what we do not find in Putnam's work, although he has produced a vast amount. For in each part can be found the energy enabling him to overcome the limitations of his own former positions, former solutions, former methods. What is satisfying about integrity and disappointing about mere consistency is that the former allows for emergence, unfolding, the gradual realization of ideas and methods. And Putnam's work is a paradigm of such growth. Each part exemplifies conviction, a driving purpose and a clear conception of its goals. So it is possible to appreciate the integrity of the whole without easy appeals to the various labels, the "-isms", under which each part can be made to fall.

Now it is one thing to say that a body of work has integrity and another to say what that integrity consists in. But it is the latter question that it is our task to explain. And, for certain reasons, this task is especially complicated in Putnam's case. The kinds of feature by which we recognize integrity in individual writings are not necessarily the same features that give rise to an impression of integrity across the body of work. This has become clear over the course of this book. One implication is that much of the consistency of Putnam's work, its integrated drive, is not available to inspection when its parts are lifted out piecemeal for individual analysis. We lose sight of the cohesive nature of his writing and proposals if we only ever treat the questions dealt with and the solutions proposed to methodical one-by-one analysis. What makes each problem or position the thing it is owes much to its context and to the subtle system of interrelations existing between it and other problems and positions. As a consequence, much of this book has been dedicated to establishing the deep connections that exist throughout Putnam's work.

Another issue complicating the question of integrity in Putnam's work is that our ideas of what such integrity consists in or entails are partly an artefact of precisely the kinds of process that it is philosophy's job to call into question. Our ideas of what constitutes a coherent point of view in philosophy, or of what turns a set of inchoate worries into a coherent philosophical problem, depend on attitudes and models that change with changing conceptions of philosophy, its aims and methods. At any one time, certain models and attitudes dominate, often by being realized in writings that have come to seem paradigmatic of the philosophical endeavour. But it is itself a philosophical question what should count as paradigmatic in this way. And Putnam has constantly addressed this question, subjecting various paradigms to searching interrogation.

Given the dependence of ideas of integrity on these deeper habits of thought, his criticism of certain paradigms raises questions about these ideas. Analytic philosophy describes itself as centrally concerned with clarity and rigour, for example. But why are they desiderata? And what counts for us as clear and rigorous? Why do some ideas and their formulations "work" for us while others do not? Why do problems have a habit of becoming suddenly pressing, or of retiring into the background without being resolved? And, deeper still, what explains the grip these influences have on us? Is it a matter of sudden taste or more stable attitudes with histories and a persuasive pedigree? So by raising these questions, Putnam's writing puts itself in question. And if we do take it for work of integrity, this should make us particularly keen to ask why we do.

My answer to this question depends on an interpretative claim. It is Putnam's constant and adaptive engagement with the question of intentionality, and the underlying stance his writing takes towards it, that accounts for the integrity of his work. To be absolutely clear: this is not to claim that he has been guided or driven from the beginning by some single explicit conception of what philosophy is, of why it is necessary, of how it should be conducted, or of what the truth of the matter is as regards the fundamental questions of philosophy. I do not suspect that he writes or ever has written from such a prior plan, nor that, on looking back, he would necessarily recognize that such a plan has determined what he has written. I would claim nevertheless that there is an underlying stance to be discerned in his work.

It is possible to hold these claims consistently because it is possible for the integrity of a body of work to become clear as such only in retrospect, and not necessarily to its author. Indeed, this is the most likely scenario in areas requiring the kinds of complexity and inventiveness characteristic of good philosophy. For the goals in relation to which the integrity of that work is recognized will often only become sufficiently clearly defined once they are achieved. And there is a proper sense of this to be distinguished here, one in which we can legitimately say "now I can see what I was aiming for", which is not at all the same as drawing a bull's-eye around an already-planted arrow. If what is produced is to be described as an integrated body of successive investigative efforts, rather than a shallow but consistent job of work, it is perhaps necessary that the ends that confer integrity on the whole are not clearly perceptible in their beginnings.

One effect of presenting Putnam's work in such a way that intentionality problems stand out is to foreground the integrity and continuity that may be perceived underlying its surface variations. It is not simply that the topics he deals with overlap, interrelate and inform one another, although this is evidently the case, as he himself often remarks.[1] His writings are united in all their variety by an underlying directedness on sets of core issues, a steadiness of focus that makes his departures and changes of course relatively less deep. This is not to assume that the finished work is perfect, nor that the development towards it consisted of various anticipations of a distant completeness. The movements of Putnam's thought reveal a struggle rather than a steady progress towards an expected result. And no account of his work could be accurate that did not also represent flaws in its nature and design, elements of incompleteness and deficiency. So our investigative task has avowedly not been to discover or create some fictitious preconceived unity immanent in Putnam's development.

But it would be equally mistaken to represent the struggle revealed by that development as detached from the search for consistency, coherence and unity. Putnam's approach has undoubtedly changed over time. But the stages of development are more like chapters of a single book than separate volumes, and so must be made to appear as such. These stages are marked by the successive examination of features he has identified as essential to the bearing that subjects have on the world and that the world has on them: in particular, the objectivity of scientific theorizing, the role of background worldviews, and the possibility of the world's disclosing itself directly in experience.

We should resist the temptation to coin an "-ism" for this gradually revealed perspective, a name that would enable the overall view to join the long list with which Putnam has been associated in the course of his career. It is not that such labels do not suggest themselves.[2] It is rather that such labelling implies that the emerging view is in *competition* with others (metaphysical realism, internal realism, etc.) when in fact it underlies his temporary advocacy of these more superficial viewpoints. A more helpful marker would identify not the developing perspective itself, but the approach by which it was achieved. As we have seen, it is Putnam's function-based approach that, applied consistently over the course of his career, gradually revealed his underlying stance. The method gives priority in any of a number of areas to the use or role of the features in question rather than, for example, to their constitution.

Intentionality

Putnam has called attention to the centrality of the intentionality problem on several occasions: its unifying significance not simply for philosophy itself, but for his own contributions to the subject. Some of the most revealing of these occasions are retrospective discussions.

In 1975, for example, looking back over twenty years' work, he stressed the extent to which his development during that period was centred on a growing appreciation of the fact that philosophy is dependent on the kinds of intentionality examined by philosophy of language. In dealing with the nature of mental phenomena, for example, we need to know how to treat words such as "pain". This means more than identifying its particular semantic category (Putnam argues here that we should take seriously the idea that "pain" is a name), more even than identifying its possible referents (sensations, in Putnam's view). We cannot answer these questions correctly without answering the deeper intentionality questions: how is it that "pain" refers, in particular; and in general, how is it that any one thing could possibly be "about" another thing? (Putnam 1975b: vii–xvii, esp. xi–xiii).

Putnam wrote another revealing retrospective account in 1978 about work he had completed in 1960 (Putnam 1978a; 1960a). At the earlier date, the main issue had seemed to be making sense of the correspondence theory of truth (that a true assertion is one that corresponds with reality). But hindsight enabled him to identify more accurately the issues most deeply at stake. Language and the concepts we use are under constant pressure from science, as scientists themselves from Galileo on have noted. This has been a crucial issue for Putnam from his earliest philosophical work on, and one that others also recognized as particularly pressing. For example, in a 1955–56 Gifford lecture given at the very time Putnam was formulating his own initial positions on these questions and with the very Putnamian title "Language and Reality in Modern Physics", the renowned German physicist Werner Heisenberg argued that it is the phenomenon of language under pressure from scientific discovery that is responsible for the "violent reaction" associated with the reception of relativity theory and of quantum theory. Moreover, he claimed that this reaction, felt especially keenly in the political arena as well as in broadly scientific and intellectual circles, shows that:

> one has not yet found the correct language with which to speak about the new situation and that the incorrect statements published here and there in the enthusiasm about the new discoveries have caused all kinds of misunderstanding. This is indeed a fundamental problem. The improved experimental

technique of our time brings into the scope of science new aspects of nature which cannot be described in terms of the common concepts. But in what language, then, should they be described?

(Heisenberg 1999: 167)

In order to answer this question – and indeed to know whether Heisenberg is even right to claim that "the common concepts" will not suffice – we need to understand more generally "how language works and how science works". Hence it is necessary to give (if one cannot simply appeal to) an account of the intentional relation in virtue of which language users relate to the world (Putnam 1978a: 3–4). And by 1960, Putnam was formulating an answer to this background question. He regarded the intentional relation as dependent on the following conditions: (i) the language speaker should be viewed as constructing a symbolic representation of his environment; (ii) doing this requires causal interaction between him and his environment; (iii) the (in)accuracy of his representation will affect the viability and success of his efforts in dealing with his environment; (iv) "thus such an account of the relation of language-speakers to the world is part of a causal model of human behaviour"; (v) for this a correspondence account of truth is required (*ibid.*: 4).

So the many topics Putnam examines have their deep point of intersection in the problem of intentionality. Similarly, it is his growing appreciation of their convergence that has shaped his treatment of each. Moreover, the issues raised by the intentionality problem are those about which he has most to say of genuine and lasting philosophical significance. But perhaps the strongest reason for recognizing the salience of intentionality to an effective consideration of Putnam's career is that the history created by his attempts to tackle the issue best captures his development. For summary purposes, these findings can be grouped in three classes.

First, subjects are to be regarded as contributing actively to experience by their capacities for reason and reflection. Our access to truth and objectivity in judgement depends not only on the way the world is, but on each other and on common norms and standards.

Secondly, experiences that purport to reveal facts about the world are to be regarded as working within a background worldview that the subject already possesses. It is only from within some conceptual scheme or other that we can have significant experience of the world, think and use language meaningfully about it. Such a scheme is in turn always to be conceived in relation to us, to language users. It is only in relation to a model or interpretation that any aspect of our worldview makes sense, and there can be many such interpretations. So it is incoherent to suppose that intentionality depends on a single determinate relation of reference between us and the world.

Thirdly, experiences that purport to reveal facts about the world are to be regarded as disclosing facts about the world directly. The mind is not a kind of organ separated from the world by some interposing material. Minds are in, and fully part of, the world. They are not even to be thought of as things that could be dependent on the world. So objectivity has to be reconceived. Standard attempts to account for intentionality rest on the unchallenged and unwarranted presupposition that we genuinely face the threat of being cut off from the world, of losing it, either in part or altogether. This presupposition is incoherent. Consequently, much of the standard apparatus used to account for intentionality and its various aspects has to be reconceived.

Analytic philosophy

On one issue at least, it may seem that Putnam has changed his mind decisively, and in such a way as to damage the supposed integrity of his approach by the creation of a deep gulf between his earlier and later self: the issue of his relationship with analytic philosophy.

It should be admitted immediately that what the later Putnam takes issue with here is not immediately obvious, for it is not (or no longer) immediately obvious what analytic philosophy itself stands for or represents. A commitment to high standards of clarity and rigour in argumentation is certainly implied by advocacy of the approach. But that is evidently not sufficient to characterize it. (This is not to say that clarity is not a necessary aim for philosophers generally; as John Austin remarked, "Clarity, I know, has been said to be not enough: but perhaps it will be time to go into that when we are within measurable distance of achieving clarity on some matter."[3]) In distancing himself from analytic philosophy, Putnam has certainly neither denounced nor renounced that obligation to be clear and rigorous for which his own work has established high standards.

The fact is that, within fifty years, "analytic philosophy" has come to mean something considerably more vague than it did when first coined to signify a particular way of doing philosophy and a particular conception of its ends. And it is to the narrower conception that

Putnam is referring, one that is more complex and considerably more controversial than that signified by current usage. In his view, there is something deeply paradoxical about recent history. Using a phrase in which we are perhaps meant to hear an echo of Paul Feyerabend's notorious pronouncement of 1970, that philosophy of science is a "subject with a great past" (1970: 172–83), he writes: "at the very moment when analytic philosophy is recognized as the 'dominant movement' in world philosophy, it has come to the end of its own project – the dead end, not the completion" (Putnam 1985a: 51). The clue explaining why the end of analytic philosophy might be a cul-de-sac or blind alley rather than the completion of its project lies in its origins. And the fact that analytic philosophy tends to pass over the historical dimension in which any notions of rationality evolve, overlooking the fact that any philosophical tradition has both a past and a future, means that it is blind to its own quandary and to the causes of that quandary (1983a: vii–viii).

Analytic philosophy identified its project early in the twentieth century when there was still a significant shortfall between the methodology of science and what that methodology could achieve. It is comparatively easy to prevent a proper respect for the rationality of science turning into veneration when the visible signs of that rationality are made manifest by remarkable theoretical advances, and almost impossible when those advances issue in astonishing technological innovations. Or so it has turned out. And it is such veneration that Putnam regards as largely responsible for poisoning the sources of analytic philosophy, guaranteeing its demise before it can achieve its ends.

Those sources emerged from a healthy dislike for any form of intellectual veneration, and specifically for the dogmatism and prejudice resulting from it. At the dawn of analytic philosophy, science was perceptibly the victim of chauvinism, largely at the hands of rationalist metaphysics and of religious bigotry. It is in the name of science that bias of this sort occurs, and most especially in analytic philosophy itself: Putnam began expressing this view in the mid-1970s and with increasing bite (Putnam 1976a (vi): 66–80). He now sees scientism expressing itself most clearly in analytic philosophy as a self-defeating empiricism, a guise which it is his job to unmask. "[W]hile paying lip service to fallibilism", a guiding principle of any scientific enterprise worthy of the name, "empiricism and its favourite moral theory, Utilitarianism, are actually dogmatic" (2004a: 6). Scientism of this sort has disastrous results, for not all modes of thought characteristic of the humanities and of the social sciences can be made to take on the form of theories in the physical sciences, their jargon and formalization. Putnam may have been expressing this latter view, a major component of his later attack on tendencies in analytic philosophy, as early as the 1960s. Towards the end of that decade, he gave the following explanation of why syntactic theory had recently made extraordinary advances while the semantic theory of natural languages had lagged behind. Semantic theory is a typical social science, and naturally characterized by "sloppiness, the lack of precise theories and laws, the lack of mathematical rigor" (Putnam 1970b: 152). But the crucial interpretative point is not wholly clear: it would be consistent with the view expressed at the time to suppose that the social sciences will one day reach maturity, having acquired the requisite precision to be counted alongside the physical sciences. This interpretation is encouraged by a reference Putnam makes to the present "infancy" of semantic theory (*ibid.*: 141). Whatever his position in the late 1960s, Putnam certainly rejected this latter view by the mid-1970s.

At this point, a new dimension enters into consideration, one that Putnam has fully expressed only latterly: "if science is a philosophy, it suffers from being all metaphysics and no ethics; and metaphysics without ethics is blind" (1975j: 92). This appeal to one half of the famous Kantian phrase ("Thoughts without content are empty, intuitions without concepts are blind") strongly suggests a way to fill out the overall view: that without metaphysics, ethics would be empty (Kant 1933: A51, 93). Philosophical reflection is so constituted that, correctly established, our modes of metaphysical thought must be informed by broadly ethical concerns. The means by which we think ethically, on the other hand, owe to metaphysical considerations. So neither has priority or is to be given preference over the other. Without metaphysics, ethics would lack subject-matter; without ethics, metaphysics would lack direction. Hence metaphysics is blind without ethics, and ethics is empty without metaphysics.[4] Putnam (2004a) contains the most developed presentation of these views to date. We should not be distracted by the fact that he speaks there of an ethics "without metaphysics" (see Putnam 2004a (i)), for he means by this an ethics that has relinquished particular *kinds* of ontology (and he marks the differentiating point by capitalizing it, "Ontology"; *ibid.*: 21); namely, those specifically associated with analytical philosophy. His main complaint against any form of Ontology (and he distinguishes between inflationary and deflationary types) is the same as his complaint against scientism: it is unwilling to take seriously ways of thinking that are indispensable to everyday life (*ibid.*: 16).

In Putnam's view, scientism leads either to distortion or to narrow-mindedness. The former occurs whenever attempts are made to answer philosophical or social scientific questions in ways that ape the jargon, formalization and theoretical apparatus of the physical sciences.[5] Such questions and the information relevant to solving them have to be skewed dramatically if there is to be even the appearance of experimental testing, of systematic data collection, of quantitative analyses and so on. When distortion of this sort becomes obvious, one has an alternative: either to give up asking such questions, or to give up trying to answer them in that way.

Scientistic narrow-mindedness occurs when the first option is taken. Putnam has constantly pointed out the effects: for example, we then have no room for literature, or become confused about what bearing literature should have on our thinking (Putnam 1975j: 81–94). His position here is nuanced and expressed using equally harsh words for those prejudiced against science and scientists as for those blind to literary worth. Putnam argues that placing a high value on the one must at the least be compatible with placing high value on the other. Indeed, his central argument for becoming sensitive to literature has an instrumental feel to it. Such sensitivity increases our imaginative resources, which in turn aids practical reasoning. Developing our sensibility through contact with literature primes us for reasoning rationally about a range of subjects, for example by strengthening our ability to withstand certain sorts of rational criticism.[6]

The second option – to give up trying to answer all questions in the scientific manner, with scientific procedures and scientific criteria of success – is the appropriate course of action. But in Putnam's view, at least in certain moods, it is too late for analytic philosophy to take it. Analytic philosophy has allowed healthy respect for science to turn into intellectual veneration. This is particularly disastrous for a mode of philosophizing founded on the preservation of respect in the face of temptations to veneration. In betraying this essential feature, analytic philosophy may have betrayed itself irredeemably.

But it would be wrong to interpret Putnam's deep concerns with analytic philosophy as the U-turn or simplistic reversal that they may immediately appear to be, given the undoubted vigour of this attack. For Putnam has continued to value much of the work done in the analytic manner, and to criticize much that has been written in the names of pragmatism and of other kinds of non-analytic or "continental" philosophy. There is no sign that he has renounced his early-expressed view that one core aim of analytic philosophy – "becoming clear on the nature and magnitude" of the difficulties facing those who would interpret hypotheses in theoretical science (such as quantum mechanics) – is a "modest but essential step" (Putnam 1965b: 130–58). In response to the standard criticism of analytic philosophy, that it is overly technical and has abdicated from concern with real problems, Putnam notes that "such complaints have always occurred precisely when philosophy was significant and vital!" (Putnam 1975i: 132). And he offers a swift diagnosis of such complaints: most non-philosophers are bored by philosophy itself or at least quite uninterested in it; however, culture requires that they profess admiration for it, so they say they are bored not by philosophy itself but by the philosophers of the current period; and this happens in every generation (Putnam 1975d: 1–32; he is particularly vexed by those who try to account for the significance analytic philosophy gives to philosophy of language as a fixation with unreal or "merely" technical questions). This bad-faith explanation of common criticisms of philosophy is to be extended, presumably. Non-philosophers are so extremely irritated with philosophy that they express their rage in the oldest and worst form of abuse: accusing its practitioners of profession-betrayal. When committed specifically by academics, the French alone seem to have a ready phrase for this crime: *trahison des clercs*.

Conversely, from the very beginnings of his publishing career, Putnam was arguing that analytic philosophy is wrong about certain of its assumptions and misguided in elements of its methodology. As early as 1957, for example, he protested against the fact that "analytic philosophers are disturbingly unanimous in regarding 2-value logic as having a privileged position . . . in the sense of having no serious rival for *logical* reasons". This is evidently a prejudice, in his view, and one that must be questioned on grounds that relate to scientific investigation, for at the time he believed the only logic that could make sense of quantum mechanics is three-value logic (Putnam 1957a: 172). Five years later, Putnam issued a corrective to "the analytical philosopher" who "misconstrues his job" when trying to advise "the logician (or any scientist) to stop what he is doing". This point was an instance of a more general principle: in so far as analytic philosophy supposes that "merely philosophical" arguments might be justified in causing someone to abandon a constructive logical venture, it is wrong-headed (Putnam 1963b: esp. 286–7).

By 1962, Putnam was regularly settling debates in analytical philosophy with the deconstructive strategy that would later become his primary tool in undermining elements of the whole approach.[7] The root of this strategy was clearly enunciated by Frank Ramsey (1903–1930), a close associate of Wittgenstein. In situations where two philosophical views oppose each other over some lengthy period without conclusive resolution in either direction:

> it is a heuristic maxim that the truth lies not in one of the two disputed views but in some third possibility which has not yet been thought of, which we can only discover by rejecting something assumed as obvious by both the disputants.
>
> ("Universals" in his 1978: 20ff.)

The strategy becomes fully deconstructive when the "something assumed as obvious" to be rejected includes the notion that the debate itself is properly established. Instead of weighing in on one side or the other, or constructing some third alternative, the deconstructivist denies there is a genuine cause for disagreement and destroys both parties to the dispute, pointing out sufficiently deep internal inconsistencies in their construction to make the positions untenable and the debate unprofitable. In his *Philosophical Investigations*, Wittgenstein gives clear expression to the strategic possibilities offered by Ramsey's maxim:

> Where does our investigation get its importance from, since it seems only to destroy everything interesting, that is, all that is great and important? (As it were all the buildings, leaving behind only bits of stone and rubble.) What we are destroying is nothing but houses of cards and we are clearing up the ground of language on which they stand. (Wittgenstein 1958: §118, 48)

Putnam adopted this strategy quite early, though only latterly has he pressed the implications for analytic philosophy as a whole. One example of the strategy in use is his response to the standard view about the role of theories in empirical science: that they rest on a dichotomy between the observational and the theoretical. What justifies this dichotomy is a certain sort of problem; so we feel the need to invent the dichotomy to solve the problem. But the problem does not exist, in Putnam's view. Hence there is no justification for the dichotomy (Putnam 1962a). Putnam himself identifies several such pseudo-debates in analytic philosophy; in so far as analytic philosophy exists to promote them, he advises that it be abandoned. Deconstructive strategies of this sort are used by a growing number of analytic philosophers, some to question the rationale for debates within the enterprise, some to question the rationale for the enterprise itself.[8] In brief, we should not exaggerate the differences between early and late Putnam. The tendency to do so is encouraged by common errors over dating. Putnam is frequently represented as coming fresh to positions that he had actually been advocating for some significant time. The two most important instances concern the nature of truth and of experience. As we have seen, Putnam's reconception of truth as epistemically constrained is frequently dated to the early or even mid-1980s when in fact it occurred in the mid-1970s, and his reconception of experience as something in whose formation concepts play a vital role is often assumed to have occurred in the 1990s when he actually espoused it in the late 1970s and early 1980s.

If there is a significant distinction to be made between different periods in Putnam's career, it is this. For much of his writing life, Putnam was concerned with redirecting analytic philosophy from inside; latterly he has stood on the margins of the enterprise, and his interventions have been characterized by the fact that it is from this direction that they emerge. His present position is not an easy rejection of analytic philosophy but an attempt to think through what has been attractive about it. Nevertheless, in order to understand Putnam's career, early and late, we need to appreciate ways in which what originally attracted him now repels him, and vice versa.

Volitional necessity

Beneath Putnam's willingness to question and change surface features of his position runs a deeper vision of what is proper to philosophizing:

> If the philosopher can contribute to the reasoned resolution of some of the problems of his or her time, that is no small achievement, and that some of her assumptions will in the future no doubt have to be qualified or even rejected is only to be expected. Our task as philosophers isn't to achieve "immortality".
>
> (Putnam 2004a: i)

This judgement gains in substance and specificity when read in the light of another remark of Putnam's: that "there are some philosophers in the history of philosophy whose importance does not very much depend upon their being *right*" (1976: 88). There are many reasons why we might defend the right of thinkers to change their minds, to modify, adapt, or even reject their own former views. For many, the basic ground is the simple right to be free from certain kinds of constraint or repression, even when (perhaps especially when) those forms of restraint are, for whatever reason, imposed on oneself by oneself. To employ this notion of freedom in order to defend the right to change is, of course, consistent with defending a thinker's right to pursue thought seriously, or to continue in the profession while renouncing the ambition to engage with pressing questions of their own time. And Putnam frankly rejects this as an option; the thinker has a calling whose purposes have to be taken seriously: "there is, God knows, irresponsibility enough in the world, including irresponsibility masquerading as responsibility, and it belongs to the vocation of the thinker, now as always, to try to teach the difference between the two" (1999 (i): 4).

This appeal to "the vocation of the thinker" is characteristic of Putnam, who does not ground the right to change one's mind in a freedom from constraint. In his view, thinkers must be free to act in the ways that their vocation constrains them to act. These actions are voluntary and under the control of thinkers. Thinkers are not coerced or compelled in so acting; nor are they acting out of some compulsion. But they are nevertheless actions that thinkers who care about their vocation feel they must perform; there is no real alternative for those who take thinking seriously. So this is a case of that volitional necessity exhibited by Martin Luther in his famous statement at the Council of Worms: "Here I stand; I can do nothing else."[9]

In order to engage thus with the problems of their time, thinkers cannot afford the high-minded retreat of those who wait to see every assumption verified, every norm of argument regulated. Moreover, in communicating with people at some particular point in time, they must make assumptions that will be subject to correction, and accept certain superficial norms that will be subject to alteration. So it is precisely not because thinkers should be unconstrained that they have the right to change their minds, to modify and to adapt. Thinkers who are serious about their profession are constrained by that calling to engage. And it is because engagement requires dealing with contingencies of various sorts that changes of mind are licensed. (At present, for example, it is a Deweyan "strategic optimism" that is required; Putnam 2004: 11). It is only by constant adaption that thinkers can carry out what their vocation requires of them, and in the way it requires it of them.

There is a particular sense, then, in which thinkers are forced to be free.[10] The possible sources for this conviction are many and various.

But the conviction itself is certainly a legacy of the logical positivists who so influenced Putnam, many of them émigrés, thinkers who resisted external constraints on the use of their intellect with a recognition of its internal demands. These are the philosophers to whom analytic philosophy is most greatly indebted for its character, of course. So we return again to the place from which we began: Putnam's relationship to analytic philosophy.

Notes

Chapter 1. Introduction

1. This standard mixed reaction is neatly captured by the definition of "Hilary" in Daniel Dennett's joking *The Philosophical Lexicon* (Newark, NJ: American Philosophical Association, 1987): "*(from* hilary term) A very brief but significant period in the intellectual career of a distinguished philosopher. 'Oh, that's what I thought three or four hilaries ago'".

2. Putnam has more recently been described as "a very *mobile* target" by W. Künne in *Conceptions of Truth* (Oxford: Oxford University Press, 2003), 406. Evidently the charge has been levelled sufficiently frequently to warrant modifying for the sake of variety.

3. Useful collections of papers focused on discussion of Putnam include: G. Boolos (ed.), *Meaning and Method* (Cambridge: Cambridge University Press, 1990); P. Clark & B. Hale (eds), *Reading Putnam* (Oxford: Blackwell, 1994); A. Pessin & S. Goldberg (eds), *The Twin-Earth Chronicles* (New York: M. E. Sharpe, 1996); J. Conant & U. M. Zeglen, *Hilary Putnam: Pragmatism and Realism* (London: Routledge, 2002); and Y. Ben-Menahim (ed.), *Hilary Putnam* (Cambridge: Cambridge University Press, 2005).

Chapter 2. Overview

1. Originally published in *The Nation*, reprinted in *The Chicago Tribune*, 28 October 1917.

2. Putnam attributes aspects of his approach to the theory of meaning to his upbringing: "as the son of a translator, I know very well that translation isn't easy" (Putnam, "The Way the World is", in *Realism with a Human Face*, J. Conant (ed.) (Cambridge, MA: Harvard University Press, 1990)). Putnam's *Realism and Reason, Philosophical Papers, Volume 3* (Cambridge: Cambridge University Press, 1983) is dedicated to his father.

3. The parallel is drawn specifically with instrumentalism in physics. A compelling argument for the view that Hilbert had a decisive influence on philosophical practice as well as on the development of mathematical philosophy is offered by M. Giaquinto, "Hilbert's Philosophy of Mathematics", *British Journal of the Philosophy of Science* **34** (1983), 119–32.

4. Although Diophantus himself accepted any solution in rational numbers, Diophantine equations refer only to those with integer solutions. A set D of

natural numbers is Diophantine if there is a polynomial P with integer coefficients (positive, negative or zero) such that $x \in D$ if and only if $(\exists y_1)(\exists y_2) \ldots (\exists y_k) \cdot P(x, y_1, y_2, \ldots y_k) = 0$. One central decision problem connected with such equations is as follows. Suppose we are given a polynomial P with integer coefficients $P(x_1, \ldots, x_n)$. Let the bound variables range over natural numbers, and let subscripts after quantifiers indicate an upper bound (so that, for example, "$(y_1)_x$" reads "for every y_1 less than or equal to x"). Is there an algorithm for determining whether $(\exists x)(\exists y_1)_x (y_2)_x \cdot P(x, y_1, y_2, \ldots, y_k) \neq 0$? Other decision problems concern *exponential* Diophantine equations, where the variables may appear not only in the exponents of power terms but in the bases and coefficients. Standard examples of these equations include $x^x y^y = z^z$, $2^y - 7 = x^z$, and $2^x + 11^y = 5^z$.

5. Where P is a polynomial with integer coefficients, and the variables range over non-negative integers, Putnam and his colleagues proved that the equation $(\exists x)(y_1)_x (y_2)_x \ldots (y_k)_x \cdot P(x, y_1, y_2, \ldots y_k) \neq 0$ is recursively unsolvable; that there is no decision method for statements of this form; that no algorithm exists by which we can always determine whether what it states is the case. Thus Putnam offers a rigorous proof of Myhill's Theorem ("An Unsolvable Problem in Number Theory", *Journal of Symbolic Logic* **25** (1960), 220–32; "The Decision Problem for Exponential Diophantine Equations" (with Martin Davis and Julia Robinson), *Annals of Mathematics* **74** (1961), 425–36). The proof for this conclusion partly depended on showing that every recursively enumerable predicate is Diophantine. In 1958 Putnam, together with Davies, showed that there are a number of recursive predicates with the property that, if they are Diophantine, then all recursively enumerable predicates are Diophantine ("Reductions of Hilbert's Tenth Problem" (with Martin Davis), *Journal of Symbolic Logic* **23** (1958), 183–7). Putnam published further results connected to this proof over the next three years. On the positive side, he showed how the Diophantine sets of positive, non-negative and arbitrary integers may be simply characterized. On the negative side, he proved that there is no algorithm for determining the answer to several further and related questions: whether or not any polynomial P with integer coefficients represents every natural number; whether or not it represents every sufficiently large natural number; whether or not it represents every integer.

6. For the mature position and arguments in its favour, see Adolf Grünbaum, *Philosophical Problems of Space and Time*, 2nd edn (Dordrecht: D. Reidel, 1973). Putnam argues that Grünbaum cannot claim Reichenbach's support; see Putnam, "What is Mathematical Truth?", in *Mathematics, Matter and Method, Philosophical Papers, Volume 1*, 60–78 (Cambridge: Cambridge University Press, 1975).

Chapter 3. Analytic philosophy

1. See G. H. von Wright, "Analytic Philosophy: A Historico-critical Survey", in *Realism, Meaning and Truth*, 2nd edn (Oxford: Blackwell, 1993). Ernest Nagel's paper "Impressions and Appraisals of Analytic Philosophy in Europe" (*Journal of Philosophy* **33**), was published in 1936 but the name did not enter common currency until the late 1940s.

2. This latter interpretation is supported by the fact that it was precisely in these first years of widening usage that W. B. Gallie's paper "The Limitations of Analytical Philosophy" (*Analysis* **9**), was published (1949). But one should

be hesitant about any explanation: the coining of philosophical names and their currency are as complex as their use.

3. Putnam recommends Reichenbach's posthumously published *The Direction of Time* (1956; republished New York: Dover, 1999) to philosophers as a book from which they can educate themselves in physical theory without losing sight of the essential conceptual questions (Putnam, "Philosophy of Physics", in *Mathematics, Matter and Method*, 87). See also: "An Examination of Grünbaum's Philosophy of Geometry", in *Mathematics, Matter and Method*, 93–129; "The Refutation of Conventionalism", in *Mind, Language and Reality, Philosophical Papers, Volume 2* (Cambridge: Cambridge University Press, 1975), 153–91; "Equivalence", in *Realism and Reason*, 26–45; "Reichenbach's Metaphysical Picture", in *Words and Life* (Cambridge, MA: Harvard University press, 1994), 99–114; "Reichenbach and the Myth of the Given", in *Words and Life*, 115–30; and "Reichenbach and the Limits of Vindication", in *Words and Life*, 131–48.

4. Putnam himself has explored connections between the Enlightenment and doctrines associated with analytic philosophy in "The Three Enlightenments" and "Skepticism about Enlightenment", in *Ethics without Ontology* (Cambridge, MA: Harvard University Press, 2004); his arguments depend partly on his interpretative position that there are three Enlightenments – one associated with Plato and Socrates; one associated with that of the seventeenth to eighteenth century; and one associated with John Dewey that "has not yet come fully to fruition" (*Ethics without Ontology*, 5).

5. Analytic philosophers who describe themselves as committed above all to argumentative rigour and to clarity usually mean to associate themselves thereby with the ideals of scientific investigation as widely promulgated in the Early Modern period. So it is not surprising to find similar locutions occurring as the primary means of self-definition for those enterprises also. The heart of Bishop Sprat's laudatory account of the early years of the Royal Society, for example, is contained in this phrase: they "exacted from all their members a close, naked, natural way of speaking" (Sprat, *The History of the Royal Society*, J. Cape (ed.) (London: Routledge, 1959), vol. I, xx.

6. G. M. Hopkins wittily expresses the good sense behind maintaining such a style by using language that illustrates the condition it is meant to replace – "plainly" at the start, "intelligible" at the end, and mounting torture in between: "Plainly if it is possible to express a subtle and recondite thought on a subtle and recondite subject in a subtle and recondite way and with great felicity and perfection, in the end, something must be sacrificed, with so trying a task, in the process, and this may be the being at once, nay perhaps even the being without explanation at all, intelligible" (*The Letters of Gerard Manley Hopkins to Robert Bridges*, C. C. Abbott (ed.) (Oxford: Oxford University Press, 1935), 265–6).

7. Recognizing this problem, some analytic philosophers have described themselves as characterized not just by their commitment to clarity and argumentative rigour, but by having as their aim "truth and knowledge, as opposed to moral or spiritual improvement" and by accommodating "a more piecemeal approach" (S. Soames, *Philosophical Analysis in the Twentieth Century*, 2 vols (Princeton, NJ: Princeton University Press, 2003), vol. I, xiv–xv). But the underlying difficulty remains: these characteristics are hardly peculiar to analytic philosophy. (That advocates often speak as if these features *are* unique to the approach is not one of its more attractive features.)

8. So another contradiction runs as follows. Consider the sentence (a) "Round squares do not exist" (true).

   (1) (a) is a true, meaningful subject-predicate sentence.

   (2) Subject–predicate sentences are true (false) iff there is an object to which the subject refers, and that object has (does not have) the property expressed by the predicate.

   (3) (Given (1)–(2)) There must be objects – round squares – to which the subject expression "round squares" refers; and these objects must have the property of not existing.

   (4) No objects have the property of not existing; if there are objects to which the subjects of these meaningful sentences refer, then they exist.

   (5) (Given (3)–(4)) Meaningful negative existentials cannot be true.

   (6) (Given (5)) Meaningful negative existentials cannot exist.

   But (6) is itself a counter-example to the argument (1)–(6): that is, it is *itself* a negative existential. Moreover, (6) is a contradiction: that is, if (6) is true, there must be at least one meaningful negative existential; so (6) must be false.

9. Mach saw himself here as rooted in a Kantian, or at least neo-Kantian, tradition. He described Kant's first critique with approval as having "banished into the realms of shadows the sham ideas of the old metaphysics" *Popular Scientific Lectures*, 1896, quoted in Passmore, *A Hundred Years of Philosophy*, 2nd edn (Harmondsworth: Penguin, 1994), 321.

Chapter 4. Structural issues

1. Grünbaum in particular used the phrase "intrinsic metric" to formulate his version of conventionalism. Putnam's suspicion that the phrase is used meaninglessly here is suggested early on (e.g. see Putnam, "Memo on 'Conventionalism'", in *Mathematics, Matter and Method*, 206–14, esp. 206) and becomes overt in his "Reply to Gerald Massey", in *Mind, Language and Reality*, 192–5. There he introduces the dummy phrase "boojum metric" to substitute for any conventionalist use of "intrinsic metric" and shows how it has a dummy denotation for reasons that Wittgenstein employs as a basic strategy in his private language argument (see *Philosophical Investigations*, 2nd edn, G. E. M. Anscombe (trans.) (Oxford: Blackwell, 1958, §§243–315)): since either there are no criteria for a manifold's possessing such a metric, or those criteria are unintelligible, the phrase itself must be bogus.

2. In "The Refutation of Conventionalism", in *Mind, Language and Reality*, 153–91, Putnam states explicitly the interpretative position only hinted at in remarks he made in papers over the previous decade: that in his view the conventionalism about geometry regularly attributed to Reichenbach is not his position at all but Grünbaum's. It is certainly worth noting that, as early as 1920, Reichenbach was arguing that Poincaré's conventionalism is incompatible with the general theory of relativity (H. Reichenbach, *The Theory of Relativity and a priori Knowledge*, M. Reichenbach (trans.) (Los Angeles, CA: University of California Press, 1965 [1920]), 3–4 and 109, n.1), although he later retracted the view. See M. Friedman, *Reconsidering Logical Positivism* (Cambridge: Cambridge University Press, 1999), Chs 3 and 4, esp. p. 82.

3. The other part was provided by economic theory: modified Turing machines were to be determined in their behaviour by the utility rule (maximize estimated utility). See in particular Putnam, "The Mental Life of Some Machines", in *Mind, Language and Reality*, 408–28.

4. "Something akin" because, anachronism aside, the claim blurs an important distinction between the sense of molecular propositions and the sense of elementary propositions. The former might be regarded as given by their truth-conditions consistently with the way the *Tractatus* conceives of such conditions; the latter could not be.

5. These are important historical points, but their relevance to our own concerns should not be exaggerated. Putnam has latterly been heavily influenced by Wittgenstein (as we shall see in the chapters that follow), but it is to the later works that he is particularly indebted, not the *Tractatus*. He has recently joined debate on the proper interpretation of Wittgenstein's early work (e.g. Putnam, "Comment and Replies", in Clark & Hale (eds), *Reading Putnam*, 1–70, and "Floyd, Wittgenstein and Loneliness", in *Loneliness*, L. Rouner (ed.), 109–14 (Notre Dame: University of Notre Dame Press, 1998), but that is not a matter of influence.

6. There is considerable disagreement about the extent to which Ayer was either reporting views or originating them, and an unfortunate tendency to damn him either way. If his main purpose was to report the views of others, then he can be blamed for misrepresenting them, but hardly for the claims and arguments themselves. If his primary aim was to originate, then he is not starkly vulnerable to charges of misrepresentation, but only to advancing false claims and weak arguments. Wherever the truth of the matter lies, Putnam himself takes issue with Ayer on the matter of misrepresentation. In his view, Ayer's work is somewhat spoilt by insufficient sensitivity to the nature and the value of Wittgenstein's functional conception of language, and of Austin's "new kind of science of language" (Putnam, "Review of *The Concept of a Person* (by A. J. Ayer)", in *Meaning and the Moral Sciences*, 132–8 (London: Routledge & Kegan Paul, 1978).

7. This identification occurs in Putnam, "The Refutation of Conventionalism", 153. Putnam goes on to describe Quine's argument for the indeterminacy of radical translation in his *Word and Object* (Cambridge, MA: MIT Press, 1960), Ch. 2, as "what may well be the most fascinating and the most discussed philosophical argument since Kant's Transcendental Deduction of the Categories" (Putnam, "The Refutation of Conventionalism", 159). A credible case might now be made for a challenge to that title: from Putnam's own "Twin-Earth" argument for externalism/anti-individualism.

8. Quine's argument is too detailed to be discussed in the text at this point while retaining flow. But since knowing exactly why Quine thought as he did is important for the discussion that follows (i.e. Putnam's views on meaning), a schematic representation is presented here for those unfamiliar with Quine's paper.

(1) If a genuine analytic–synthetic distinction can be drawn, it must be possible to define analyticity in a non-circular way (i.e. without appealing to analyticity).

(2) Any definition of analyticity must account for the supposed analyticity of sentences such as "All bachelors are unmarried".

(3) (The best candidate) A statement S is analytic iff S is *immediately* a logical truth or *mediately* a logical truth (i.e. S can be turned into a logical truth by putting synonyms for synonyms).

(4) S is a logical truth iff it is a substitution instance of a schema all of the substitution instances of which are true (where a schema is a formula

such as "either *S* or not *S*", or "All *F*s who are *G* are *G*" and a substitution instance is the sentence resulting from replacing schematic letters with linguistic expressions, for example, "either Quine is alive or Quine is not alive"; "All males who are unmarried are unmarried").

(5)   Now "All bachelors are unmarried" is *immediately* a substitution instance of the schema "All *F*s are *G*"; not all of the substitution instances of that schema are true (e.g. "All males are English"), so it is not immediately a logical truth. By (3), if it is analytic, it must be mediately a logical truth (i.e. capable of being turned into a logical truth by replacing synonyms with synonyms). This works: if "males who are unmarried" is synonymous with "bachelors", then we obtain "All males who are unmarried are unmarried", which is a substitution instance of a schema ("All *F*s who are *G* are *G*") all of whose instances are true. So it appears (3) satisfies (2); but there is unfinished business.

(6)   If there are mediately logical truths, then any definition of analyticity must account for the supposed synonymy of substitution instances (e.g. "males who are unmarried" for "bachelors").

(7)   (The best candidate) An expression *A* is synonymous with an expression *B* iff *A* can be substituted for *B* in all sentences in which *B* occurs without that sentence changing truth-value.

(8)   These "*A*" expressions (*a definite description*: the planet seen in the morning sky; *a proper name*: Ben Franklin; *a predicate*: is a creature with kidneys) can be substituted for these "*B*" expressions (the planet seen in the evening sky; the first postmaster general of the US; is a creature with a heart) in all sentences in which the "*B*" expressions occur without that sentence changing truth-value.

(9)   (Given (3) and (7)) Sentences such as "For any object, it is the evening planet iff it is the morning planet"; "Any relative of Benjamin Franklin is a relative of the first postmaster general of the US"; "Every creature with a heart is a creature with kidneys" are mediately logical truths, and hence analytic; but evidently they are not – they cannot be known to be true simply by knowing the meaning of the words contained; they are contingent; so either (3) or (7) fails. The only solution is to place the operator "It is necessary that" before each sentence: then these sentences turn out true where true (e.g. that necessarily Ben Franklin was Ben Franklin) and false where false (e.g. that necessarily Ben Franklin was the first postmaster general of the US); but this opens up new business.

(10) If the notion of mediately logical truths requires the notion of necessary truths, then any definition of analyticity must account for necessary truths.

(11) (The best candidate) A statement *S* is a necessary truth iff *S* is analytic. And this is evidently circular: to explain analyticity, we must explain synonymy; to do that we must explain necessity; and to do that we must explain analyticity.

(12) (Given (1) and (11)) No genuine analytic–synthetic distinction can be drawn.

Chapter 5. Core issues

1. The review was written in the 1960s but remained unpublished until its inclusion in the retrospective collection (Putnam, *Mind, Language and Reality*).

2. It is not clear exactly how much of an ally Putnam takes Austin to be in his 1960s review. Austin would certainly not have agreed that philosophy itself is simply continuous with science, either at the general level or in specific instances ("The philosophy of physics is continuous with physics itself"; Putnam, "Philosophy of Physics", 79). This point is implicit in Ryle's comment: in so far as Austin's quasi-botanical classifications were meant to contribute to a *Principia Grammatica*, he understood them as contributing to science *rather than* to philosophy. But this difference of opinion between Austin and Putnam is consistent with coincidence over what counts as good practice. And it is particularly worth noting in this regard G. J. Warnock's comment, that Austin "wanted us to think of philosophy as more like a science than an art, as a matter of finding things out" and that, in his view, the correct aim is "a more empirical, 'objective' way of doing philosophy, offering the hope of getting things actually settled by patient industry" (Warnock, "Saturday Mornings", in *Essays on J. L. Austin*, I. Berlin *et al.* (eds), 31–45 (Oxford: Clarendon Press, 1973), 43).

3. This final principle explains Putnam's underlying reason for thinking that verificationism in any form must fail. For some explicit endorsements of these principles, see in particular Putnam ("Language and Reality", "Introduction" and "Language and Philosophy", in *Mind, Language and Reality*). Even in his earliest papers, Putnam gave special attention to common speech; this is made clear quite dramatically in "Three-valued Logic", in *Mathematics, Matter and Method*, 166–73, where he argues that we should reject the prejudice in favour of two-valued logic partly on the grounds that "3-valued logic corresponds to a certain way of speaking" ("Three-valued Logic", 172).

4. An early example of Putnam's use of the widely applicable function-based approach is his intervention in the debate on how to distinguish statements that are true for mathematical reasons from other kinds of statement: by their use, and not by some specious appeal to "mathematical objects" (see Putnam, "Truth and Necessity in Mathematics", in *Mathematics, Matter and Method*, 1–11). It is particularly important to note the difference between functionalism (i.e. Putnam's one-time position in the philosophy of mind) and a function-based approach (i.e. his underlying strategy), because it is possible to say that the former was arrived at and then discarded by the latter. Putnam himself is happy to use the term "functionalism" to denote the broad approach, rather than a narrow position that could be achieved (or disposed of, as Putnam would later show) by employing it. This was so even in the 1960s when he was developing the views in the philosophy of mind whose widespread adoption ensured that the standard use of the term would be narrow and denote a particular position: "a synthetic hypothesis about the nature of mental states" (Putnam, *Mind, Language and Reality*, xiii). An early example of this usage is his reference to Wittgenstein's functionalist conception of language (Putnam, "Review of *The Concept of a Person*"). In order to avoid confusion, however, I will continue to distinguish the approach from the position by using "a function-based approach" to refer to the former and "functionalism" to refer to the latter.

5. This contrast may be too stark – between the static, one-to-one representational relation of the *Tractatus* and the dynamic, function-based conception of representation in Wittgenstein's later work (though its crudity certainly reflects something of Wittgenstein's own take on these matters), for there may be signs of a rudimentary use theory in the *Tractatus*'s conception of names. What object a name stands for depends on its "logico-syntactic

employment", the way it behaves in propositions. Names without such employment are regarded as meaningless; those with the same such employment are held to be synonyms of each other (see Wittgenstein, *Tractatus Logico-Philosophicus*, C. K. Ogden & F. P. Ramsey (trans.) (London: Routledge, 1922), §§3.326ff.). But it is overly generous and probably just misleading to call this even a rudimentary use theory, given the severely limited role it offers to the use of a name. What determines the meaning of a name is not its use on the *Tractatus* conception; it is the combinatorial possibilities of the object for which the name stands which are responsible for doing that; the use of the name merely shows or displays these possibilities, the combinations responsible for determining its meaning.

Chapter 6. Intentionality

1. See in particular his *Ethics without Ontology*, which argues that ethics is possible without ontology (understood in a certain, explicitly restricted sense; see pp. 15–22) on grounds provided by a particular approach to intentionality: that there is and can be no scheme-independent set of uniquely determinate relations in ethics or in any other area of thought and language in virtue of which what we think and say is "about" what it is about.

2. For example, that the way to investigate the nature of some entity E is to analyse sentences in which "E" (i.e. the word for E) occurs (see A. Kenny, *Frege* (Harmondsworth: Penguin, 1995), 211); or that a philosophical account of thought can, and can only, be achieved by a philosophical account of language (see M. Dummett, *Origins of Analytical Philosophy* (London: Duckworth, 1993), 4).

3. So analytic philosophers came to self-recognition as such by agreeing on the *nature* of the issues underlying philosophical problems, identifying them as fundamentally intentionality issues. J. A. Coffa, *The Semantic Tradition from Kant to Carnap: To the Vienna Station* (Cambridge: Cambridge University Press, 1991) and others – including Dummett and his critics – are supportive of this proposal. Dummett spoils the picture by going one step too far: claiming that analytic philosophers are identified as such by agreement also on the *method* for solving intentionality issues.

4. Russell himself muddies the waters by making a number of innocuous-seeming moves that, together, amount to a substantive position: supposing that to think of a particular item is (a) to have it "before the mind", where that means (b) being acquainted with it, or directly present to it, where that in turn means (c) being incapable of being wrong about it (see in particular "Knowledge by acquaintance and knowledge by description" in his *Mysticism and Logic and Other Essays* (London: Longmans Green and Co., 1918), 209–32). If we accept this line of thought, then we will suppose that what it is to think about some particular thing does indeed after all come down to knowing about it – at least to the extent of being ascribed knowledge of which thing is meant. But we certainly need not accept (c) as entailed by (a), and perhaps not (b) either. It can seem that we do not need an argument because (b)–(c) present themselves as a mere gloss on (a). But they gloss a specific sense in which (a) might be understood that we need not accept without argument. Perhaps having something before the mind just means thinking it, where we are agnostic about whether thinking something requires it to be directly present to the mind or not.

5. The relevant occasions being: (i) Frege's "Context Principle": "Only in the context of a proposition do words mean something" (Frege, *The Foundations of Arithmetic*, 2nd edn, J. L. Austin (trans.) (Oxford: Blackwell, 1953), §60; see also §§61–2, 106); (ii) Russell's insistence that a proposition be regarded as the value of a propositional function; and (iii) Wittgenstein's argument that it is only in the context of propositions that names have meaning (*Tractatus*, §§3.3, 3.314). Wittgenstein drew this conclusion from the claim that names only have meaning in structural combination with others, i.e. all names are unsaturated (*Tractatus*, §§3.1431–3.1432). For the background to this departure from Frege (who thought names of objects ("Reichenbach"), unlike names of functions ("is the teacher of Putnam"), were saturated), see *Tractatus*, §§2.0121–2.0131.
6. Although contested, this is far from a novel interpretation. In his "Introduction", commonly thought to be quite uncomprehending, Russell certainly gets the priorities straight: "Starting from the principles of Symbolism and the relations which are necessary between words and things in any language, [the *Tractatus*] applies the result of this inquiry to various departments of traditional philosophy" (*Tractauts*, 7). And G. E. M. Anscombe writes in her mid-century interpretative essay: "It is clear enough from this that the principal theme of the book is the connection between language, or thought, and reality" (*An Introduction to Wittgenstein's Tractatus* (London: Hutchinson, 1959), 19).
7. Unsurprisingly, commentators who have missed the fact that the metaphysical picture of the *Tractatus* proceeds from and is justified by its account of intentionality have expressed frank amazement at that otherwise strange and apparently un-argued-for vision of indestructible and eternal simple objects. This misinterpretation, apparently based on the naive assumption that the order of presentation in the *Tractatus* must be the order of justification, has proved resilient (for the most recent example, see Soames, *Philosophical Analysis*, vol. 1, 195–253, esp. 200–201, 212–13).
8. As Strawson & Grice ("In Defense of a Dogma", *Philosophical Review* **65** (1956), 141–58) point out, it is actually rather unclear whether Quine holds (the strong view) that there is no distinction between so-called "analytic" and "synthetic" statements, or (the weaker view) that although there may be such a distinction, philosophers have certainly failed to formulate it correctly, and may have misunderstood it. Passages such as the following contain this ambiguity: "a boundary between analytic and synthetic statements simply has not been drawn [weak view]. That there is such a distinction to be drawn at all is an unempirical dogma of empiricists, a metaphysical article of faith [strong view]" ("Two Dogmas of Empiricism", in *From a Logical Point of View* (Cambridge, MA: Harvard University Press, 1953), §4). Since Putnam identifies Quine with the strong view, we shall ignore the possible weaker interpretation.
9. Putnam defends the more general position here: that "a speaker's knowledge of the rules of his native language is implicit and not explicit"; that "only the very sophisticated speaker can verbalize even (some of) the *syntactical* rules of his native language"; that linguistic rules have an "unconscious character" (Putnam, "How Not to Talk about Meaning", in *Mind, Language and Reality*, 127; see also "What Theories are not", in *Mathematics, Matter and Method*, 225; and "Philosophy of Physics", 235).
10. It may not be wrong to characterize this conception as standard, but it is certainly demanding. Some have argued that there is a more modest and

fallibilist version of the notion, one that would not be threatened by either Quine's or Putnam's arguments (see for example L. Bonjour, *In Defense of Pure Reason* (Cambridge: Cambridge University Press, 1998), 115–20; T. Burge, *Truth, Thought, Reason* (Oxford: Oxford University Press, 2005), 62–4, 340ff., 346ff.

11. Earlier in his career, Putnam looked more sympathetically on the notion of the absolutely *a priori*. For example, in his 1956 discussion of colour incompatibilities, he claimed that the statement "nothing is both red and green" has such status (Putnam, "Reds, Greens and Logical Analysis", *Philosophical Review* **65** (1956), 206–17). This is so even if by "red" we mean not specific shades but broad classes of such shades, so long as it is true that no matter which shade of red or green we choose, nothing is both that shade of red and that shade of green (*ibid.*: 211). Putnam was correct to reconsider this claim since it is subject to various sorts of counter-example. Suppose the Labour Party picks red (the broad colour) as its emblem; no matter which shade of the colour picked by the party for its emblem and which shade of green we choose, nothing is both that shade of the former and that shade of the latter; nevertheless it is obviously not *a priori* that "nothing is both the colour picked by the Labour Party for its emblem and green". See C. Peacocke, *The Realm of Reason* (Oxford: Oxford University Press, 2004), 185–6).

12. Putnam at one time argued that subjects such as mathematics, which have been supposed to reveal such truths, actually depend on a hypothetico-deductive methodology and hence on inferences that should be regarded as "quasi-empirical"; indeed, mathematics itself should be regarded as a quasi-empirical science. He uses the discovery of the existence of real numbers and their one-to-one preserving correspondence to points on the line as his example: this was first postulated and then shown to be sufficiently fertile in physics and mathematics to be justified (Putnam, "What is Mathematical Truth?", 64–9). This paper is also notable for its playful use of a thought experiment (imagine what a "Martian mathematics" which depended on "quasi-empirical" methodology would look like) which turns out to be a deliberate hoax: it is the actual mathematical methodology of "us humans, right here on earth" that has been described (*ibid.*, 61–4).

13. See also Putnam, "Two Dogmas Revisited", in *Realism and Reason*, 87–97, where Putnam distinguishes his own position by contrast with Quine's onslaught on analyticity. The significant and correct part of his attack was against the notion that there might be statements which are confirmed (or confirmable) *no matter what*, rather than against the linguistic notion of analyticity (i.e. that any attempt to define what is analytic about a statement must fail due to circularity problems). His attack was successful, but not against the targets he had chosen: that is, his arguments undermine the notion that there is a useful *a priori–a posteriori* distinction, not that there is a useful analytic–synthetic distinction. See also Putnam, "Analyticity and Apriority: Beyond Wittgenstein and Quine", in *Realism and Reason*, 115–38.

Chapter 7. Mind

1. Putnam himself has described his early work as fundamentally a reaction to positivism and verificationism (*Mathematics, Matter and Method*, vii–xiv; *Mind, Language and Reality*, vii–xvii). This part of the book can be viewed as an attempt to make good on this interpretative claim.

2. It is indicative of the strength of his overall preferential option towards simplicity that, as he expresses the maxim ("*without* necessity"), it shaves even

more closely than usual, for "praeter" in the phrase *entia non sunt multiplicanda praeter necessitatem* is perhaps more accurately, and certainly more commonly, translated as "beyond". Aspects of the difference this makes come out if we ask what a parent would or should say in advising their student-child: for example, would/should Polonius say to Laertes: "don't live *beyond* the means available to you" or "*without* the means available to you"?

3. Putnam has drawn particular attention to the way a fellow scientific realist, Richard Boyd, connects his advocacy of that position with analysis of the defects of verificationism and positivism (Putnam, *Mind, Language and Reality*, xi; "Language and Reality", in *Mind, Language and Reality*, 290). In the mid-1970s Putnam was happy to adopt Boyd's phrase for the position he then advocated: philosophy of science is normative description of science ("Reply to Gerald Massey", 194). For the relevant aspects of Boyd's view, see in particular his "Scientific Realism and Naturalistic Epistemology", *Philosophy of Science Association* **II** (1980), 6113–39.

4. The weaknesses and merits of the theoretical–observational distinction are discussed in Chapter 9.

5. For discussion of arguments in this direction and others closely related – for example, are androids conscious? What is there to the notion of artificially created life-forms? – see Putnam, "Robots: Machines or Artificially Created Life?", in *Mind, Language and Reality*, 386–407.

6. So critics standardly point to the "qualia" that certain mental states are supposed to have – features of what it is like to be in those states variously described as "subjective", "inner", "intrinsic" and "qualitative" – as counterexamples to functionalism: they are (a) *bona fide* mental phenomena, but (b) inert with respect to the relevant causal mediations. Justly or otherwise, Putnam's version of functionalism certainly overlooks these alleged mental phenomena.

Chapter 8. Science

1. "*Qual è 'l geomètra che tutto s'affige / . . . e non ritrova, / pensando, quel principio ond' elli indige*" [my translation].

2. Michael Dummett has championed this view; see in particular his *Truth and Other Enigmas* (London: Duckworth, 1978), essays 1, 10–14, 21. Putnam began paying serious attention to Dummett's anti-realist semantics (what Putnam preferred to call "verificationist semantics", since he regarded it as consistent with at least one form of realism – the form he was then advocating, i.e. internal realism) in the early and mid-1970s; see in particular Putnam, "Realism and Reason", in *Meaning and the Moral Science*, 121–40. For a retrospective account of that influence, see Putnam, "The Face of Cognition", in *The Threefold Cord: Mind, Body, and World* (New York: Columbia University Press, 1999).

3. Poincaré, for example, allows for two different "aspects" under which the laws of motion (e.g. the generalized inertial principle) manifest themselves: (a) as "truths founded on experiment and approximately verified so far as concerns almost isolated systems"; (b) as "postulates applicable to the totality of the universe and regarded as rigorously true" (H. Poincaré, *Science and Hypothesis*, G. B. Halsted (trans.) (New York: Science Press, 1905), 98).

4. It is as well to be cautious about implying that this way of telling the story is consistent with the conventionalist approach because, by introducing empirical considerations, actual advocates can modify the result. Thus, given his distinction (described in the note above) between the two aspects under which

laws function within systems, Poincaré can allow that, as well as functioning as conventions that define geometric terms such as "length", they are empirical generalizations approximately confirmed for more or less isolated systems.

Chapter 9. Language

1. Carnap himself does not make his position on this important question overt, but I believe it is clear enough. Putnam takes him to be restricting observational entities to those perceptible without the aid of instruments (Putnam, "What Theories are not", 217), but the paper to which he himself alludes (R. Carnap, "Testability and Meaning", in *Readings in the Philosophy of Science*, H. Feigl & M. Brodbeck (eds), 47–92 (New York: Appleton-Century-Crofts, 1956)) certainly does not support this contention unequivocally and the implicature contained within at least one passage undermines it. For the purpose of reconstructing the language in which observation statements find their place, Carnap says "*it seems convenient* to take some properties for which the test procedure is extremely simple" (my emphasis); these are "directly observable" properties, ones that can be observed without instruments like "finding out whether a thing is blue or hissing or cold" (*ibid.*, 63). If he had supposed that *only* such entities could be called "observational", matters of convenience would have been quite irrelevant. If they *are* relevant and Carnap is not simply misleading us here, then it must have been *possible-but-inconvenient* to have considered indirectly perceptible properties. And hence such properties are to be regarded as *bona fide* examples of observational entities.

2. As Putnam uncharitably puts it, theoretical statements are conceived of as drawing up a kind of partial meaningfulness "by osmosis" from the observation statements with which they are associated (Putnam, "What Theories are not", 216). Bridge-principles are essential to the two-layer view since, without them, theoretical terms would remain uninterpreted. And it is these principles, not just the positivists' need to regard them as analytic, that are the natural point of attack for Putnam's account of empirical terms.

3. For an argument suggesting that observation reports must be parasitic upon theoretical statements, see Feyerabend's observations concerning the ascription of colours to self-luminescent objects (P. Feyerabend, "An Attempt at a Realistic Interpretation of Experience", *Proceedings of the Aristotelian Society* **58** (1958)). Karl Popper's arguments showing how agreement between theories and observational evidence could always be achieved by a variety of strategies (modifying the rules by which theory and evidence correspond, rejecting the evidence, adding auxiliary hypotheses, etc.) persuaded many that the relations between them must be ones of interdependence; see in particular his *The Logic of Scientific Discovery* (New York: Basic Books, 1959).

4. In his "Explanation and Reference", in *Mind, Language and Reality*, 196–214, Putnam acknowledges "a large debt" to Kripke for his work on proper names (mainly heard second-hand), and in particular "for suggesting the idea of causal chains as the mechanism of reference" (*ibid.*, 198, see also 203–4; and Putnam, "The Meaning of 'Meaning' ", in *Mind, Language and Reality*, 215–71, esp. 230–35, 241, 246). At one point, Putnam summarizes the relationship thus: Kripke introduced a causal theory of reference for proper names, and Putnam extended this theory to natural kind and physical magnitude terms (Putnam, "The Meaning of 'Meaning' ", 246). But we should not

let this generosity distract us from the main argument of this chapter: that Putnam was developing the components and the background rationale for his theory of meaning and reference at least a decade before presenting it in its official form in the early 1970s.

5. For the fullest defence of the claim, with elaborations on how it can and should be interpreted, see Putnam, "The Meaning of 'Meaning'"; for his identification of the basic problems at issue, see pp. 216–22; for his summary solutions, see pp. 268–71.

6. The term "stereotype" was introduced by Putnam in lectures given in 1968; Putnam, "Is Semantics Possible?", in *Mind, Language and Reality*, 139–52, esp. 148, is the first published use; the notion to which it refers is developed in his "Explanation and Reference"; the four components of meaning are discussed at length and in relation to each other in "The Meaning of 'Meaning'".

Chapter 10. Intentional states

1. Since Putnam argues that there is an indexical element in natural kind talk, there is another sense in which, at least from his perspective, these cases are not so dissimilar.

Chapter 11. Reality

1. I have consciously avoided framing Putnam's changes of mind in the way he himself recorded them: by appeal to various labels such as "metaphysical realism", "internal realism" and so on. This is partly because, as he himself became vividly aware, the content of these terms was liable to misconstrual; partly because their value changed over the course of time, even in his own usage; but mainly because, as noted above, such labelling exaggerates the importance of relatively superficial stances which Putnam advocated only temporarily and thus blinds us to the significance of the underlying structures and genuinely directive movements of his thought.

2. Meyer Schapiro's "Einstein and Cubism: Science and Art", in his *The Unity of Picasso's Art*, 49–149 (New York: George Braziller, 2000) offers a deeply suggestive monograph-length treatment of what is similar and dissimilar about twentieth-century scientific and artistic attempts to accomplish this.

3. Austin is referring specifically here to the way A. J. Ayer prepares the ground for his account of perception based on a particular notion of what "sense-data" are (Austin, *Sense and Sensibilia* (Oxford: Oxford University Press, 1962), 6).

4. The effects of an aesthetic that removes the artist from the representation can be felt as acutely by the audience. One of the preconditions of gaining knowledge about how things are from entering into relations with a work of art is that one know whether the person responsible for the artistic representation is being straightforward, or ironic, or pleasing; whether their intention is to amuse, to anger, or to warn; whether they are acting out of delight, or fear, or scorn, and so on. So it requires knowing a good deal about the artist, and particularly about their relationship to their own work. (A particularly helpful discussion of these points occurs within Stanley Cavell's discussion of Jean-Luc Godard, and specifically his diagnoses of Godard's failings as a film director; Cavell, *The World Viewed*, enlarged edn (Cambridge, MA: Harvard University Press, 1979), 96–101.)

5. See also Putnam, "Reference and Understanding", in *Meaning and the Moral Sciences*, 95–119, where he compares and contrasts his own position at some length with Dummett's. One main cause of difference is whether understanding

a language consists in being able to use it (Putnam thinks so; Dummett does not). Another is what follows from rejecting the correspondence theory of truth. Putnam at one time thought it led to identifying truth with "an idealization of justification", simultaneously (and erroneously) ascribing to Dummett the view that truth is to be identified with justification *simpliciter* ("Reference and Truth", in *Reason and Realism*, 84; Putnam describes Dummett's position more cautiously in *Reason and Realism*, xvi–xviii, acknowledging that they both recognize the possibility of "a gap" between truth and justification). For a retrospective account of Dummett and his influence on Putnam, see Putnam, "The Face of Cognition".

6. This self-description is still common: Soames, *Philosophical Analysis*, vol. I, xiii–xvi.

7. Putnam acknowledges his debts to Nelson Goodman for the arguments that follow (Putnam, "Realism and Reason", 132). For Goodman's developed position, see his *Ways of Working* (Indianapolis, IN: Hackett, 1978). Goodman memorably describes the world we risk losing touch with as a result of conceiving it in the ways just described as "a world well lost" (*ibid.*, 4).

8. Putnam's discussion at these points closely follows Quine's doctrine of "ontological relativity", a consequence of that scepticism about meaning expressed by his thesis of the indeterminacy of translation. Call the range of objects which must exist if a theory is to be true the ontology of that theory. In Quine's view, there can be no fact of the matter about what the ontology of any theory is that is non-relative. For just to count as such, the ontology of a theory must be stated relative to at least two entities: a background language and a translation manual. See Putnam, "Two Dogmas Revisited", 87–97; "Analyticity and Apriority", 115–39; "Why Reason can't be Naturalized", in *Realism and Reason*, 229–47; *Realism and Reason*, vii–xviii; and "Meaning Holism", in *Words and Life*, 278–302. For a provocative connection between Quine's indeterminacy thesis and deconstruction as a literary theory, see Putnam, "Is there a Fact of the Matter about Fiction?", in *Realism with a Human Face*, 209–13).

9. Putnam rejects the conclusions Quine himself draws from similar arguments (i.e. ontological relativity): namely, that there are correspondence relations between what we think and say, and reality but no *unique* relation of that type. In Putnam's view, this leads directly to a Kantian portrayal of intentionality (as a relation between what we think and say, and a noumenal world) which is finally unintelligible; see Putnam, "Why Reason can't be Naturalized"; *Realism and Reason*, vii–xviii; and "Meaning Holism", 278–302.

Chapter 12. Reference

1. In Putnam's view, Tarski's theory falls to this criticism: Tarski offers "a perfectly correct account of the formal logic of the concept 'true'" (Putnam, *Meaning and the Moral Sciences*, 4) – it satisfies his own criterion of adequacy: that a definition of "true" as a sentence in *L* (for some language, e.g. English) should entail that "snow is white" is true as a sentence of *L* if and only if snow is white. But the formal logic of the concept cannot be all there is to the notion of truth. In order "to understand how language works and how science works", we need to be told that (and how it can be that) a sentence is true if and only if it bears some specifiable relation to extra-linguistic facts (or intra-linguistic facts in the special case where the assertions are about language). And Tarski's semantical conception does not

tell us this or explain it to us; we need to appeal to the correspondence theory instead. At best, Tarski's theory suggests how to achieve certain supposedly desirable effects; namely, how to make uses of "true" eliminable in certain contexts. See Putnam, "Do the Assertions Correspond to Reality?", in *Mathematics, Matter and Method*, 70–84.

2. This is Field's own characterization of his proposal; see the "Postscript" to "Tarski's Theory of Truth" in H. Field, *Truth and the Absence of Fact* (Oxford: Oxford University Press, 2001), 29. In this reconsideration, Field acknowledges that the argument he offers for a physicalist reduction of truth is mistaken if the central role of truth is as a device of generalization (a view argued for by D. Grover, J. Camp and N. Belnap in their "A Prosentential Theory of Truth", *Philosophical Studies* 27 (1975), 73–125), and which Field regards as "essentially correct" (Field, *Truth and the Absence of Fact*, 29).

3. The passage captures a fundamental characteristic of much of Putnam's writing. Other writers carefully edit their thoughts so that the reasons for which one would be justified in holding the conclusions they draw are carefully separated from the reasons that formed part of the process by which they actually arrived at those conclusions. Putnam frequently offers both, usually in combination (as in the quoted passage). So we are given an intuitively appealing picture leading to the assertion of a bold claim; the scrutiny of that claim; its rethinking and trimming; finally, its restatement in a modified form that leads to further intuitively appealing pictures and the same revision process. This is an example in miniature of Putnam's working method – the boldly outlined sketch followed by infilling and the occasional correction. Once we appreciate this fact about his style, it is easier to see how the continuities in his work might be regarded as basic to it; the changes of opinion, although apparently dramatic, are by comparison quite superficial.

4. Putnam himself leaves the claim unmodified: the speaker will *utter* the appropriate sentence when a certain state of affairs obtains ("Reference and Understanding", 103). But this is evidently too strong. Unless in very particular circumstances, it is no mark against a person's *reliability* that they do not say what they think; they may keep their knowledge entirely to themselves, or manifest it practically without speaking (e.g. getting up to feed the cat they perceive as hungry). Hence endorsement, or "accepting-as-true" is a better fit for the argument at this point.

Chapter 13. Truth

1. Philosophers usually skip over the difficulties with translating ordinarily (as opposed to radically) second languages, but Putnam sees commonality. "As the son of a translator, I know very well that translation isn't easy" ("Meaning and Knowledge", in *Meaning and the Moral Sciences*, 55.) The difficulties exist in the ordinary case as well as the radical, and the solution he proposes in the latter case is an extension of the solution generally adopted for the former: interest-relativity.

2. Quine offered various arguments to this conclusion; the one presented has been called the "argument from below" because its force derives from the alleged indeterminacy of sub-sentential expressions (i.e. putatively referring terms) rather than from the indeterminacy of whole sentences. See Quine, *Word and Object*, 51–5, 68–79; *Ontological Relativity and Other Essays* (New York: Columbia University Press, 1969), 1–6, 30–35).

3. And two sub-routes open up here in turn. In Quine's view, the observable facts that the translators go on are a matter of the "stimulus meaning" associated

with sentences in a language: the ordered pair consisting of various stimulations to the subject's sensory receptors and assent to or dissent from a particular sentence. And we can respond by pointing out that either side of this pairing is unjustifiably parsimonious. So on the one side, experience may be held to consist of more than the stimuli of behaviourist psychology; on the other, what experiences typically prompt or cause may be held to consist of more than assent and dissent. The first option is taken by those who claim that experiences cannot simply be a matter of sensory receptor stimulation if they are to stand in the kind of rational relation to the translators' hypotheses that would be necessary to count as supporting or offering evidence for them (see J. H. McDowell, *Mind and World* (Cambridge, MA: Harvard University Press, 1994), Afterword I). The alternative sub-route is taken by those who insist with the later Wittgenstein on the great variety of uses to which whole sentences are put. Often it is not assent/dissent that is prompted; this is true even of declarative sentences, let alone those used to express commands, requests, questions and so on. And as regards those sentences to which experience *does* prompt assent/dissent, often that is not *all* that is prompted.

4. Putnam himself does not enter the caveat concerning subsequent actions and concurrent thoughts (see Putnam, "Meaning and Knowledge", 44–5). It is necessary because the hunter might consistently say "rabbithood" and then act in the ways described – for example, if his spoken comment was a quasi-poetic observation and his wordless actions were quite pragmatic. The former would then concern one kind of thing (the property of being a rabbit) and the latter would reflect thoughts about another (the instance of that property realized in a particular rabbit).

5. Wolfgang Künne has offered the most recent and apparently exhaustive treatment of what he dubs Putnam's "interim period". But since he ignores Putnam's John Locke lectures ("Meaning and Knowledge") and his APA Presidential Address ("Realism and Reason"), his account passes over the early periods of change, making Putnam's development overall seem curiously unmotivated and out of synch with the rest of his emerging views. Künne (*Conceptions of Truth*, 404–5) dates the "interim period" from the early 1980s until 1992; it actually began in the mid-1970s as we are seeing. Putnam himself recognizes this and is explicit about the timing; see his *Realism and Reason*, viii.

6. The proposition has been modified to include "ideal" since it is being used to illustrate a different claim from the one for which Putnam himself introduced it.

7. Putnam aligns himself with a neo-Humean view: that is, one that surrenders Hume's own particular theory of the nature and existence of mental phenomena, but retains the Humean point that it is only ever with other words, images, beliefs and judgements that the mind compares words, images, beliefs and judgements. "The idea of a comparison of words or mental representations with objects is a senseless one" (Putnam, *Realism and Reason*, viii).

Chapter 14. Experience

1. Several commentators have attempted to chart Putnam's changes of opinion concerning the ways in which the nature of truth should be regarded as epistemically constrained (see C. Wright, *Truth and Objectivity* (Cambridge, MA: Harvard University Press, 1992), 38–44; Künne, *Conceptions of Truth*, 404–24). But there is significant disagreement between them (in both senses; it is striking that such substantial disagreements exist), particularly

on the question of whether his account is Peircean (a true belief is one that would be verified by all investigators under ideal conditions of enquiry and at its ideal end), neo-Peircean, or non-Peircean.

2. That degree will be determined differently by different subsequent accounts, but on any plausible account will allow for the rational acceptability of some experiential beliefs that are inconsistent with the way the world is; namely, those false experiential beliefs that it is nevertheless rational to hold.

3. It is often assumed that Putnam only came to the recognizably Kantian view that concepts play a vital role in the formation of experience much later, and under the particular influence of John McDowell (especially his *Mind and World*). But although Putnam's work in the late 1990s (particularly his *The Threefold Cord*) represents the highwater mark of his advocacy of the position and its subtle development, it remains the case that his advocacy goes back to the late 1970s and early 1980s when the foundations of the more refined system were laid. Putnam is explicit about this Kantian connection as early as his *Reason and Truth* (Cambridge: Cambridge University Press, 1981), 60–66.

4. For subsequent debates on the relations between concepts and perceptual content which highlighted and helped define the issues to be settled, see in particular G. Evans, *The Varieties of Reference* (Oxford: Oxford University Press, 1982), 123–4; C. McGinn, *Mental Content* (Oxford: Blackwell, 1989), 58–62); C. Peacocke, *A Study of Concepts* (Cambridge, MA: MIT Press, 1992) and "Non-conceptual Content Defended", *Philosophy and Phenomenological Research* **58** (1998), 381–8; and McDowell, *Mind and World*.

5. This picture would be identified by those who reject it as "the myth of the given", or perhaps more properly a structural variation on a theme since different philosophers have described the fundamental issue differently (as blurring the distinction between sapience and sentience; as extending "the space of reasons" beyond "the space of concepts"; as assuming non-epistemic facts about knowers could possibly entail epistemic facts about them). See in particular W. Sellars, *Empiricism and the Philosophy of Mind*, reprinted (Cambridge, MA: Harvard University Press, 1997); R. Rorty, *Philosophy and the Mirror of Nature* (Oxford: Blackwell, 1980); and McDowell, *Mind and World*.

6. The relevant assumption made by Locke, Berkeley and Hume is that the human mind has an innate ability to be aware of certain determinate repeatables or sorts (such as the colour *red*), and that it is aware of them simply by virtue of having sensations. Russell took this view to be so obvious and commonsensical that he incorporated it into knowledge of the world so certain that no reasonable person could doubt it (*The Problems of Philosophy* (Oxford: Oxford University Press, 1967 [1912]), 3–5); the example he used to make the point (perceiving the shaded parts of a table) was sufficiently effective that Putnam remembered it as his "most memorable encounter with the argument" (Putnam, "The Importance of Being Austin: The Need for a Second Naïveté, in *The Threefold Cord*, 39).

7. Putnam himself clearly rejects the former option; he notes that the problem with the correspondence theory "is not that correspondences between words or concepts and other entities don't exist, but that *too many* correspondences exist. To pick out just *one* correspondence between words or mental signs and mind-independent things we would have already to have referential access to the mind-independent things" (Putnam, *Reason, Truth and History*, 72–3).

8. Putnam himself uses the terminology of "internalism" and "externalism" to denote these contrasting accounts of intentionality (see Putnam, *Reason, Truth and History*, 49–74 *passim*); the names are kept in inverted commas to mark the fact that they denote something different from the internalism–externalism we have examined in the theory of semantic content.

9. Putnam's explicit concentration on the openness intrinsic to *perceptual experience*, as opposed to that openness intrinsic to intentional modes quite generally, explains why his troubled search for a label to denote the approach (he has at different times used "direct realism", then exchanged it for "natural realism", and then for "commonsense realism"; see his remarks in "The Antimony of Reason", in *The Threefold Cord*, 10; "Are Psychological Conditions 'Internal States'?", in *The Threefold Cord*, 101; and *The Threefold Cord*, 182–3, nn. 36, 41) has been restricted to names that recall its perceptual focus. This is the most telling marker of the distance between his stance and that taken most notably by John McDowell, for all the commonalities of argument style and metaphor (both are keen to deny either that experience is an "interface" between the subject and the world, or that experience is the "highest common factor" between veridical and non-veridical situations; see Putnam, "The Face of Cognition", in *The Threefold Cord*, 43; "Are Appearances Qualia?", in *The Threefold Cord*, 152–4; and McDowell, "Criteria, Defeasability and Knowledge", in *Meaning, Knowledge and Reality*, 228–59 (Cambridge, MA: Harvard University Press, 1998)). In *Mind and World*, McDowell has stressed the wide and extra-perceptual competence of the openness model in accounting for intentionality. This distinction is reflected also in what either regards as the challenge to openness about intentionality: McDowell directs his attention broadly; Putnam to sense-datum theories of perception (Putnam, *The Threefold Cord*).

10. McDowell uses the term for a similar purpose in his "Criteria, Defeasability and Knowledge", 393, n.45. A little later he describes the problematic view using the metaphor of a "gulf", which it is the role of experience to "bridge" ("Singular Thought and the Extent of Inner Space", reprinted in *Meaning, Knowledge and Reality*, 237).

11. Putnam regards Jaegwon Kim as offering the best, because "most intelligently defended", version of the semi-Cartesian position (the materialist interface); Kim is the focus of Putnam's attention in "An Automatic Sweetheart", "Are Psychological Conditions 'Internal States'?" and "Psychophysical Correlation", all in *The Threefold Cord*.

12. This point is worth emphasizing since a false supposition is still unfortunately commonplace: that for experience to be conceptual it must be a propositional attitude of some type, perhaps even a form of believing–judging, or a form that entails beliefs–judgements (it is assumed, for example, by the so-called "belief-independence" argument against concept-dependence about experience; see Evans, *Varieties of Reference*). This evidently does not follow from the only claim being put forward here: that concepts are constituents of the way experiences, beliefs and judgements all represent the world as being.

Chapter 15. Conclusion: an integrated vision

1. Putnam often uses commonality of argument-form as an interpretative strategy when analysing the work of other philosophers, justifying the practice by appeal to the axiomatic method in mathematics: "the same proof may occur in what look like totally different areas . . . once we see the structure of an . . . argument, we may often see that the conclusion

depended on very little that was specific to one ... domain as opposed to another" (Putnam, "The Refutation of Conventionalism", 155). Examples of this interpretative tactic abound in his work; one particularly bold instance is the wholesale transference of form (from linguistic theory to facts about space) entailed by his diagnosis that a "single argument underlies" two superficially very different positions taken on two very really different subjects: Quine on radical translation and Grünbaum on the nature of geometry.

2. Given Putnam's emphasis on experience and the transcendental form of his argumentation, "transcendental empiricism" is immediately appealing as a description of the viewpoint with which he might be identified (notwithstanding either his own recent very negative observations concerning an extreme position that he labels, simply, "empiricism" (*Ethics without Ontology*, 6), or the fact that the phrase is logically rather comical, at least if "transcendental" is used in Kant's strict sense, to refer to experience, for it would seem to mean a philosophical position taken by any who stress the primary importance of experience for experience). John McDowell is one philosopher currently courting this label ("Transcendental Empiricism", unpublished manuscript), although he may have negotiated the reef of redundancy by aligning himself more cautiously with "a minimal empiricism, transcendentally slanted" (McDowell, "Responses", in *Reading McDowell*, N. H. Smith (ed.) (London: Routledge, 2002), 287).

3. "A Plea for Excuses" in his *Philosophical Papers*, 3rd edn, J. O. Urmson & G. J. Warnock (eds), 175–204 (Oxford: Oxford University Press, 1979), 189. Note that this is rather a backhanded compliment to analytic philosophy: if this style of philosophizing has chosen to pursue the right goal, it is because that goal has been nowhere unachieved. Many advocates might say: clarity is the right final goal, and we have achieved it in many cases. Austin seems to be saying: clarity may not be the right final goal, but it is a necessary goal if we are to achieve anything else; at any rate, in no case have we achieved it.

4. For his comments on just why it is that ontology flourishes in analytic philosophy even after the positivists had banished "metaphysics", see Putnam, "Ontology: An Obituary", in *Ethics without Ontology*, 78ff. It turns out that Quine (and in particular his paper "On What There is") is largely to blame: he promoted the assumption that "there is, somehow fixed in advance, a single 'real', a single 'literal' sense of 'exist' " (Putnam, "Ontology: An Obituary", 84–5). This historical interpretation builds on direct criticisms of Quine that Putnam had sketched much earlier; see Putnam, "Why Reasons can't be Naturalized", 229–47, and *Realism and Reason*, xii–xiii.

5. Putnam's characteristic way of expressing the point is hortatory; for example, "Let us try to preserve our humanity by, among other things, taking a humane view of ourselves and our self-knowledge" (Putnam, "Meaning and Knowledge", lecture vi, in *Meaning and the Moral Sciences*, 77). The phrasing may exaggerate the point, although it is possible that "humanity" is indeed being used here in such a way as to denote something that could be lost, and hence in need of preserving. It is possible, in other words, that scientism is being viewed not as an innocently misguided attempt to represent the human, but as actually *inhumane*.

6. There are several points where we may draw instructive parallels between Putnam's interventions in philosophy and literary criticism; in particular, certain structural commonalities regarding the space of various positions confronted, and certain shared features of argumentative line in dealing with

them. The best example of this is realism as it occurs in philosophy and in literature. So Putnam's critique of his previously held model of realism may be summed up thus: in its attempt to ground itself on scheme-independent and uniquely determinate correspondence-relations, "the conventions of realism are not being abolished but, on the contrary, exhausted, overworked. Appropriately, then, one's objections should not be made at the level of verisimilitude but at the level of morality: this style of [thinking] is not to be faulted because it lacks reality – the usual charge – but because it seems evasive of reality while borrowing from realism itself." This is an acute description of Putnam's own current position; but the passage is actually taken from a critique by James Woods of "Hysterical Realism", a trend in recent fiction exemplified by Salman Rushdie, Thomas Pynchon, Don DeLillo, David Foster Wallace and Zadie Smith (J. Woods, *The Irresponsible Self: On Laughter and the Novel* (London: Jonathan Cape, 2004), 168). Replacing "writing" with "thinking" in the square brackets was the only modification necessary.

7. This is a term of art; it is not used here in a way that equates exactly with strategies in literary theory associated with Jacques Derrida and others (strategies, incidentally, to which Putnam is alive; he has, for example, noted connections between them and Quine's indeterminacy thesis (Putnam, "Possibility and Necessity", in *Realism and Reason*, 209–13)).

8. For a book-length treatment of the former sort, devoted specifically to the debate between realist and anti-realist analytic philosophers, see S. Blackburn, *Essays in Quasi-Realism* (Oxford: Oxford University Press, 1993). For a treatment at similar length of the latter sort, see my interpretation of John McDowell in *John McDowell* (Cambridge: Polity, 2004).

9. The phrase is due to Harry Frankfurt; see his *Necessity, Volition and Love* (Cambridge: Cambridge University Press, 1999), 129–41, 155–80.

10. Putnam has become steadily more interested in uncovering the various complexities relating to the volitional necessities of serious thought (see in particular his *Ethics without Ontology*; but he made his commitment to the basic claim explicit early in his career (see for example Putnam, "Probability and Confirmation", in *Mind, Language and Reality*, 304).

Bibliography

Cited works by Hilary Putnam

The aim of this reference section is to assist those wishing to research the book's interpretative claims. So it is designed primarily with the needs of readers of this text in mind, and not scholars who require a complete record in full bibliographical detail of Putnam's writings. Choosing the interpretative perspective unavoidably affects what follows in form and content, so it is worth drawing attention to idiosyncratic features.

(a) The section picks out from the complete list of Putnam's publications those cited in the text.

(b) When sufficient information makes available a choice about the chronological ordering of individual items, the criteria used are those that make most sense for readers whose primary concern is the kind of critical interpretation offered in this book. For example, Putnam's doctoral thesis appears against its year of defence (1951) rather than its year of publication (1990); his "Reply to Gerald Massey" appears against the year it was delivered (1974) rather than the year it was published (1975); and so on.

(c) Page numbers refer to volumes of collected papers whenever material has appeared there, and to the places of first publication whenever not.

(d) Information about individual papers relates to their first publication in English, or to the circumstances of their presentation if they appeared unpublished before compilation in the volumes of collected papers. Most chapters in Putnam's more integrated volumes are nevertheless as distinct from each other as independent papers on related themes. Since they have been treated accordingly in the text, as individual items as well as part of a collective work, each has been cited separately here.

1951. *The Meaning of the Concept of Probability in Application to Finite Sequences*. New York: Garland. Published in 1990 with "An Introduction" some years later.

1954a. "Synonymity and the Analysis of Belief Sentences". *Analysis* **14**, 114–22.

1954b. "A Definition of Degree of Confirmation for Very Rich Languages". *Philosophy of Science* **23**, 58–62.

1956. "Reds, Greens, and Logical Analysis". *Philosophical Review* **65**, 206–17.
1957a. "Three-valued Logic". *Philosophical Studies* **8**. Reprinted in Putnam (1975a), 166–73.
1957b. "Decidability and Essential Undecidability". *Journal of Symbolic Logic* **22**, 39–54.
1957c. "Psychological Concepts, Explication and Ordinary Language". *The Journal of Philosophy* **54**, 94–9.
1957d. "Red and Green all over again: A Rejoinder to Arthur Papp". *Philosophical Review* **66**, 100–103.
1958. (with Martin Davies) "Reductions of Hilbert's Tenth Problem". *Journal of Symbolic Logic* **23**, 183–7.
1959. "Memo on 'Conventionalism'", privately circulated by the Minnesota Center for the Philosophy of Science. Reprinted in Putnam (1975a), 206–14.
1960a. "Do True Assertions Correspond to Reality?" Talk presented at Oxford. Reprinted in Putnam (1975b), 70–84.
1960b. "Minds and Machines". In *Dimensions of Mind*, S. Hook (ed.). New York: New York University Press. Reprinted in Putnam (1975b), 362–85.
1960c. "An Unsolvable Problem in Number Theory". *Journal of Symbolic Logic* **25**, 220–32.
1961a. "Some Issues in the Theory of Grammar". *Proceedings of Symposia in Applied Mathematics* **12**. Reprinted in Putnam (1975b), 85–106.
1961b. (with Martin Davies and Julia Robinson) "The Decision Problem for Exponential Diophantine Equations". *Annals of Mathematics* **74**, 425–36.
1962a. "What Theories are not". In *Logic, Methodology and Philosophy of Science*, E. Nagel, P. Suppes & A. Tarski (eds). California: Stanford University Press. Reprinted in Putnam (1975a), 215–27.
1962b. "It Ain't Necessarily So". *The Journal of Philosophy* **59**. Reprinted in Putnam (1975a), 237–49.
1962c. "The Analytic and the Synthetic". In *Minnesota Studies in the Philosophy of Science, III*, H. Feigl & G. Maxwell (eds). Minneapolis, MN: University of Minnesota Press. Reprinted in Putnam (1975b), 33–69.
1962d. "Dreaming and 'Depth grammar'". In *Analytical Philosophy First Series*, R. Butler (ed.). Oxford: Basil Blackwell. Reprinted in Putnam (1975b), 304–24.
1963a. "An Examination of Grünbaum's Philosophy of Geometry". In *Philosophy of Science, The Delaware Seminar, 2*, B. Baumring (ed.). New York: Interscience Publishers. Reprinted in Putnam (1975a), 93–129.
1963b. "'Degree of Confirmation' and Inductive Logic". In *The Philosophy of Rudolf Carnap*, P. A. Schilpp (ed.). La Salle, IL: Open Court. Reprinted in Putnam (1975a), 270–92.
1963c. "Probability and Confirmation", *The Voice of America, Forum Philosophy of Science* (US Information Agency). Reprinted in Putnam (1975a), 293–304.
1963d. "Brains and Behavior". In *Analytical Philosophy Second Series*, R. Butler (ed.). Oxford: Basil Blackwell. Reprinted in Putnam (1975b), 325–41.
1964a. "Truth and Necessity in Mathematics". Public Lecture, Vienna. Reprinted in Putnam (1975a), 1–11.
1964b. "Robots: Machines or Artificially Created Life?". *The Journal of Philosophy* **61**. Reprinted in Putnam (1975b), 386–407.
1964c. "Discussion: Comments on Comments on Comments: A Reply to Margenau and Wigner". *Philosophy of Science* **31**(1). Reprinted in Putnam (1975a), 159–65.

1965a. "Philosophy of Physics". In *Aspects of Contemporary American Philosophy*, F. H. Donnell, Jr. (ed.). Würzburg: Physica-Verlag, Rudolf Liebing K. G. Reprinted in Putnam (1975a), 79–92.

1965b. "A Philosopher Looks at Quantum Mechanics". In *Beyond the Edge of Certainty*, R. G. Colodny (ed.). Englewood Cliffs, NJ: Prentice-Hall. Reprinted in Putnam (1975a), 130–58.

1965c. "Craig's Theorem", *The Journal of Philosophy* **62**. Reprinted in Putnam (1975a), 228–36.

1965d. "How Not to Talk about Meaning". *Boston Studies in the Philosophy of Science, Volume II*, R. Cohen & M. Wartofsky (eds). New York: Humanities Press. Reprinted in Putnam (1975b), 117–31.

1965e. (with J. S. Ullian) "More about 'About'". *The Journal of Philosophy* **62**, 305–10.

1967a. "The Thesis that Mathematics is Logic". In *Bertrand Russell, Philosopher of the Century*, R. Schoenman (ed.). London: Allen and Unwin. Reprinted in Putnam (1975a), 12–42.

1967b. "Mathematics without Foundations". *The Journal of Philosophy* **64**. Reprinted in Putnam (1975a), 43–59.

1967c. "Time and Physical Geometry". *The Journal of Philosophy* **64**. Reprinted in Putnam (1975a), 198–205.

1967d. "The 'Innateness Hypothesis' and Explanatory Models in Linguistics". *Synthese* **17**. Reprinted in Putnam (1975b), 107–16.

1967e. "The Mental Life of Some Machines". In *Intentionality, Minds and Perception*, H. Castaneda (ed.). Detroit: Wayne State University Press. Reprinted in Putnam (1975b), 408–28.

1967f. "The Nature of Mental States". First published as "Psychological Predicates", in *Art, Mind and Religion*, W. H. Capitan & D. D. Merrill (eds). Pittsburgh: University of Pittsburgh Press. Reprinted in Putnam (1975b), 429–40.

1968. "The Logic of Quantum Mechanics". First published as "Is Logic Empirical?", in *Boston Studies in the Philosophy of Science, 5*, R. Cohen & M. Wartofsky (eds). Dordrecht: D. Reidel. Reprinted in Putnam (1975a), 174–97.

1969. "Logical Positivism and the Philosophy of Mind". In *The Legacy of Logical Positivism*, P. Achinstein & S. Barker (eds). Baltimore: Johns Hopkins University Press. Reprinted in Putnam (1975b), 441–51.

1970a. "On Properties". In *Essays in Honor of Carl G. Hempel*, N. Rescher (ed.). Dordrecht: D. Reidel. Reprinted in Putnam (1975a), 305–22.

1970b. "Is Semantics Possible?". In *Languages, Belief and Metaphysics*, H. Kiefer & M. Munitz (eds). New York: SUNY Press. Reprinted in Putnam (1975b), 139–52.

1971. *Philosophy of Logic*. New York: Harper and Row. Reprinted in Putnam (1975a), 323–57.

1973a. "Explanation and Reference". In *Conceptual Change*, G. Pearce & P. Maynard (eds). Dordrecht: D. Reidel. Reprinted in Putnam (1975b), 196–214.

1973b. "Philosophy and our Mental Life". Symposium, Berkeley. Reprinted in Putnam (1975b), 291–303.

1973c. "Reductionism and the Nature of Psychology". *Cognition* **2**. Reprinted in Putnam (1994a), 428–40.

1974a. "The 'Corroboration' of theories". In *The Philosophy of Karl Popper*, P. A. Schilpp (ed.). La Salle, IL: Open Court. Reprinted in Putnam (1975a), 250–69.

1974b. "Language and Reality". Lecture, Princeton. Reprinted in Putnam (1975b), 272–90.

1974c. "Reply to Gerald Massey", American Philosophical Association colloquium. Reprinted in Putnam (1975b), 192–5.

1975a. *Mathematics, Matter and Method, Philosophical Papers, Volume 1* (2nd edn 1979). Cambridge: Cambridge University Press. With "Introduction: Science as Approximation to Truth", vii–xiv.

1975b. *Mind, Language and Reality, Philosophical Papers, Volume 2*. Cambridge: Cambridge University Press. With "Introduction: Philosophy of Language and the Rest of Philosophy", vii–xvii.

1975c. "What is Mathematical Truth?". In Putnam (1975a), 60–78.

1975d. "Language and Philosophy". In Putnam (1975b), 1–32.

1975e. "The Refutation of Conventionalism". In *Semantics and Meaning*, M. Munitz (ed.). New York: New York University Press. Reprinted in Putnam (1975b), 153–91.

1975f. "The Meaning of 'Meaning'". In *Language, Mind and Knowledge*, K. Gunderson (ed.). Minneapolis, MN: University of Minnesota Press. Reprinted in Putnam (1975b), 215–71.

1975g. "Other Minds". In Putnam (1975b), 342–61.

1975h. "What is 'Realism'?". *Proceedings of the Aristotelian Society* **76**, 177–94. Expanded version in Putnam 1976a (ii),(iii), 18–45.

1975i. "Review of *The Concept of a Person* (by A. J. Ayer)", written in the 1960s. In Putnam (1975b), 132–8.

1975j. "Literature, Science and Reflection". *New Literary History* **7**. Reprinted in Putnam (1978a), 81–94.

1976a. "Meaning and Knowledge", the John Locke Lectures. Reprinted in Putnam (1978a), 9–80. (i) Lecture I; (ii) Lecture II; (iii) Lecture III; (iv) Lecture IV; (v) Lecture V; (vi) Lecture VI.

1976b. "Reference and Understanding". Reprinted in Putnam (1978a), 95–119.

1976c. "Realism and Reason". Address, Boston. Reprinted in Putnam (1978a), 121–40.

1976d. "'Two Dogmas' revisited". In *Contemporary Aspects of Philosophy*, G. Ryle (ed.). Oxford: The Oriel Press. Reprinted in Putnam (1983a), 87–97.

1978a. *Meaning and the Moral Sciences*. London: Routledge and Kegan Paul. With "Introduction", 1–6.

1978b. "There is at Least One a priori Truth". *Erkenntnis* **13**. Reprinted in Putnam (1983a), 98–114.

1979a. "Analyticity and Apriority: Beyond Wittgenstein and Quine". In *Midwest Studies in Philosophy, Volume IV*, P. French (ed.). Minneapolis, MN: University of Minnesota Press. Reprinted in Putnam (1983a), 115–38.

1979b. "Reflections on Goodman's *Ways of Worldmaking*". *The Journal of Philosophy* **76**. Reprinted in Putnam (1983a), 155–69.

1979c. "The Place of Facts in a World of Values". In *The Nature of the Physical Universe*, D. Huff & O. Prewett (eds). New York: John Wiley and Sons. Reprinted in Putnam (1990a), 142–62.

1979d. "Philosophy of Mathematics: Why Nothing Works". In *Current Research in Philosophy of Science*, P. D. Asquith & Henry Kyburg, Jr (eds). East Lansing, MI: Philosophy of Science Association. Reprinted in Putnam (1994a), 499–512.

1980. "Models and Reality". *Journal of Symbolic Logic* **45**. Reprinted in Putnam (1983a), 1–25.

1981a. *Reason, Truth and History*. Cambridge: Cambridge University Press. (i) "Brains in a Vat"; (ii) "A Problem about Reference"; (iii) "Two Philosophical

Perspectives"; (iv) "Mind and Body"; (v) "Two Conceptions of Rationality"; (vi) "Fact and Value"; (vii) "Reason and History"; (viii) "The Impact of Science on Modern Conceptions of Rationality"; (ix) "Values, Facts and Cognition".

1981b. "Philosophers and Human Understanding". In *Scientific Explanation*, A. F. Heath (ed.). Oxford: Oxford University Press. Reprinted in Putnam (1983a), 184–204.

1981c. "Quantum Mechanics and the Observer". *Erkenntnis* **16**. Reprinted in Putnam (1983a), 248–70.

1981d. "Convention: A Theme in Philosophy". *New Literary History* **13**. Reprinted in Putnam (1983a), 170–83.

1981e. "Beyond Historicism". In Putnam (1983a), 287–303.

1982a. "Why there isn't a Ready-made World". *Synthese* **51**. Reprinted in Putnam (1983a), 205–28.

1982b. "Why Reason can't be Naturalized". *Synthese* **52**. Reprinted in Putnam (1983a), 229–47.

1982c. "A Defense of Internal Realism". Symposium, Eastern American Philosophical Association. Reprinted in Putnam (1990a), 30–42.

1982d. "Beyond the Fact/Value Dichotomy". *Critica* **14**. Reprinted in Putnam (1990a), 135–41.

1982e. "Peirce the Logician". *Historia Mathematica* **9**. Reprinted in Putnam (1990a), 252–60.

1982f. "Three Kinds of Scientific Realism". *The Philosophical Quarterly* **32**. Reprinted in Putnam (1994a), 492–8.

1983a. *Realism and Reason, Philosophical Papers, Volume 3*. Cambridge: Cambridge University Press. With "Introduction: An Overview of the Problem", vii–xviii.

1983b. "Equivalence". In Putnam (1983a), 26–45.

1983c. "Possibility and Necessity". In Putnam (1983a), 46–68.

1983d. "Reference and Truth". In Putnam (1983a), 69–86.

1983e. "Computational Psychology and Interpretation Theory". In Putnam (1983a), 139–54.

1983f. "Vagueness and Alternative Logic". In Putnam (1983a), 271–86.

1983h. "How not to Solve Ethical Problems". Lecture, Kansas. Reprinted in Putnam (1990a), 179–92.

1983i. "Taking Rules Seriously". *New Literary History* **15**. Reprinted in Putnam (1990a), 193–200.

1983j. "Is there a Fact of the Matter about Fiction?". *Poetics Today* **4**. Reprinted in Putnam (1990a), 209–13.

1983k. "Nelson Goodman's *Fact, Fiction, and Forecast*", Foreword. Reprinted in Putnam (1990a), 303–8.

1983l. "On Truth". In *How Many Questions? Essays in Honor of Sidney Morgenbesser*, L. S. Cauman, I. Levi, C. Parsons & R. Schwartz (eds). Indianapolis, IN: Hackett. Reprinted in Putnam (1994a), 315–29.

1983m. "Probability and the Mental". In *Human Meanings and Existence*, D. P. Chattopadhyaya (ed.). New Delhi: Macmillan India. Reprinted in Putnam (1994a), 376–88.

1984a. "Is the Causal Structure of the Physical Itself something Physical?" In *Midwest Studies in Philosophy, volume IX*, P. French (ed.). Minneapolis, MN: University of Minnesota Press. Reprinted in Putnam (1990a), 80–95.

1984b. "The Craving for Objectivity". *New Literary History* **15**. Reprinted in Putnam (1990a), 120–31.

1984c. "Models and Modules: Fodor's *The Modularity of Mind*". *Cognition* **17**. Reprinted in Putnam (1994a), 403–15.

1985a. "After Empiricism". In *Post-Analytic Philosophy*, J. Rajchman & C. West (eds). New York: Columbia University Press. Reprinted in Putnam (1990a), 43–53.

1985b. "Reflexive Reflections". *Erkenntnis* **22**. Reprinted in Putnam (1994a), 416–27.

1986a. "The Way the World is". Talk, Harvard. Reprinted in Putnam (1990a), 261–7.

1986b. "Meaning Holism". In *The Philosophy of W. V. Quine*, L. E. Hahn & P. A. Schilpp (eds). La Salle, IL: Open Court. Reprinted in Putnam (1990a), 278–302.

1986c. "How Old is the Mind?". In *Exploring the Concept of Mind*, R. M. Caplan (ed.). Iowa City: University of Iowa Press. Reprinted in Putnam (1994a), 3–21.

1986d. "A Comparison of Something with Something Else". *New Literary History* **17**. Reprinted in Putnam (1994a), 330–50.

1986e. "Information and the Mental". In *Truth and Interpretation: Perspectives on the Philosophy of Donald Davidson*, E. Lepore & J. Leplin (eds). Oxford: Basil Blackwell.

1987a. *The Many Faces of Realism*, The Paul Carus Lectures. La Salle, IL: Open Court. (i) "Is there Still Anything to Say about Reality and Truth?"; (ii) "Realism and Reasonableness"; (iii) "Equality and our Moral Image of the World"; (iv) "Reasonableness as a Fact and as a Value".

1987b. "Realism with a Human Face". Lecture, Stanford. Reprinted in Putnam (1990a), 3–29.

1987c. "Truth and Convention". *Dialectica* **41**. Reprinted in Putnam (1990a), 96–104.

1987d. "Scientific Liberty and Scientific License". *Grazer Philosophische Studien* **13**. Reprinted in Putnam (1990a), 201–8.

1987e. "The Diversity of the Sciences". In *Metaphysics and Morality*, P. Pettit, R. Sylvan & J. Norman (eds). Oxford: Basil Blackwell. Reprinted in Putnam (1994a), 463–80.

1988a. *Representation and Reality*. Cambridge, MA: MIT Press. (i) "Meaning and Mentalism"; (ii) "Meaning, Other People, and the World"; (iii) "Fodor and Block on 'Narrow Content'"; (iv) "Are there such Things as Reference and Truth?"; (v) "Why Functionalism didn't Work"; (vi) "Other Forms of Functionalism"; (vii) "A Sketch of an Alternative Picture".

1988b. "James' Theory of Perception". Presentation, Texas. Reprinted in Putnam (1990a), 232–51.

1988c. "The Greatest Logical Positivist". *London Review of Books* **10**. Reprinted in Putnam (1990a), 268–77.

1988d. "Artificial Intelligence: Much Ado about not very much". *Daedalus* **117**. Reprinted in Putnam (1994a), 391–402.

1989a. "William James' ideas". *Raritan* **8**. Reprinted in Putnam (1990a), 217–31.

1989b. "Model Theory and the 'Factuality' of Semantics". In *Reflections on Chomsky*, Alex George (ed.). Oxford: Basil Blackwell. Reprinted in Putnam (1994a), 351–75.

1990a. *Realism with a Human Face*, J. Conant (ed.). Cambridge, MA: Harvard University Press.

1990b. "Is Water Necessarily H$_2$O?". In Putnam (1990a), 54–79.

1990c. "Why is a Philosopher?". In Putnam (1990a), 105–19.

1990d. "Objectivity and the Science/Ethics Distinction". In Putnam (1990a), 163–78.

1990e. "Dewey's *Logic*: Epistemology as Hypothesis. First published as "Epistemology as hypothesis", *Transactions of the Charles S. Peirce Society* **26**. Reprinted in Putnam (1994a), 198–220.

1990f. "The Idea of Science". In *Midwest Studies in Philosophy, volume XV*, P. French, T. Uehling & H. Wettstein (eds). Notre Dame: University of Notre Dame Press. Reprinted in Putnam (1994a), 481–91.

1991a. "Logical Positivism and Intentionality". In *A. J. Ayer Memorial Essays*, A. Phillips Griffiths. Cambridge: Cambridge University Press. Reprinted in Putnam (1994a), 85–98.

1991b. "Reichenbach's Metaphysical Picture". *Erkenntnis* **35**. Reprinted in Putnam (1994a), 99–114.

1991c. "Reichenbach and the Myth of the Given". Lecture, Harvard. Reprinted in Putnam (1994a), 115–30.

1991d. "Does the Disquotational Theory of Truth Solve all Philosophical Problems?". *Metaphilosophy* **22**. Reprinted in Putnam (1994a), 264–78.

1992a. *Renewing Philosophy*, The Gifford Lectures. Cambridge, MA: Harvard University Press. (i) "The Project of Artificial Intelligence"; (ii) "Does Evolution Explain Representation?"; (iii) "A Theory of Reference"; (iv) "Materialism and Relativism"; (v) "Bernard Williams and the Absolute Conception of the World"; (vi) "Irrealism and Deconstruction"; (vii) "Wittgenstein on Religious Belief"; (viii) "Wittgenstein on Reference and Relativism"; (ix) "A Reconsideration of Deweyan Democracy".

1992b. *Pragmatism: An Open Question*. Originally published in Italian. Published in English in 1995 (Oxford: Blackwell). (i) "The Permanence of William James"; (ii) "Was Wittgenstein a Pragmatist?"; (iii) "Pragmatism and the Contemporary Debate".

1992c. "Changing Aristotle's Mind". In *Essays on Aristotle's De Anima*, M. Nussbaum & A. Rorty (eds). Oxford: Oxford University Press. Reprinted in Putnam (1994a), 22–61.

1992d. "Pragmatism and Relativism: Universal Values and Traditional Ways of Life". First published as "The French Revolution and the Holocaust: Can Ethics be Ahistorical?". In *Culture and Modernity*, E. Deutsch (ed.). Honolulu: University of Hawaii Press. Reprinted in Putnam (1994a), 182–97.

1992e. "Why Functionalism Didn't Work". First published as "Why Functionalism Failed". In *Inference, Explanation, and Other Philosophical Frustrations*, J. Earman (ed.). Berkeley, CA: University of California Press. Reprinted in Putnam (1994a), 441–59.

1992f. "Replies to 'The Philosophy of Hilary Putnam'". *Philosophical Topics* **20**, 347–408.

1993a. "Aristotle after Wittgenstein". In *Modern Thinkers and Ancient Thinkers*, R. W. Sharples (ed.). London: UCL Press. Reprinted in Putnam (1994a), 62–81.

1993b. "Reichenbach and the Limits of Vindication". In *Proceedings of the Ninth International Congress of Logic, Methodology, and Philosophy of Science*. Amsterdam: Elsevier. Reprinted in Putnam (1994a), 131–48.

1993c. "Education for Democracy". *Educational Theory* **43**. Reprinted in Putnam (1994a), 221–41.

1993d. "Realism without Absolutes". *International Journal of Philosophical Studies* **1–2**. Reprinted in Putnam (1994a), 279–94.

1993e. "The Question of Realism". Lecture, London. Reprinted in Putnam (1994a), 295–312.

1993f. "The Cultural Impact of Newton: Pope's *Essay on Man* and those 'Happy Pieties'". In *Pursuits of Reason: Essays in Honor of Stanley Cavell*, T. Cohen,

P. Guyer & H. Putnam (eds). Lubbock, TX: Texas Tech University Press. Reprinted in Putnam (1994a), 513–22.

1994a. *Words and Life*. Cambridge, MA: Harvard University Press.

1994b. "Pragmatism and Moral Objectivity". In Putnam (1994), 151–81.

1994c. "Rethinking Mathematical Necessity". In Putnam (1994a), 245–63.

1994d. "Sense, Nonsense and the Senses. An Inquiry into the Powers of the Human Mind". The John Dewey Lectures. *The Journal of Philosophy* **91**. Reprinted in Putnam (1999), 1–70.

1994e. "Comments and Replies". In *Reading Putnam*, P. Clark & B. Hale (eds). Oxford: Basil Blackwell, 242–95.

1998. "Floyd, Wittgenstein, and Loneliness", in "The Uncaptive Eye: Solipsism in Wittgenstein's Tractatus". In *Loneliness*, L. Rouner (ed.), 109–14. Notre Dame: University of Notre Dame Press.

1999. *The Threefold Cord: Mind, Body, and World*. New York: Columbia University Press. (i) "The Antinomy of Reason"; (ii) "The Importance of Being Austin: The Need for a 'Second Naïveté'"; (iii) "The Face of Cognition"; (iv) "I Thought of What I Called 'An Automatic Sweetheart'"; (v) "Are Psychological Conditions 'Internal States'?"; (vi) "Psychophysical Correlation"; (vii) "Causation and Explanation"; (viii) "Are Appearances 'Qualia'?".

2000. (with Juliet Floyd) "A Note on Wittgenstein's 'Notorious Paragraph' about the Gödel Theorem". *The Journal of Philosophy* **97**, 624–32.

2001. *Enlightenment and Pragmatism*, the Spinoza Lectures. Assen: Koninklijke Van Gorcum. Reprinted in Putnam (2004), 89–129.

2002a. *The Collapse of the Fact/Value Dichotomy and Other Essays*. Cambridge, MA: Harvard University Press. (i) "The Empiricist Background"; (ii) "The Entanglement of Fact and Value"; (iii) "Fact and Value in the World of Amartya Sen"; (iv) "Sen's Prescriptivist Beginnings"; (v) "On the Rationality of Preferences"; (vi) "Are Values Made or Discovered?"; (vii) "Values and Norms"; (viii) "The Philosophers of Science's Evasion of Values".

2002b. "Comments". In *Hilary Putnam: Pragmatism and Realism*, J. Conant & U. M. Zeglen (eds). London: Routledge, *passim*.

2004a. *Ethics without Ontology*. Cambridge, MA: Harvard University Press. (i) "Ethics Without Metaphysics"; (ii) "A Defense of Conceptual Relativity"; (iii) "Objectivity without Objects" (iv) "'Ontology': An Obituary" (v) "The Three Enlightenments"; (vi) "Skepticism about Enlightenment".

2004b. "Sosa on Internal Realism and Conceptual Relativity". In *Ernest Sosa and his Critics*, J. Greco (ed.), 233–48. Oxford: Blackwell.

Cited works by other authors

Anscombe, G. E. M. 1959. *An Introduction to Wittgenstein's Tractatus*. London: Hutchinson.

Atlas, J. 2000 *Bellow: A Biography*. New York: Random House.

Austen, J. 1990. *Northanger Abbey*, J. Davie (ed.), reissue. Oxford: Oxford University Press.

Austin, J. L. 1962. *Sense and Sensibilia*. Oxford: Oxford University Press.

Austin, J. L. 1979. *Philosophical Papers*, 3rd edn, J. O. Urmson & G. J. Warnock (eds). Oxford: Oxford University Press.

Ayer, A. J. 1946. *Language, Truth and Logic*, 2nd edn. London: Victor Gollancz.

Bellow, S. 1995 *The Adventures of Augie March*. London: Everyman.

Ben-Menahim, Y. (ed.) 2005. *Hilary Putnam*. Cambridge: Cambridge University Press.

Blackburn, S. 1993. *Essays in Quasi-Realism*. Oxford: Oxford University Press.

Bonjour, L. 1998. *In Defense of Pure Reason*. Cambridge: Cambridge University Press.

Boolos, G. (ed.) 1990. *Meaning and Method*. Cambridge: Cambridge University Press.

Boyd, R. 1980. "Scientific Realism and Naturalistic Epistemology". *Philosophy of Science Association* **II**, 613–39.

Burge, T. 2005. *Truth, Thought, Reason* Oxford: Oxford University Press.

Carnap, R. 1956. "Testability and Meaning". Reprinted in *Readings in the Philosophy of Science*, H. Feigl & M. Brodbeck (eds), 47–92. New York: Appleton-Century-Crofts.

Carnap, R. 1955. "Foundations of Logic and Mathematics". In *International Encyclopedia of Unified Science*, vol. I, no. 3, O. Neurath, R. Carnap & C. Morris (eds), 1–70. Chicago, IL: University of Chicago Press.

Carnap, R. 1956. "The Methodological Character of Theoretical Concepts". In *Minnesota Studies in the Philosophy of Science*, H. Feigl, M. Scriven & G. Maxwell *et al.* (eds), 1–74. Minneapolis, MN: University of Minnesota Press.

Cavell, S. 1979. *The World Viewed*, enlarged edn. Cambridge, MA: Harvard University Press.

Church, A. 1972. "Review of Hilary Putnam 'An Unsolvable Problem in Number Theory'". *Journal of Symbolic Logic* **37**, 601–2.

Clark, P. & B. Hale (eds) 1994. *Reading Putnam*. Oxford: Blackwell.

Coffa, J. A. 1991. *The Semantic Tradition from Kant to Carnap: To the Vienna Station*. Cambridge: Cambridge University Press.

Coleridge, S. T. 1896. *Aids to Reflection*, new rev. edn. Edinburgh.

Conant, J. & U. M. Zeglen 2002. *Hilary Putnam: Pragmatism and Realism*. London: Routledge.

Davis, M. 1962. "Applications of Recursive Function Theory to Number Theory". In *Proceedings of Symposia in Pure Mathematics: American Mathematical Society* **5** (Providence), 135–8.

Davis, M. 1963. "Extensions and Corollaries of Recent Work on Hilbert's Tenth Problem". *Illinois Journal of Mathematics* **7**, 246–50.

Davis, M. 1973. "Hilbert's Tenth Problem is Unsolvable". *American Mathematical Monthly* **80**, 233–69.

Dedmon, E. 1953. *Fabulous Chicago*. New York: Random House.

Dennett, D. (ed.) 1987. *The Philosophical Lexicon*. Newark, NJ: American Philosophical Association.

Donnellan, K. 1962. "Necessity and Criteria". *The Journal of Philosophy* **59**(22), 647–58.

Doyle, A. C. 1981. *The Adventures of Sherlock Holmes*. Harmondsworth: Penguin.

Dummett, M. 1978. *Truth and Other Enigmas*. London: Duckworth.

Dummett, M. 1993. *Origins of Analytical Philosophy*. London: Duckworth.

Einstein, A. 1922. *Sidelights on Relativity*. London.

Einstein, A., B. Podolsky & N. Rosen 1935. "Can Quantum Mechanical Description of Reality be Considered Complete?". *Physical Review* **47**, 777–80.

Evans, G. 1982. *The Varieties of Reference*. Oxford: Oxford University Press.

Feigl, H. 1958. "The 'Mental' and the 'Physical'". In *Minnesota Studies in the Philosophy of Science, II*, H. Feigl, M. Scriven & G. Maxwell (eds), 370–497. Minneapolis, MN: University of Minnesota Press.

Feigl, H. 1981. *Herbert Feigl: Inquiries and Provocations, Selected Writings 1929–1974*, R. S. Cohen (ed.). Dordrecht: D. Reidel.
Feyerabend, P. 1958. "An Attempt at a Realistic Interpretation of Experience". *Proceedings of the Aristotelian Society* **58**.
Feyerabend, P. 1970. "Philosophy of Science: A Subject with a Great Past". In *Historical and Philosophical Perspectives of Science*, R. Stuewer (ed.), 172–83. Minneapolis, MN: University of Minnesota Press.
Field, H. 2001. *Truth and the Absence of Fact*. Oxford: Oxford University Press.
Fowler, A. 2003. *Renaissance Realism*. Oxford: Oxford University Press.
Fraassen, Bas C. van 1980. *The Scientific Image*. Oxford: Oxford University Press.
Frankfurt, H. G. 1999. *Necessity, Volition and Love*. Cambridge: Cambridge University Press.
Frege, G. 1953. *The Foundations of Arithmetic*, 2nd edn, J. L. Austin (trans.). (Oxford: Blackwell.
Friedman, M. 1992. *Kant and the Exact Sciences*. Cambridge, MA: Harvard University Press.
Friedman, M. 1999. *Reconsidering Logical Positivism*. Cambridge: Cambridge University Press.
Friedman, M. 2000. *A Parting of the Ways: Carnap, Cassirer, and Heidegger*. Chicago, IL: Open Court.
Gallie, W. B. 1949. "The Limitations of Analytical Philosophy". *Analysis* **9**.
Gaynesford, M. de 2004. *John McDowell*. Cambridge: Polity.
Garfinkel, A. 1981. *Forms of Explanation*. New Haven, CT: Yale University Press.
Gellner, E. 2005. *Words and Things*, 2nd rev. edn. London: Routledge.
Giaquinto, M. 1983. "Hilbert's Philosophy of Mathematics". *British Journal of the Philosophy of Science* **34**, 119–32.
Glock, H.-J. (ed.) 1997. *The Rise of Analytic Philosophy*. Oxford: Blackwell.
Goodman, N. 1968. *Languages of Art*. Indianapolis, IN: Hackett.
Goodman, N. 1978. *Ways of Worldmaking*. Indianapolis, IN: Hackett.
Grover, D., J. Camp & N. Belnap 1975. "A Prosentential Theory of Truth". *Philosophical Studies* **27**, 73–125.
Grünbaum, A. 1973. *Philosophical Problems of Space and Time*, 2nd edn. Boston Studies in the Philosophy of Science, vol. XII. Dordrecht: D. Reidel.
Hacker, P. 1996. *Wittgenstein's Place in Twentieth-Century Analytic Philosophy*. Oxford: Blackwell.
Hazlitt, W. 1991. *The Spirit of the Age*, 2nd edn, E. D. Mackerness (ed.). Plymouth: Northcote House.
Hempel, C. G. 1949. "The Logical Analysis of Psychology". In *Readings in Philosophical Analysis*, H. Feigl & W. Sellars (eds). New York: Appleton Century Crofts.
Heisenberg, W. 1949. *The Physical Principles of the Quantum Theory*. New York: Dover.
Heisenberg, W. 1999. *Physics and Philosophy*. New York: Prometheus.
Hilbert, D. 1967. "The Foundations of Mathematics". Reprinted in *From Frege to Gödel*, J. van Heijenoort (ed.). Cambridge, MA: Harvard University Press.
Hopkins, G. M. 1935. *The Letters of Gerard Manley Hopkins to Robert Bridges*, C. C. Abbott (ed.). Oxford: Oxford University Press.
Horwich, P. 1998. *Truth*, 2nd edn. Oxford: Oxford University Press.
Hylton, P. 1990. *Russell, Idealism and the Emergence of Analytic Philosophy*. Oxford: Oxford University Press.
Innes, M. 1958. *Death at the President's Lodging*. Harmondsworth: Penguin.

Kant, I. 1933. *Critique of Pure Reason*, 2nd edn, N. Kemp Smith (trans.). London: Macmillan.

Kenny, A. 1995. *Frege*. Harmondsworth: Penguin.

Keynes, J. M. 1949. *Two Memoirs*. London: Rupert Hart-Davis.

Kripke, S. 1972. "Naming and Necessity". In *The Semantics of Natural Language*, G. Harman & D. Davidson (eds), 254–355. Dordrecht: Kluwer.

Künne, W. 2003. *Conceptions of Truth*. Oxford: Oxford University Press.

Langer, S. 1957. *Philosophy in a New Key*, 3rd edn. Cambridge, MA: Harvard University Press.

Laudan, L. 1977. *Progress and its Problems*. Berkeley, CA: University of California Press.

Laudan, L. 1984. "A Confutation of Scientific Realism". In *Scientific Realism*, J. Leplin (ed.), 218–49. Berkeley, CA: University of California Press.

Leavis, F. R. 1948. *The Great Tradition: George Eliot, Henry James, Joseph Conrad*. London: Chatto & Windus.

Lewis, C. I. 1956. *Mind and the World Order*. New York: Dover.

Locke, J. 1975. *An Essay Concerning Human Understanding*, P. H. Nidditch (ed.). Oxford: Oxford University Press.

Malcolm, N. 1984. *Ludwig Wittgenstein: A Memoir*, 2nd edn. Oxford: Oxford University Press.

McDowell, J. H. 1982. "Criteria, Defeasibility and Knowledge". Reprinted in McDowell (1998), 369–94.

McDowell, J. H. 1986. "Singular Thought and the Extent of Inner Space". Reprinted in McDowell (1998), 228–59.

McDowell, J. H. 1998. *Meaning, Knowledge, and Reality*. Cambridge, MA: Harvard University Press.

McDowell, J. H. 1994. *Mind and World*. Cambridge, MA: Harvard University Press.

McDowell, J. H. 2000. "Transcendental Empiricism", unpublished manuscript, Pittsburgh.

McDowell, J. H. 2002. "Responses". In *Reading McDowell*, N. H. Smith (ed.), 269–305. London: Routledge.

McGinn, C. 1977. "Charity, Interpretation and Belief". *Journal of Philosophy* **74**, 521–35.

McGinn, C. 1989. *Mental Content*. Oxford: Blackwell.

Menand, L. 2001. *The Metaphysical Club*. London: HarperCollins.

Moore, G. E. 1962. *Philosophical Papers*. London: Collier.

Moore, G. E. 1993. *Principia Ethica*, rev. edn, T. Baldwin (ed.). Cambridge: Cambridge University Press.

Morris, C. 1946. *Signs, Language and Behavior*. New York: George Braziller.

Nagel, E. 1936. "Impressions and Appraisals of Analytic Philosophy in Europe". *Journal of Philosophy* **33**, 5–24.

Nagel, E. & J. R. Newman 1959. *Gödel's Proof*. London: Routledge & Kegan Paul.

Nagel, E. 1961. *The Structure of Science*. New York: Harcourt, Brace and World.

Neurath, M. & R. S. Cohen (eds) 1973. *Neurath, Empiricism and Sociology*. Dordrecht: Kluwer.

Oppenheimer, J. R. 1989 *Atom and Void*. Princeton, NJ: Princeton University Press.

Passmore, J. 1994. *A Hundred Years of Philosophy*, 2nd edn. Harmondsworth: Penguin.

Peacocke, C. 1992. *A Study of Concepts*. Cambridge, MA: MIT Press.

Peacocke, C. 1998. "Non-conceptual Content Defended". *Philosophy and Phenomenological Research* **58**, 381–8.

Peacocke, C. 2004. *The Realm of Reason*. Oxford: Oxford University Press.

Peirce, C. S. 1933. *Collected Papers. Vol. V: Pragmatism and Pragmaticism*, C. Hartshorne & P. Weiss (eds). Cambridge, MA: Harvard University Press.

Pessin, A. & S. Goldberg (eds) 1996. *The Twin-Earth Chronicles*. New York: M. E. Sharpe.

Plato 1973. *Theaetetus*, translated with notes by J. McDowell. Oxford: Oxford University Press.

Poincaré, H. 1905. *Science and Hypothesis*, G. B. Halsted (trans.). New York: Science Press.

Popper, K. 1959. *The Logic of Scientific Discovery*. New York: Basic Books.

Quine, W. V. O. 1953. *From a Logical Point of View*. Cambridge, MA: Harvard University Press.

Quine, W. V. O. 1960. *Word and Object*. Cambridge, MA: MIT Press.

Quine, W. V. O. 1969. *Ontological Relativity and Other Essays*. New York: Columbia University Press.

Ramsey, F. P. 1978. *Foundations: Essays in Philosophy, Logic, Mathematics and Economics*, D. H. Mellor (ed.). London: Routledge and Kegan Paul.

Reichenbach, H. 1944. *Philosophic Foundations of Quantum Mechanics*. Los Angeles, CA: University of California Press.

Reichenbach, H. 1947. *Elements of Symbolic Logic*. New York: The Free Press.

Reichenbach, H. 1949. *Experience and Prediction*. Chicago, IL: University of Chicago Press.

Reichenbach, H. 1958. *The Philosophy of Space and Time*, M. Reichenbach & J. Freund (trans.). New York: Dover.

Reichenbach, H. 1965. *The Theory of Relativity and a priori Knowledge*, M. Reichenbach (trans.). Los Angeles, CA: University of California Press.

Reichenbach, H. 1999. *The Direction of Time*. New York: Dover.

Ricks, C. 1984. *The Force of Poetry*. Oxford: Oxford University Press.

Robinson, J. 1972a. "Review of Martin Davis and Hilary Putnam 'Reductions of Hilbert's Tenth Problem'". *Journal of Symbolic Logic* **37**, 602.

Robinson, J. 1972b. "Review of Martin Davis 'Applications of Recursive Function Theory to Number Theory'". *Journal of Symbolic Logic* **37**, 601.

Rorty, R. 1980. *Philosophy and the Mirror of Nature*. Oxford: Blackwell.

Russell, B. 1918. *Mysticism and Logic and Other Essays*. London: Longmans Green and Co.

Russell, B. 1959. *My Philosophical Development*. London: Allen & Unwin.

Russell, B. 1967 [1912]. *The Problems of Philosophy*. Oxford: Oxford University Press.

Ryle, G. 1971. *Collected Papers*. London: Hutchinson.

Schapiro, M. 2000. *The Unity of Picasso's Art*. New York: George Braziller.

Searle. J. 1992. *The Rediscovery of the Mind*. Cambridge, MA: MIT Press.

Segal, G. 2000. *A Slim Book about Narrow Content*. Cambridge, MA: MIT Press.

Sellars, W. 1997. *Empiricism and the Philosophy of Mind*, reprinted. Cambridge, MA: Harvard University Press.

Soames, S. 2003. *Philosophical Analysis in the Twentieth Century*, 2 vols. Princeton, NJ: Princeton University Press.

Sprat, B. 1959 [1667]. *The History of the Royal Society*, J. Cape (ed.). London: Routledge.

Strawson, P. F. & P. Grice 1956. "In Defense of a Dogma". *Philosophical Review* **65**, 141–58.

Strawson, P. F. 1959. *Individuals*. London: Methuen.

Strawson, P. F. 2004. *Logico-Linguistic Papers*, 2nd edn. Aldershot: Ashgate.

Tarski, A. 1983. "The Concept of Truth in Formalized Languages". Reprinted in his *Logic, Semantics and Metamathematics*, 2nd edn. Indianapolis, IN: Hackett.

Trilling, L. 2000. *The Moral Obligation to be Intelligent: Selected Essays*, L. Wieseltier (ed.). New York: Farrar, Straus & Giroux.

Warnock, G. 1973. "Saturday Mornings". In *Essays on J. L. Austin*, I. Berlin *et al.* (eds), 31–45. Oxford: Clarendon Press.

Williams, B. 1972. "Knowledge and Reasons". In *Problems in the Theory of Knowledge*, G. H. von Wright (ed.). The Hague: Nijhoff.

Williams, B. 1993. *Shame and Necessity*. Berkeley. CA: University of California Press.

Wittgenstein, L. 1922. *Tractatus Logico-Philosophicus*, C. K. Ogden & F. P. Ramsey (trans.), Introduction by Bertrand Russell. London: Routledge.

Wittgenstein, L. 1958. *Philosophical Investigations*, 2nd edn, G. E. M. Anscombe (trans.). Oxford: Blackwell.

Wittgenstein, L. 1975. *Philosophical Remarks* of 1929–30, R. Rhees (ed.), R. Hargreaves & R. White (trans.) Oxford: Blackwell.

Woods, J. 2004. *The Irresponsible Self: On Laughter and the Novel*. London: Jonathan Cape.

Woolf, V. 1931. *The Waves*. London: Harcourt.

Wright, C. 1992. *Truth and Objectivity*. Cambridge, MA: Harvard University Press.

Wright, C. 1993. *Realism, Meaning and Truth*, 2nd edn. Oxford: Blackwell.

Wright, G. H. von 1993. *The Tree of Knowledge and Other Essays*. Leiden: Brill.

Index